Teaching and Learning in
Inclusive Classrooms

How can you develop effective teaching strategies so that *all* the children in your classroom are included in meaningful and enriching learning experiences?

What can you do to help young people from diverse backgrounds achieve their full potential?

Addressing the wide variety of issues of diversity and inclusion routinely encountered in today's classrooms, this comprehensive text provides both a theoretical background and practical strategies.

Chapters from leading figures on inclusive education present and analyse the latest debates, research studies and current initiatives, including considerations for teaching and learning, and conclude with key questions for reflection and additional resources.

Moving beyond simple theory about diversity, to what this means for real teachers' practice, the contributions focus on issues relating to values and professional practice for teachers, emphasising inclusive approaches and the importance of understanding the perspectives of learners. Topics discussed include:

- understanding inclusive education
- ethnic and cultural diversity
- challenging behaviour
- bullying
- gender identity and sexuality
- gifted and talented learners
- Gypsy, Roma and Traveller children
- special educational needs
- collaborative working in school
- the perspective of parents.

Designed to stimulate and strengthen teachers' professional understanding, the book also reflects on legislative duties, personal values, and the importance of listening to the voices of individuals who experience disadvantage in educational settings.

Teaching and Learning in Diverse and Inclusive Classrooms is a key resource for teachers, supporting their learning throughout their initial training and early professional development. It will also be of interest to more experienced teachers interested in diversity and inclusion, particularly those mentoring NQTs through their induction and Master's-level studies.

Gill Richards is Director of Professional Development at the School of Education, Nottingham Trent University. She teaches on the MA in Inclusive Education at NTU and delivers the new National Award for SEN Co-ordination and CPD courses for teachers, in partnership with Nottinghamshire Local Authority.

Felicity Armstrong is Professor of Education at the Institute of Education, University of London. She is course leader for the MA in Inclusive Education and leader of the Inclusive Education Special Interest Group.

Teaching and Learning in Diverse and Inclusive Classrooms

Key issues for new teachers

Edited by
Gill Richards and Felicity Armstrong

Routledge
Taylor & Francis Group

LONDON AND NEW YORK

This first edition published 2011
by Routledge
2 Park Square, Milton Park, Abingdon, Oxon OX14 4RN

Simultaneously published in the USA and Canada
by Routledge
270 Madison Avenue, New York, NY 10016

Routledge is an imprint of the Taylor & Francis Group, an informa business

© 2011 Gill Richards and Felicity Armstrong for selection and editorial
material. Individual chapters, the contributors.
The right of Gill Richards and Felicity Armstrong to be identified as editors of
this work has been asserted by them in accordance with sections 77 and 78 of
the Copyright, Designs and Patents Act 1988.

Typeset in Bembo by Taylor & Francis Books
Printed and bound in Great Britain by TJ International Ltd, Padstow, Cornwall

British Library Cataloguing in Publication Data
A catalogue record for this book is available from the British Library

Library of Congress Cataloging in Publication Data
Teaching and learning in diverse and inclusive classrooms : key issues for new
teachers / edited by Gill Richards and Felicity Armstrong.
       p. cm.
    1. Inclusive education–Great Britain. 2. Special education–Great Britain. 3.
Multicultural education–Great Britain. 4. Special education teachers–Training
of–Great Britain. I. Richards, Gill. II. Armstrong, Felicity.
    LC1203.G7T43 2011
    371.9'0460941–dc22
                          2010015922

ISBN13: 978-0-415-56462-5 (hbk)
ISBN13: 978-0-415-56463-2 (pbk)
ISBN13: 978-0-203-84091-7 (ebk)

Contents

Contributors

Vikki Anderson has taught in schools and further education colleges, and in higher education. She works as a Learning Support advisor at the University of Birmingham and delivers continuing professional development. She has published research on listening and responding to the voice of the learner and supporting students with specific learning difficulties in higher education.

Felicity Armstrong is Emeritus Professor of Education at the Institute of Education, University of London, and co-founder of the MA in Inclusive Education and the Inclusive Education Special Interest group at the Institute. She is on the editorial board of *Disability and Society* and the *International Journal of Inclusive Education*.

Steve Bartlett has published widely on education studies issues and teacher research methods. His research interests are in practitioner research, working with networks of teachers developing their classroom evaluations. He has also been involved with the development of Education Studies as a subject in HE and in reviewing the Education Studies Subject Benchmarks for QAA, and has been chair of the British Education Studies Association.

Diana Burton is Professor of Education and Pro-Vice Chancellor at Liverpool John Moores University. Her research interests centre on applications of education psychology to the professional contexts of pupil learning and teacher education. She is a fellow of the Royal Society for the Arts, and a member of the British Education Research Association, the Higher Education Academy, and the Universities Council for the Education of Teachers' management forum.

Mano Candappa is a Senior Research Officer at the Institute of Education, University of London, UK. Her research focuses on childhoods, migration and education, and she has conducted extensive research on social policy and the experiences of refugees and asylum-seeking families. Recent publications include *Education, Asylum and the 'Non-Citizen' Child: the politics of compassion and belonging* (2010, co-authored).

Chris Derrington is an independent consultant who previously held positions as a Traveller education service manager, a head teacher and a Senior Lecturer in Inclusive Education. Over the past 15 years, she has undertaken research studies for the Department for Children, Schools and Families, the Training and Development Agency, and the National Foundation for Educational Research, and has published widely in the field of Traveller education.

Neil Duncan's research field is bullying and gender identity in high schools, and is unique in that it falls outside the traditional theoretical camps of sexual harassment and educational psychology. His work has attracted international interest from Finland, Australia and the USA. Neil has been a contributor to TV programmes in Australia and the UK, appearing and advising on homophobic bullying.

Roger Moltzen is Professor of Education at the University of Waikato, New Zealand. He is a former teacher and principal with a particular interest in inclusive, and gifted and talented education. His most recent research investigated the life stories of eminent adults. In 2005 he was awarded the New Zealand Prime Minister's Supreme Award for Tertiary Teaching Excellence.

Michele Moore works on the global agenda for inclusive education in association with the Institute of Education, University of London and the University of Nizwa in Oman. She is Editor of the leading international journal *Disability & Society* and a member of the Editorial Team of the journal *Community Work & Family*.

Alison Patterson has taught in primary schools, where she was also a SENCO, and for two years within a special school. She currently works for Nottinghamshire County Council as a Specialist Teacher for the Early Years Inclusion Support Service, and is also employed as a visiting lecturer at Nottingham Trent University.

Gill Richards works at Nottingham Trent University in the School of Education as Director of Professional Development, having previously worked in schools and further education colleges. She is involved with a range of projects for student teachers, NQTs and SENCOs on inclusive practice, and her research interests focus on 'learner voice' and inclusive education.

Raphael Richards is Head of Sheffield's Ethnic Minority and Traveller Achievement Service. His work involves supporting schools, young people and local communities to work together to raise minority ethnic pupils' attainment and promote community cohesion. He has extensive experience in developing and managing mentoring programmes in education, social justice and business settings.

Richard Rieser has been a teacher and advisory teacher for 30 years in inner-city Hackney. He was founder and director of Disability Equality in Education for 17 years, and represented the UK Disabled Peoples' Movement in the negotiations towards the UN Convention on the Rights of Persons with Disabilities. Richard is an internationally renowned advocate of inclusive education.

Jackie Scruton has always worked with learners for whom the term inclusion is relevant. This has been in a number of educational settings, including nurseries, special schools and further education colleges. She is currently a senior lecturer at Nottingham Trent University in the School of Education, working across a range of programmes helping students to explore the concepts of inclusion and diversity. She is also a specialist member of the Special Educational Needs and Disability Tribunal (SENDIST) and a regional tutor for Makaton. Her interests lie in the fields of inclusion, diversity, equality and, particularly, communication.

Marjorie Smith has taught throughout the age range and also in special and higher education settings. She is an educational psychologist and has worked in teacher education as well as contributing to research on gender and learning, and gender and special education needs. Her long term research interests embrace human rights in education and inclusive practice. More recently, she has taken up a specific interest in young people with issues around their gender identity or sexual orientation, and campaigns for an education system that acknowledges their needs and their rights.

Foreword

Teaching and Learning in Diverse and Inclusive Classrooms is a twenty-first-century book about inclusion, and Gill Richards and Felicity Armstrong are to be congratulated for it. If you look at many books about inclusion from the 1990s, or about 'integration', which was the concern of policy makers and commentators 20 years ago, you will find something very different from this book. You will find discussion of 'special educational needs' that occludes an understanding of where children and young people lie in relation to the education system: there is almost a disembodiment of the child. The resolute emphasis on 'special educational needs' somehow depersonalises the child.

By particularising the difficulties that children experience at school, Richards and Armstrong reintroduce the person to the scene. With an unusually well written collection of contributions, they create a tableau of characters whom educators have difficulty dealing with, and in doing so they effectively combine the theoretical with the practical – always a difficult task. They offer not only understanding, but guidance on learning and teaching for these young people.

I very much like the idea – running right through the book – of focusing on communities of learners. This is a thoroughly contemporary approach to learning: it is about the ways in which people identify with learning and with what goes on in schools. We all learn every minute of the day, but if our identity is not as a member of a community that shares the aspirations and the motivations of others, then we fail to share the cultural richness of the wider community of which we are part. This is surely what school is all about. By looking at areas such as ethnicity, gender and sexuality, and at Gypsy, Roma and Traveller children, the book's contributors show how alienation happens and point to ways in which participation is possible. In doing this they show how 'diversity' can be more than simply a buzzword. They also implicitly deconstruct 'special educational needs'.

This focus on communities of learning is combined very nicely with a review of important national initiatives and developments for promoting inclusion and diversity, and these help the reader to understand what can be done and where to go in seeking help.

I am really pleased to see the publication of this book. It marks a turning point in the way that we think about inclusion, participation and diversity.

Gary Thomas
Professor of Inclusion and Diversity
School of Education, University of Birmingham

Acknowledgements

We would like to thank Alison Foyle, Senior Commissioning Editor (Education) and Claire Westwood (Editorial Assistant), and the team at Routledge, for their encouragement and invaluable support in the production of this book. We would also like to thank Claire Smith, Subject Co-ordinator in the School of Education at Nottingham Trent University, for vital support, again, with the administrative work associated with the final stages of this book.

Introduction

Felicity Armstrong and Gill Richards

This book is dedicated to all those starting out on a teaching career in challenging times – and we also hope it will be useful and interesting to experienced teachers. Our focus is on inclusive education, and the particular interpretations and challenges relating to this concept from a number of different perspectives. For us, inclusive education has multiple meanings and reaches into all aspects of education, but it is based on some fundamental principles, as outlined by Tony Booth:

> We see inclusion as concerned with reducing all exclusionary pressures in education and society, thus providing a dynamic relationship between the two concepts. We view inclusion in education as concerned with *increasing participation in, and reducing exclusion from, the learning opportunities, cultures and communities of the mainstream.* Inclusion is a never-ending process, working towards an ideal when all exclusionary pressures within education and society are removed.
>
> (Booth 2003: 2)

This approach, far from being utopian, recognizes that social and cultural change requires both ideals through which to frame it, and an understanding of the breadth, depth and complexity of social relationships and policy making in education. Working towards inclusive education requires a continuous commitment to critical examination of our own values, assumptions and practices, as well as of those of others in the wider context of school and society. It also requires an understanding of the many ways in which children and young people can experience exclusion and discrimination in education. This book aims to explore some of these, and to suggest ways in which teachers and schools can try to prevent barriers to participation from occurring. For us, understanding must include, where possible, listening to the voices of 'insiders' who have direct experience of questions relating to the issues under discussion. We have tried to ensure that the voices of insiders are reflected in some of the contributions that make up this book.

Some chapters focus specifically on groups – such as Gypsy, Roma and Traveller children, or asylum-seeking and refugee children. Others focus on broader areas such as bullying, working with parents behaviour, and teachers and teaching assistants working together for inclusion. You will also find chapters that raise fundamental issues for inclusive education, such as human rights, and the relationships between families, communities and schools. One purpose of this book is to explore questions of diversity and inclusion in relation to teaching and communities of learners, rather than focusing on a particular group of learners. Our concern has been to provide a collection of chapters that challenge the dominant notion that inclusive education is primarily the domain of 'special educational needs'. On the contrary – inclusive education is concerned with all school members, regardless of difference, and with the wider communities of which schools are a part. Difficulties in learning and barriers to participation can arise for many different reasons, but the primary cause is the failure of societies and of education systems to respond in positive ways to diversity – not failures or deficits on the part of individual learners. In order to begin to understand the barriers to participation, we cannot underestimate the importance of *listening* to the voices of those who are primarily affected and excluded by those barriers, and we need to think about what meaningful listening involves.

Tony Booth argues that:

> The identification of inclusion with an aspect of student identity such as impairment or ethnicity is self-defeating since students are whole people, with multiple, complex identities. When it is associated with a devaluing label such as 'a child *with special educational needs*' it involves a particular contradiction. The inclusion in education of a child categorized as '*having special educational needs*' involves their de-categorization. Inclusion has to be connected to the recognition to all aspects of diversity.
>
> (Booth 2003: 2)

We agree with this position and also recognize that some groups in society experience very particular kinds of discrimination and marginalization, which need to be understood and addressed. So inclusive education concerns everybody in and around school communities. Within these communities, there are some children and young people whose identification with a particular group, their appearance, situation or lifestyle, their prior experiences and aspirations, may be misunderstood or constructed by others in particular ways that may be negative and may lead to the creation of barriers to their full participation and sense of wellbeing and belonging. We believe that teachers need to understand, as far as possible, the perspectives and experiences of all learners as individuals and as members of their communities, and we hope this book will prove to be a valuable contribution in developing this understanding.

The chapters in this book represent different interpretations of inclusion and different understandings of the underlying barriers to participation and approaches to overcoming these. These interpretations reflect our individual perspectives as editors and those of the individual authors, and mirror some of the differences, and even contradictions, that are evident in recent policies and practices. We are united, however, in wanting to explore and understand the conditions and processes that contribute to inequalities and marginalization in the classroom as they affect individuals, groups and school communities. This is not a book that seeks to present a 'unified view' on issues, but it represents the diversity of values, preoccupations and experiences that we, as a group of contributors, bring to our writing. We have not used our editorial powers to smooth over differences and impose our own voices on contributions. Nevertheless, during the process of editing this book, the question of the use of labels and their effects has arisen frequently. This has led us to an increased awareness of the embeddedness of labels and how they have become a kind of globalizing shorthand in many sectors, which lumps groups of children together on the basis of a defining characteristic as perceived by powerful others. We have had many discussions about this between ourselves as editors, and with individual contributors by email, and questions and new insights have emerged about the language we use to describe others, and about why some ways of talking about others have more negative connotations than others.

Contributors were invited to review some important debates, research studies and recent initiatives relating to their area, with a focus on developing new teachers' understanding of issues, classroom practice, and considerations for teaching and learning. Each chapter concludes with two or three questions for teachers to reflect upon and a short list of additional resources for further study. We seek to move beyond broad discussions of 'diversity' and inclusive education, to a focus on what these mean for schools and for teachers' practices in the classroom. Diversity and inclusion are not issues that can simply be taught as subjects; they involve reflection on personal values and professional understanding and engagement.

We hope this book will provide a key resource for teacher education and, in particular, provide support for new teachers. In reading it, you may find your own prior assumptions challenged – but this can be a positive and fruitful experience in opening up new insights and possibilities for happier and more equitable relationships in the classroom and in the community.

Structure and content

Teaching and Learning in Diverse and Inclusive Classrooms is made up of 14 chapters, which address different aspects of, and issues relating to, inclusive education diversity, and teaching and learning.

In **Chapter 1**, Felicity Armstrong discusses the meanings and principles of inclusive education, and the ways in which these can be translated into school cultures, teaching and learning. She draws out some of the difficulties and constraints that schools and teachers have to negotiate, and considers some core values that are necessary for the development of inclusive thinking and practices.

In **Chapter 2**, Marjorie Smith explores sexuality and gender identity in relation to children and young people, and their experience of education. Drawing on some examples, she shows how this area of inclusion presents special challenges for schools and teachers, yet it is an area where comparatively small shifts in attitude and practice can bring about extraordinary benefits in the achievements and wellbeing of a significant number of individuals. 'Sexuality' is routinely ignored in debates about inclusive education, and this chapter makes a powerful contribution to addressing this important and invisible subject.

Chapter 3, by Neil Duncan, explores bullying from the perspective that schools are powerful systems that can inadvertently support, or even produce, bullying behaviours. Neil argues that teachers need to move beyond a common but simplistic way of looking at bullying that focuses entirely on children as the problem. The chapter considers some of the implications of this, and suggests ways of reducing the negative impact of schooling on pupils' social relations.

In **Chapter 4**, Chris Derrington introduces questions relating to inclusive education in relation to Gypsy, Roma and Traveller children and young people and their communities. She explains the importance of understanding cultural differences, and explores some of the possible barriers to participation that can arise in schools, particularly in relation to these communities, and ways in which these can be overcome.

Chapter 5, by Steve Bartlett and Diana Burton, covers a brief review of research and past initiatives relating to boys' and girls' aspirations and achievement. It explores a range of current gender-specific initiatives and the impact these can have on pupils. It reflects on current curriculum and social issues that affect participation and achievement, identifying considerations for teachers as they plan for their learners.

Chapter 6, by Raphael Richards, explores the ethnic diversity that exists in classrooms across Britain today. The chapter starts by considering the needs of Black and minority ethnic children and those with English as an additional language, drawing out issues of community and personalization of lessons. Much of 'Not in my image' is about building positive relationships, so readers are called upon to reflect on what they, as individuals, will bring to the classroom. The chapter seeks to help new teachers to enter the classroom ready to be champions for young people from diverse ethnic backgrounds.

Chapter 7, by Mano Candappa, is about asylum-seeking and refugee children and their experiences in British schools. The chapter explains how these students are among the most marginalized in our society, and even among their peers at school. They are often 'invisible' within schools, yet they desperately need the school's support to help them get on with their lives. The challenge for schools is how best to support them whilst not taking agency away from them. The chapter argues that the inclusive school that adapts in order to respond to the diversity of its community is the most supportive environment for asylum-seeking and refugee students.

In **Chapter 8**, Gill Richards considers issues of teaching and learning raised by the increasing inclusion of learners identified as having 'special educational needs' in mainstream classrooms. It reviews the need for such labels in inclusive schools and the impact these have on teachers' expectations and practice. The chapter draws on recent initiatives, reflecting on the impact these have on new teachers, and explores strategies for increasing teachers' confidence.

Chapter 9, by Roger Moltzen, introduces the concept of 'gifted and talented' and discusses how some students who may be categorized in this way are potentially vulnerable and underachieving. It reviews different strategies used by schools to meet their learning needs, in particular exploring how these learners can successfully be included within ordinary classrooms, and how teachers can provide positive, inclusive support.

In **Chapter 10**, Jackie Scruton presents a brief review of research, legislation and policies concerning students who are perceived as 'challenging' within educational settings. She explores barriers that contribute to young people's disenfranchisement, and considers the role of teachers and schools within this. The chapter draws on a range of initiatives currently used in schools to respond to behaviour that is seen to be difficult, using these to suggest ways in which teachers can work positively with learners and other professionals.

In **Chapter 11**, Vikki Anderson briefly traces the historical development of teaching assistants in educational settings, and explores the current range of roles they undertake in schools. She considers the working relationship between teachers and teaching assistants, focusing on recent studies and policy initiatives. In particular, she examines how this key relationship may affect the quality of learners' experiences, identifying implications for teachers' roles.

Chapter 12, by Alison Patterson, briefly explores the range of educational agencies that support teachers in schools, and then focuses on the key roles involved in supporting inclusion. It considers expectations different educational professionals have of each other and how these link to individual responsibilities and affect children's inclusion. The chapter draws on a study of the expectations teachers and support service staff have of each other to make suggestions for working effectively in partnership.

In **Chapter 13**, Michele Moore examines the positioning of parents as allies in the new teacher's project of advancing inclusion. She provides an insider's perspective, exploring how relationships between parents and teachers can be understood from her own point of view as a parent of two children with impairments. She reflects on her experiences as a parent seeking to work closely with teachers who are willing to see parents as allies, but she also writes from the viewpoint of a professional working with teachers on best practice in inclusive education. The approach Michele puts forward in this chapter is, she argues, effective in building positive relationships with parents of all children at risk of, and at risk from, exclusion.

Chapter 14, by Richard Rieser, examines some of the main issues facing teachers in thinking about the values and practices that underpin inclusive education from a global perspective, particularly in relation to disability. However, in adopting a human rights and international perspective, a powerful argument is developed that links all children and young people together as having shared rights to participation in education in inclusive schools. The chapter explores the relationships of the social and medical models of disability with different educational structures and practices, demonstrating that a 'deficit view' of children has serious consequences in terms of the failure to respect children's rights. The argument is put forward that a firm understanding of the issues involved in responding to, and celebrating, difference is essential to the development of effective inclusive teaching.

Reference

Booth, T. (2003) 'Inclusion and exclusion in the city: concepts and contexts', in Potts, P. (ed.) *Inclusion in the City: Selection, Schooling and Community*, London: RoutledgeFalmer.

Chapter 1

Inclusive education

School cultures, teaching and learning

Felicity Armstrong

> To be asked to show that inclusion works is like being asked to show that equality
> works. To promote inclusion involves judgments based on values, and there is no
> reason to be apologetic about this.
>
> (Thomas and Glenny 2002: 366)

Inclusive education is one of the most important, yet elusive, concepts to
emerge in the UK and internationally in recent years.[1] It is an important
concept because, in its full interpretation, it represents a potentially profound
shift away from policies and practices based on selections according to perceptions about ability, which have traditionally sanctioned the exclusion of
many learners from mainstream education. Inclusive education rests on the
belief that all members of the community have the right to participate in, and
have access to, education on an equal basis. However, it is an elusive concept
because it is the subject of many different interpretations, depending on who
is using the term, in what context, and for what purpose.

There is a persistent mismatch, in the UK context, between the apparent
intentions of one set of policies and what actually happens in practice (Dyson
and Gallannaugh 2007). This phenomenon should not be understood in some
crude sense as, for example, a 'gap between policy and practice'. Rather, it
draws attention to the very complex nature of policy making and interpretation,
especially in the light of conflicting national and global policy agendas. Official
policy documents use the term 'inclusion' inconsistently, often linking it
specifically to policies relating to students with 'special educational needs', and
this is how the term is sometimes used in schools. In contrast, for others the
use of the term 'inclusive education' reflects the principle that inclusion concerns everybody – all learners, and all members of the school, college and
wider community. Inclusion is

> ... fundamentally about issues of human rights, equity, social justice and
> the struggle for a non-discriminatory society. These principles are at the
> heart of inclusive policy and practice.
>
> (Armstrong and Barton 2007: 6)

Tony Booth describes participation in the inclusive classroom in the following terms:

> It ... implies learning alongside others and collaborating with them in shared lessons. It involves active engagement with what is learnt and taught and having a say in how education is experienced. But participation also means being recognised for oneself and being accepted for oneself: I participate with you when you recognise me as a person like yourself and accept me for who I am.
>
> (Booth 2003: 2)

These two perspectives complement each other. They are both underpinned by a view of inclusive education as concerning *all* learners – not just one group of students deemed to be 'vulnerable' or as 'having special needs'. Tony Booth emphasizes the importance of recognition as well as participation. Recognition is concerned with ' ... injustices which are understood to be cultural (and) rooted in social patterns of representation, interpretation and communication' (Fraser 1999). Participation is about being a part of, and belonging to, communities, and having equal access and rights with others. Inclusive education demands both – that every child and young person has a right to attend their local school or college (that is, all participate), and that all members of the school and college, and of the wider community, have the right to recognition in terms of who they are, their culture and beliefs, appearance, interests, lifestyle and uniqueness. Inclusion recognizes, and is responsive to, diversity and the right 'to be oneself' in an open, shared and democratic community. Inclusion, therefore, is a rather different concept from integration, which focuses on how individual learners, or a group of learners, might 'fit in' to a school or a class. Inclusive education implies a transformation in the social, cultural, curricular and pedagogic life of the school, as well as its physical organization. Integration has, traditionally, referred to concepts and practices relating to learners labelled as having special educational needs. In the English context, the key difference between the concept of inclusion and the concept of integration is that integration focuses on the perceived deficits in the child as creating barriers to participation, whereas inclusion situates the barriers to participation within the school or college, and within social attitudes, policies and practices.

A major contribution to thinking in this area over the past decade has been made by the work of the Centre for Studies on Inclusive Education and through the *Index for Inclusion* (Booth and Ainscow 2002). The *Index for Inclusion* provides materials that support schools in critically examining their policies and practices, and guides them through a process of development towards inclusive education. It is 'about building supportive communities and fostering achievement for all staff and students' (*ibid.*). The *Index for Inclusion* is not a blueprint or a checklist, but is an invitation to schools to engage with where they are now, and to move forward in a process of positive change. The *Index* describes the processes involved as follows.

- Valuing all students and staff equally.
- Increasing the participation of students in, and reducing their exclusion from, the cultures, curricula and communities of local schools.
- Restructuring the cultures, policies and practices in schools so that they respond to the diversity of students in the locality.
- Reducing barriers to learning and participation for all students, not only those with impairments or those who are categorized as 'having special educational needs'.
- Learning from attempts to overcome barriers to the access and participation of particular students to make changes for the benefit of students more widely.
- Viewing the difference between students as resources to support learning, rather than as problems to be overcome.
- Acknowledging the right of students to an education in their locality.
- Improving schools for staff as well as for students.
- Emphasizing the role of schools in building community and developing values, as well as in increasing achievement.
- Fostering mutually sustaining relationships between schools and communities.
- Recognizing that inclusion in education is one aspect of inclusion in society.

(Booth and Ainscow 2002)

The importance of transforming school cultures lies at the heart of these processes. In the context of discussions about inclusive education, the notion of school culture refers to the principles and practices that inform relationships, curricula, pedagogy and the organization of schools and their connections with, and recognition of, the communities they serve.

Inclusive practices and values

When thinking about particular contexts, such as policy making and inter-pretation in a local authority or school, there are some key questions which we need to ask in relation to the development of inclusive education.

- How and where are policies made in relation to teaching and learning, by whom, and with what outcomes?
- Is inclusion understood as an 'outsider coming in', or is it seen as involving a transformation of school and institutional cultures so that all comers are accepted on a basis of equality?
- How can we identify and challenge the embedded cultural structures and practices that sustain exclusion and bring about change in the social and cultural relations of schooling?

In this chapter, the principles and practices of inclusive education are approached from the perspective of school cultures and the notion of 'inclusive pedagogy'. One of the most deeply embedded expressions of school culture is the way in which teaching and learning are understood. We need therefore to think about the values and processes involved in pedagogy, and to measure these against the principles of inclusion. This involves asking the questions: to what extent do teaching practices and the curriculum exclude, marginalize or demean any groups of learners or individuals; and to what extent do they recognize and draw on students' own rich 'funds of knowledge' (Andrews and Yee 2006) and experience?

Here it is helpful to think about the meaning of 'pedagogy'. As Jenny Corbett has pointed out (Corbett 2001), pedagogy is often used to refer to how teachers transmit a curriculum to learners. It can also refer to the particular teaching strategies they adopt in response to different contexts and learning styles. In contrast, inclusive pedagogy involves the following:

- a recognition of individual differences;
- a valuing of cultural diversity;
- a conscious and visible commitment to fostering and promoting inclusive values in all aspects of the life of the school, as well as in the classroom;
- a recognition and celebration of what the local community has to offer in terms of supporting education and inclusion.

Of course, all the above are open to interpretation. Terminology such as 'inclusion', 'participation' and 'citizenship' can be used in very diverse and often contradictory ways, and for different purposes. It reflects contextual variations and concerns – cultural, geographical, economic and autobiographical. It is the values that are at work and that underpin these variations which are important. This involves, therefore, trying to define what we mean by 'inclusive values', and any definition must be framed in cultural terms.

Inclusive values will take on different meanings in a monocultural, bicultural or a multicultural setting – although even these descriptors are too simplistic to encompass the complexities and heterogeneities that make up any 'community'. Similarly, the concept of inclusion will have particular meanings in contexts such as nurseries, special schools, young offenders' institutions, inner-city schools, fee-paying private schools, and rural community colleges. To suggest that inclusion only has meaning in the context of ordinary schools, which welcome all members of the community regardless of difference, is, in the present social and political context, to marginalize other settings in which some teachers, support staff, children and young people may find themselves. The implication of this would be to exclude some of the most marginalized groups in society from the wider struggle for inclusion which, by definition, has to encompass all members of society, regardless of the particular setting they attend, or to which they are assigned.

When carrying out research or a critical analysis of a school, researchers and practitioners who focus first on issues relating to processes of inclusion and exclusion in schools will try to understand the social and cultural nature of the school, and to explore how this is translated into classroom practice. We could describe this as starting at the macro level and moving to the micro level, to see how broad contours and features translate into rich details – rather like using the *Google Earth* navigation engine. At the micro level, there is a need to examine critically how the values that are apparently espoused at the macro level are translated and communicated at the level of the classroom, and their impacts on the relationships and opportunities available to individual learners. We also need to ask questions that explore inclusive values from a number of different vantage points. The following section presents examples of two schools, based on research in an inner city, in which an apparent commitment to inclusive education and equal opportunities is confronted by a number of contradictory values and practices. These two small studies illustrate how pressures and constraints at work at the macro level outside the school can work their way through to different levels of school life.

Acorn Community School

Acorn School is a large comprehensive school, which prides itself on being an inclusive community school with an 'open door' policy for 'all'. It is situated on a large, economically deprived housing estate on the edge of an industrial city. The buildings are accessible to disabled people. In response to being put under 'special measures' following an Ofsted (Office for Standards in Education) inspection, the school has introduced a finely graded system of setting across subjects, based on selection according to attainment, in an attempt to 'raise standards'. There is an active policy of 'including' students who are seen as having behaviour problems in their attainment group and ensuring that the lowest sets don't become receptacles for those who disturb lessons. Examination results are improving in the A–C band. A group of 11- and 12-year-olds spoke about their learning. Some in the group complained that only the 'top' sets in Science 'got to do experiments'; if you were in a lower set, you watched the teacher carry out the experiment or copied notes and diagrams from the board (surely a more abstract and therefore more demanding mode of learning than the hands-on approach, for children of this age). One child who was in a top set commented: 'I like Science practical. You work in a group and it's fun and you want to do it. Anything that's not fun, you don't learn because it's boring.' In the same school, it emerged that students in the top sets in their final GCSE year were given course texts so they could study at home; these were not provided for students in lower sets. Are these practices inclusive, and what are the reasons underlying disparities and inequalities that may have an impact on students' learning?

I raised some of these questions with a member of the senior management team, who explained that if children were allowed to do practical experiments in Science, they had to be 'highly responsible' and 'careful' or 'valuable materials could be wasted or damaged'. A similar explanation was put forward for the policy on provision of course texts for home study: these are expensive and there was 'always a risk of books getting lost or damaged at home', but, he added, perhaps in the future more students would be able to take books home. Embedded in these arguments are a number of factors that need to be critically examined, including the possible effects of under-resourcing, and pressure to increase the numbers of A–C grades at GCSE, on approaches to teaching and learning and the strategic rationing of resources. But are these constraints ever a justification for abandoning principles of fairness and equity? A further element in the justifications provided for the unequal distribution of resources in Acorn School is attitudinal; there is an implicit assumption that students who are not in top sets will be less careful with equipment, or even that their homes are more likely to be conducive to losing or damaging books. This raises questions about how students' identities are formed on the basis of assumptions made about their home life linked to their academic performance.

These examples may be fairly typical of the kinds of contradictory attitudes and practices that occur routinely in schools in which policies at the macro level, which are apparently inclusive in terms of stated policies on equality issues, are contradicted at the less-visible micro levels of teaching and learning and the provision of learning resources. These contradictions raise difficult and uncomfortable questions, but the purpose of raising them is not to vilify schools, which are often struggling to develop more equitable policies and practices within an increasingly competitive and unforgiving system. On the contrary, it is to shed light on some difficult issues that arise as a result of the profound social inequalities and conflicting values that work their way through schools and communities.

Sharrow School, Sheffield

In England, schools that claim, and demonstrate, a serious commitment to inclusion and equality, and do not operate formal or informal selection policies, are often to be found in the least economically advantaged areas, and they tend to perform poorly in national tests in comparison with schools in wealthier areas. Inclusive schools such as Sharrow Primary School in Sheffield (Abram *et al.* 2009) have an 'open-door' policy, and welcome all members of the community regardless of disability or level of attainment. Its population includes children 'in transition', who are refugees, seeking asylum, or living in temporary accommodation, and reflects the diversity of the area, with only 8% of children in the school who speak English as a first language. The increase in cultural and linguistic diversity, especially in towns and cities, is one of many outcomes of globalization which are transforming many schools and colleges in the UK.

Sharrow School is fully accessible, and there is a serious engagement with transforming curricula and pedagogical practices so that every child receives a meaningful education. Scores in national tests are low and, although Ofsted has praised the school for its inclusive response to diversity and its close links with the local community, this praise is overridden by criticism of the school's performance in national tests, which are regarded in public reports as the only 'real' indicators of 'achievement'.

The new school building, which the school moved into in September 2007, leaving behind its original, inaccessible Victorian building, was designed in consultation between the architects, school and community members, including pupils, who visited other schools and contributed ideas. It is entirely accessible to disabled children and adults, both from the outside and internally, with a central lift area and careful gradations between levels making ramps unnecessary.

The school places much emphasis on equal opportunities policies, including anti-racism policies, and runs regular pupil-led campaigns on, for example, bullying and healthy eating, which all members of the school community are involved in. There is a school council run by elected representatives from each class, which meets regularly and reports back to its constituents. A current campaign being run by the council concerns complaints about the quality of school dinners, which are provided by a private company, and children have organized protests against the poor quality of the food and small portions. The practices of inclusion and equity are embedded in the daily life of the school. For example, there is a system of 'playground friends' to ensure children are not left out or victimized in the playground or in other aspects of school life.

Disabled children are welcomed into the school as a matter of course, and there are policies and practices in place to ensure all children are able to participate fully in learning and in every aspect of the life of the school. These include developing supportive collaborative learning practices between groups of children. There is a teacher with special responsibility for inclusion in the school, although it is clear that all members of the school are collectively and individually 'responsible' for inclusion.

In a sense, schools such as Sharrow Primary School function at the periphery of the main system, often developing creative responses to diversity in their local communities which, while enhancing opportunities for participation and the creation of equitable school cultures, come into conflict with the demands of the national curriculum and assessment. Research studies have shown how pressures to improve scores on national tests have distorted the work of schools, especially those seeking to promote inclusive policies and practices (Florian and Rouse 2005; Ainscow et al. 2006). This is, perhaps, an important indication of the ways in which schools themselves are left to develop strategies in response to government policies that are potentially contradictory – some of which appear to support 'inclusion' while others are driven by a more powerful agenda – that of performance in the global arena.

Inclusive pedagogy and learning theory

Let us turn now to the life of the classroom. Are there any theories of learning, or ideas relating to education in general, that we can draw on to help us develop understanding about our own teaching practices and attitudes? You may have some ideas about this question based on your own prior learning and experience. A possible theoretical framework that may be helpful in thinking about inclusive pedagogy is that of social constructivism. This approach is often presented as a theory of learning that is in opposition to theories based on a transmission approach, in which the teacher possesses – or 'owns' – the knowledge, and their task is to transmit some of this knowledge to the learner. This may be reinforced by systems of rewards and disincentives (or punishments). Many teachers and commentators observe that the transmission approach is being reinvented, with a greater emphasis on the production of planned and measurable outcomes expressed in the form of examination grades. Since the 1980s, there has been a return to approaches to teaching and learning that focus primarily on content and measurable outcomes rather than process. In contrast, in constructivist teaching, the learner is regarded as

> A self-activated maker of meaning, an active agent in his [sic] own learning process. He is not one to whom things merely happen; he is the one who, by his own volition, causes things to happen. Learning is seen as the result of his own self-initiated interaction with the world: the learner's understanding grows during a constant interplay between something outside himself – the general environment, a pendulum, a person – and something inside himself, his concept-forming mechanisms ...
>
> (Candy 1989: 107)

The Russian psychologist Vygotsky developed a version of social constructivism as a model of learning in which the existing knowledge, experience and context was of prime importance. Learning was understood as a process of constructing new insights and concepts through interaction with the environment and intervention of the 'teacher', who could be a more experienced person, a sibling or playmate (although in Vygotsky's examples the assumption seems to be that the teacher will usually be an adult). The 'expertise' of the teacher is actively engaged with the learner's own knowledge, experience and thought processes and existing level of competence or 'zone of proximal development' (Vygotsky 1962, cited in Wood 2003). Instructional support, or 'scaffolding', is provided by the teacher to help the learner move on to a different level or kind of understanding (Bruner 1979; Wood 2003).

Thus, constructivism in education is concerned with two things: how learners *construe* (or interpret) events and ideas, and how they *construct* (build or assemble) structures of meaning. The constant dialectical interplay between construing and constructing is at the heart of a constructivist approach to education ...

(Candy 1989: 108)

This theoretical framework has a number of possible implications and opportunities for developing an inclusive pedagogy – or, rather, inclusive pedagogies, since there is no suggestion that one model or approach – however flexible and learner-centred – will necessarily fit all circumstances. Indeed, no theory should be taken as providing a blueprint for teaching and learning. Social constructivism does, however, provide a possible theoretical framework within which the potentially awkward mismatch between the knowledge, experience and expectations of the teacher and those of the learner may be resolved.

While some of Vygotsky's ideas may seem to us rather formulaic and counter-intuitive in terms of the assumptions made about how much teachers can fully understand the learner's 'internal course of development', his work opens up some important principles for exploration and interpretation. Theories can be seen as getting in the way of innovative transformation of practice if we let them work as straightjackets on our thinking, but they can also be used as catalysts for creativity if we are prepared to interpret them imaginatively so that they are sensitive and relevant to particular contexts and issues. A number of researchers and teachers have developed Vygotsky's ideas. Bruner, for example, insists on the importance of understanding the cultural influences involved in the process of learning:

Begin with the concept of culture itself – particularly its constitutive role. What was obvious from the start was perhaps too obvious to be appreciated, at least by us psychologists who by habit and by tradition think in rather individualistic terms. The symbolic systems that individuals used in constructing meaning were systems that were already in place, already 'there', deeply entrenched in culture and language. They constituted a very special kind of communal tool kit whose tools, once used, made the user a reflection of the community.

(Bruner 1990, in Pollard 2002)

The approaches suggested by this framework can be extended and reinterpreted to encompass peers working together in groups in a process of collaborative co-construction of learning, creating active and vibrant communities of learners in the classroom.

If we put together some of these ideas, the process of teaching and learning involves understanding, and giving recognition to, both the uniqueness of the individual, their history and existing knowledge, and the collective cultural knowledge and practices of the learner's social context. A learner, then, is an individual in a social world. Communities of learners are made up of individual learners who exchange knowledge and experiences, collaborate and hypothesize, argue, build and create, to develop understanding and knowledge.

This might seem too obvious to mention, yet if we consider these arguments in the light of recent top-down approaches to teaching, learning and assessment, in which knowledge is defined as a particular kind of curriculum, and learning is measured in terms of particular outcomes and behaviours, the conflicts and apparent failure of the education system to provide equal opportunities for individual and collective development at the community level are, at least partially, explained.

Building on, summarizing and interpreting some of the ideas we have touched on, there are a number of positive implications for developing inclusive approaches to teaching and learning that we might consider.

- Learners are all individuals with their own unique history and experience.
- Learners bring with them to the learning process particular kinds of socially and culturally constructed knowledge, which will interact with the curriculum and teaching practices of the school (learners are not blank slates or empty vessels).
- This knowledge gives us the capacity to transform, reinterpret or expand on what is being taught.
- Learning is a two-way or collaborative process, in which the 'teacher' seeks to understand and take into account prior learning, preferred learning style, and social context.
- Collaborative exploration in the classroom, in which students share knowledge as a means of problem solving and hypothesizing, is a form of 'scaffolding'.
- 'Pedagogy' cannot be separated from 'curriculum' in that approaches to teaching and learning reflect what is recognized and valued as 'knowledge'.
- Inclusive pedagogy rests on recognition of the uniqueness of every student and the importance of social and cultural factors in influencing responses to curriculum and pedagogy.

Conclusion

In this chapter I have introduced some issues and questions for consideration within a wider set of concerns relating to the nature and culture of schools and teaching generally, rather than in terms of some 'special' conditions and qualities.

In seeking to gain a more informed understanding of such factors, and, importantly, their interrelationship, we support the use of a framework in which a critical engagement can take place in terms of what we say we do and what we actually do as practitioners, and the tensions and dilemmas this raises in relation to specific encounters in schools and classrooms or other institutional contexts. Arenas such as schools, colleges and universities reflect the wider social conditions and relations, including inequalities, of the society in which they are placed in overt, subtle, complex and often contradictory ways. Schools are involved in important political and social functions involving the inculcation of particular values and the encouragement of specific forms of thinking and behaving. How schools and teachers engage with the contradictory pressures from external forces, including governments, is a crucial question for inclusive education. An essential aspect of inclusive thinking and the desire for developing inclusive practice is the necessity of raising critical questions such as those listed below.

Reflection on values and practice

Think about the context in which you work, or a context with which you are familiar, and ask yourself the following questions.

- What is the local authority's policy in terms of actively promoting inclusion?
- Does the school or college on which you are focusing have active policies on equal opportunities that challenge racism, sexism, heteronormativity, bullying and discriminatory practices of all kinds, and what action does the school take when these policies are disregarded by pupils or staff?
- What is the relationship between the school and the wider community, including minority groups?
- Are there disabled students at the school/college, and are they a full part of the community, sharing lessons and activities with their peers?
- Does the school welcome children and young people seeking asylum?
- How is learning facilitated for students who do not speak English well?

Note

1 There is a full discussion of the emergence of inclusive education as a global movement, and related policies, in Chapter 14: 'Disability, human rights and inclusive education, and why inclusive education is the only educational philosophy and practice that makes sense in today's world'.

Resources

Alliance for Inclusive Education (ALLFIE): www.allfie.org.uk
Centre for Studies on Inclusive Education (CSIE): www.csie.org.uk
Enabling Education Network (EENET): www.eenet.org.uk
Booth, T., Nes, K. and Strømstad, M. (eds) (2003) *Developing Inclusive Teacher Education*, London: RoutledgeFalmer.

References

Abram, E., Armstrong, F., Barton, L. and Ley, L. (2009) 'Diversity, democracy and change in the inner city: understanding schools as belonging to communities', in Lavia, J. and Moore, M. (eds) *Decolonizing Community Contexts: Cross-cultural Perspectives on Policy and Practice*, London: Routledge.

Ainscow, M., Booth, T. and Dyson, A. (2006) *Improving Schools, Developing Inclusion*, London: Routledge.

Andrews, J. and Yee, Wan Ching (2006) 'Children's "funds of knowledge" and their real life activities: two minority ethnic children learning in out-of-school contexts in the UK', *Educational Review*, 58(4): 435–49.

Armstrong, F. and Barton, L. (2007) 'Policy, experience and change and the challenge of inclusive education the case of England', in Barton, L. and Armstrong, F. (eds) *Policy, Experience and Change: Cross-cultural Reflections on Inclusive Education*, London: Springer.

Booth, T. (2003) 'Inclusion and exclusion in the city: concepts and contexts', in Potts, P. (ed.) *Inclusion in the City: Selection, Schooling and Community*, London: Routledge.

Booth, T. and Ainscow, M. (2002) *Index for Inclusion: Developing Learning and Participation in Schools*, Bristol: Centre for Studies on Inclusive Education. www.csie.org.uk/publications/inclusion-index-explained.shtml

Bruner, J. (1979) '*On Knowing, Essays for the Left Hand*', London: Belknap Press of Harvard University.

Candy, P. (1989) 'Constructivism and the study of self-direction in adult learning', *Studies in the Education of Adults*, 21(2): 95–116.

Corbett, J. (2001) '*Supporting Inclusive Education: A Connective Pedagogy*', London: Routledge-Falmer.

Dyson, A. and Gallannaugh, F. (2007) 'National policy and the development of school practices: a case study', *Cambridge Journal of Education*, 37(4): 473–88.

Florian, L. and Rouse, M. (2005) 'Inclusive practice in English secondary schools: lessons learned', in Nind, M., Rix, J., Sheehy, K. and Simmons, K. (eds) *Curriculum and Pedagogy in Inclusive Education: Values into Practice*, London: RoutledgeFalmer.

Fraser, N. (1999) 'Social justice in the age of identity politics: redistribution, recognition and participation', in Ray, L.J. and Sayer, R.A. (eds) *Culture and Economy after the Cultural Turn*, London: Sage.

Pollard, A. (2002) *Readings for Reflective Teaching*, London: Continuum.

Thomas, G. and Glenny, G. (2002) 'Thinking about inclusion. Whose reason? What evidence?', *International Journal of Inclusive Education*, 6(4): 345–69.

Vygotsky, L.S. (1962) *Thought and Language*, Cambridge, MA: Harvard University Press.

Wood, D. (2003) '*How Children Think and Learn: The Social Contexts of Cognitive Development*', Oxford: Blackwell.

Chapter 2

Half a million unseen, half a million unheard

Inclusion for gender identity and sexual orientation

Marjorie Smith

Who matters?

The 'Every Child Matters' agenda (DfES 2003) set out to ensure that young people should be 'safe and healthy' and that they should 'enjoy and achieve', but the experience of some falls far short of this ideal. They are children and young people with gender identity and sexuality issues, most of whom will eventually come out as lesbian, gay, bisexual or transgender[1] (LGBT). There are about half a million of these young people in our schools, two or three in every class of 30.[2]

Compared with others, these young people are more likely to:

- self-harm, consider or attempt suicide, become involved in substance abuse, experience mental health problems such as anxiety or depression (Rivers 2000; DH 2007)
- experience domestic abuse from either parent or even siblings (Yip 2004; Wilson and Rahman 2005)
- experience homelessness
- have been bullied at school (Rivers 1995; Stonewall 2006)
- take time off school (Rivers 2000)
- choose to leave full-time education at 16, despite having the qualifications to stay on (Rivers 2000).

This list is a terrible indictment. Until we do more to nurture the wellbeing of these young people, they will continue to pay for our society's shortcomings with their happiness, their health and their lives.

Section 28 of the Local Government Act 1988 cast a long shadow of ignorance and misinformation. It stated that local authorities should not:

> ... intentionally promote homosexuality ... or ... promote the teaching ... of the acceptability of homosexuality as a pretended family relationship.

Douglas *et al.* (1997), ten years on from the introduction of Section 28, reported confusion as to what was permissible in schools, and found examples where work on homophobic bullying had been removed from the curriculum. Despite the efforts of some, parts of our education system remain 'eerily unresponsive' to the needs of LGBT young people (DePalma and Jennett, 2007: 22).

Recent work on reducing homophobic bullying in schools (DCSF 2008) aims to make schools safer places, but a focus on eliminating hostile reactions can result in a culture of 'silent tolerance' rather than acceptance (Epstein 1994; Epstein *et al.* 2003; DePalma and Jennett 2007; DePalma and Atkinson 2009: 3). Inclusion, based on human rights, offers an alternative perspective and seeks to ensure that all young people feel a sense of belonging in their educational settings. This involves challenging the way in which society and its schools construct gender and sexuality. Schools and classrooms are not gender-neutral places. Stereotypical gender norms ensure that only certain expressions of gender are acceptable, and gender-atypical behaviour is noticed and regulated. Including those young people whose gender expression is unusual means challenging gender norms and providing educational spaces where all children feel comfortable. The view of human relationships presented in our classrooms is almost exclusively heterosexual (Epstein *et al.* 2003). Where heterosexuality is presented as the only acceptable model of human sexuality, this is called 'heteronormativity'. Epstein (1994) describes hetero-normativity as exclusionary because same-sex relationships are ignored or constructed as deviant. Inclusion, in contrast, acknowledges the reality of sexual diversity and teaches that non-heterosexual relationships have the same legitimacy as heterosexual ones. An inclusive approach also recognizes the educational and social needs of LGBT people and their families.

Introducing ...

Many of the 'half a million' will remain hidden and silent throughout their school careers, but some will be noticed. These are young people I have encountered through my work, and their experiences raise issues for teachers to consider.

Aysha

Aysha is 16. She became withdrawn in school and started to avoid eating lunch. A teacher, concerned that Aysha might be anorexic, talked to her. Aysha eventually admitted that she thought she was a lesbian but she was frightened of telling anyone. The school helped her to come out to her parents, who were very supportive.

It is common for young people to be fearful of coming out to their family. Many also react badly to the realization of their sexuality. This troubled young woman found a way to harm herself, but there are many ways in which young people express their distress, including withdrawal, anger and acting-out behaviour.

Question: The school played a significant part in helping to resolve the problem, but what could it have done to support the developing sexuality of its LGBT students in years 7–11?

Ben

Ben is 12. He has a wide range of interests, including classical music and ballet. At primary school he was often on his own at playtimes because he did not like football. When he started at secondary school and it became known that he did ballet, he experienced some gay name-calling. He was followed home by other boys and on one occasion was knocked to the ground.

Ben is vulnerable in a number of ways. He has unusual interests, which leads others to make assumptions about his sexuality. He is also more prone to bullying because he is quite solitary (Crowley *et al.* 2001).

Question: What could the primary school have done to support Ben at break times? What could the secondary school do to help Ben in forming positive relationships with other students?

Charlie

Charlie is four. He is a popular little boy who loves drawing and make-believe play. He plays exclusively with girls and ignores boys completely. When he arrives at nursery, he goes straight to the dressing-up rail, puts on his favourite pink bridesmaid's dress, and wears it all day. This behaviour has persisted throughout four terms in nursery, and is accepted both by nursery staff and by Charlie's parents.

There is absolutely nothing wrong with Charlie. He is happy, sociable and in a context where he is completely accepted. Given the persistence of his behaviour, he could be said to be displaying gender identity issues, which are a normal part of human diversity. Nevertheless, life could be hard for Charlie in contexts that are not as inclusive as his nursery.

Question: The nursery supports Charlie's behaviour. What do you think this means in terms of everyday actions? What might the nursery do to ease Charlie's transition into school?

Danielle

Danielle is 10. She dresses like a boy, and all her friends are boys. She is very competitive with them, wanting to be better at the things that boys do than all her friends. Danielle is causing problems in her class. She has a strong personality and is the ringleader of some gay name-calling.

Like Charlie, Danielle also has gender identity issues. In her bullying of gentle, quiet boys, she is drawing attention to her own masculinity.

Question: What could Danielle's class teacher do in this situation? Who could she turn to for help and ideas?

Elliott

Elliott is 13. He stopped attending his dance and drama group without explanation. Eventually he told a learning support assistant at school that his father made him stop because it was 'gay'. Elliott also disclosed that his father has hurt him and that he is frightened of him. As a result, Social Services became involved.

Most parents are supportive of their child's sexuality, but some (both mothers and fathers) find it hard to accept gender-atypical behaviour or homosexuality. LGBT and gender-atypical young people are likely to need close monitoring, and schools need to be alert to possible abuse at home as well as in school.

Question: How can school staff (including non-teaching staff) be supported in carrying out their responsibilities towards this vulnerable group of young people?

Finn

Finn is 16 and was assigned female at birth. At the age of 15 he told his mother that he did not feel like his assigned birth gender, and instead felt male. He approached his school and asked if he could attend wearing male uniform after his sixteenth birthday, when Finn changed his name by deed poll. The school agreed to the uniform change and he now uses the disabled toilet, which he finds easier, as it is private and also gender neutral. Finn has friends who have stood by him, but he has nevertheless been subjected to name-calling and harassment from other pupils who are ignorant of gender identity issues.

While the number of young people who transition from one gender to another is very small, that number is increasing as parents and young people become more aware of the availability of psychological and medical help.

Question: The school was supportive in agreeing to practical arrangements. How might this school address the issue of other students' behaviour?

Gender identity and sexual orientation

Some children and young people do not conform to gender norms. Even a boy who dislikes football, or a girl who refuses to wear a skirt, may need back-up in a context where only stereotypical expressions of masculinity and femininity are considered acceptable. More significant gender identity issues can be apparent from an early age, or may become more pronounced later on. Charlie's behaviour, where he chooses the 'girliest' dress to almost 'outgirl' the girls, is fairly typical. Gender identity issues may disappear as a child gets older, but they may persist, as with Danielle, or take different forms as time goes on. Some people feel a mismatch between the gender they feel themselves to be and the gender they were assigned at birth. Medical help may be sought where this causes extreme unhappiness. A small number, four times as many boys as girls, will be diagnosed with gender dysphoria (Brill and Pepper 2008). Some will make the decision to transition, which is not necessarily a permanent course of action in younger children.

Gender identity is different from sexual orientation, which refers to sexual attraction. There is an overlap between the two groups, in that some young people with gender identity issues will eventually come out as LGBT (Wilson and Rahman 2005), although this is by no means invariably the case. Some LGBT adults will report having experienced gender identity issues as children, but the majority will not. Despite the overlaps, these are two different groups with some individuals in both. Conflating the two ignores the experiences of children with gender identity issues, who tend to encounter prejudice earlier in their lives (Airton 2009). It also leads to confusion about the roots of negative reactions. A little boy may be called 'gay' because he wants to play with girls, but the reason for this name-calling is his gender-atypical behaviour, not his sexuality. LGBT young people are more likely to encounter discrimination based on assumptions about sexual activity or religious bigotry. Inclusive schools will be challenging both sources of discrimination.

Creating diversity-friendly environments

Starting young

Groundbreaking work by the 'No Outsiders' research project began in 2006 (DePalma and Atkinson 2009), and has explored ways of addressing LGBT rights at age-appropriate levels in primary schools. This project has given us our first taste of what effective work in primary schools might look like. Through discussion, literature, drama and visitors, children were taught the correct meanings of terms and encouraged to recognize and think about gender stereotyping and heteronormativity. This early work is essential in developing a diversity-aware, diversity-friendly culture in schools. Homophobia does not appear overnight, and secondary schools cannot take effective action without the foundations built at primary level.

Nurseries and primary schools cater for children with same-sex parents or LGBT family members, and need to find ways of openly acknowledging and welcoming these children's families.

Some LGBT adults report that they were aware of their difference at primary school age, and 6% of children who call ChildLine about sexual orientation or homophobic bullying are under 11 (www.nspcc.org.uk). Those who realize their difference at an early age may not communicate their feelings for several years: ' ... the gap between self-realisation and disclosure' (DePalma and Jennet 2007: 24). Without the vocabulary or the concepts to help them, these troubled children are silenced. Schools and nurseries need to develop the age-appropriate language, policies, curricular responses and resources that will ensure these children experience a growing awareness of their identity.

Professional development of staff

Including those with gender identity and sexuality issues is an important aspect of the continuing professional development of all adults who work with children and young people. For schools, the best approach is whole-school training involving everyone who works in the school, including school governors. Ellis and High (2004) found that while Section 28 silenced some teachers, it gave free rein to others to express homophobic views. Stonewall (2009) discovered a range of attitudes among school staff, suggesting that senior managers should provide an unambiguous steer on respect for pupils' identities. Class teachers and subject teachers need to provide a firm lead to adults who work in their classrooms.

Some teachers may feel a tension between their religious beliefs and their professional responsibilities in the context of same-sex relationships. Teachers have every right to their views. Expressing beliefs in school, however, must be consistent with the guidance provided on Religious Education (RE) and Sex and Relationships Education (SRE). It would not be either professional or inclusive to voice political, moral or religious beliefs in ways that might cause distress to any young person or exploit their vulnerability. A recent study by Stonewall (2008) has shown that many people of faith are accepting of lesbian and gay people and co-exist with them in harmony. Schools, especially faith schools, can build on these expressions of hope. Most of the major religions now have followers who are working towards a more respectful approach to homosexuality. These groups are an important resource for teachers of faith and faith schools.

Many LGBT young people are people of faith themselves, and may be seeking ways of rationalizing their sexuality with their spirituality. Unfortunately, in this instance, religion can be: 'a source of conflict rather than solace' (ChildLine, www.nspcc.org.uk). As educators, we must rise to the challenge of helping these young people cope with the diverse and often contradictory messages they will be receiving from their faith communities.

The formal and informal curriculum

By far the best way of building an inclusive school environment and challenging homo/transphobia is to include work on gender identity and sexual orientation in the formal curriculum, perhaps in Citizenship, Personal Social and Health Education (PSHE), or other subjects such as Art, English or Religious Education. Providing safe spaces for young people to discuss these issues would counter the myths and ignorance that prevail in places where there are 'moral interventions' from individual teachers (Ellis and High, 2004: 223) or simply silence. The Labour government (1997–2010) tried but failed to ensure that age-appropriate work on diversity was part of the National Curriculum. We await any revisions the Coalition government may make to the curriculum. Whether or not this work is undertaken is currently the decision of individual schools. Faith schools will need to establish inclusive ways of teaching about gender identity and sexual orientation alongside their religious perspective.

Where SRE is taught as part of PSHE, it should be taught inclusively. Ellis and High (2004) reported that where homosexuality is taught as a 'one-off' lesson, alongside social ills such as drugs and sexually transmitted infections, young LGBT people feel even more marginalized. Buston and Hart (2001: 100) identified inclusive practice in lessons where diversity in sexual orientation was: 'recognised and normalised', and information for same-sex relationships was provided alongside that for heterosexual relationships. Teaching materials should include information for all students, regardless of their sexual identity.

Some young LGBT people grow up in ignorance, thinking that they are the 'only one'. Others, brought up in homes or communities where homophobic attitudes prevail, may be repeatedly exposed to negative views about their identity. It is important that all young people regularly encounter positive LGBT images. LGBT people have succeeded in a multitude of areas, including the arts, science and sport – but these high achievers can only be role models where their sexuality or gender identity is acknowledged and discussed as part of a lesson. Positive images can also be provided through posters, Pride notice-boards, speakers in assemblies and 'out' teachers in school. Providing images of LGBT people from the black and ethnic minority community, and those with disabilities, is particularly important.

Young LGBT people are not sure what they can aspire to in later life because of the invisibility of role models, and may opt for careers traditionally seen as 'safe'. They, and other students, would benefit from encountering examples that challenge assumptions, such as gay police officers, lesbian MPs and transgender lawyers.

LGBT History Month is an opportunity for schools to focus attention on gender identity and sexuality as whole-school themes. Assemblies can be used to inform pupils, to raise important issues for discussion, or to invite external contributors. Some secondary schools have successfully encouraged LGBT young people to present assemblies themselves.

There is an increasing selection of books for primary-age children that challenge gender stereotypes and provide images of families with same-sex parents. Secondary school libraries, too, could include an LGBT section with appropriate fiction, non-fiction and information books.

Language is an important part of the informal curriculum and, as responsible adults, we must reclaim the words 'gay', 'lesbian', 'bisexual' and 'transgender', which are taboo precisely because children do not hear us using them. Atkinson (2007) suggests that teachers tend to wait until an opportunity arises to discuss these issues, but it is vital to make those conversations happen in order to persistently underline the legitimacy of gender and sexuality difference.

The school's response to bullying

Homophobic bullying (regardless of the actual sexuality of the victim) is one of the most prevalent forms of bullying in British schools. Anti-bullying policies should specifically include homophobic and transphobic bullying. Reasons for bullying can be a reflection of society's prejudices. Punishing an act of bullying is a hollow exercise where there is no work done to address the ignorance and misinformation that underlies it. Successful schools have worked hard, not only to educate the entire school community, but also to empower their LGBT pupil population by creating an environment where they feel safe to speak up and speak out.

Relationships with parents and the wider school community

The principle of including young people with gender identity and sexuality issues can conflict with attitudes held in the wider school community. Schools need to take parents with them on their journey, starting with the clear message that children and young people who do not conform to gender stereotypes, and those with sexuality issues, will be positively supported using a wide range of strategies in school. For nurseries and primary schools, this also means communicating a firm message to parents and carers that homo/transphobic language will not be accepted in the playground. Schools should be proud of the work they undertake in this field. Routinely informing parents about policies and practice through the school prospectus and the school website underlines the legitimacy of this work.

Support for individuals

Sometimes schools have to manage life-changing events. A young person coming out or transitioning may not happen every day, but every teacher in every school needs to plan to manage such a situation thoughtfully and sensitively, and to establish in advance where to go for guidance.

When a young person comes out in school, it is not the job of the school to inform his or her parents. Even though young LGBT people are more resilient in tackling the difficulties they have to face if they have the unconditional support of their family, this support will not necessarily be forthcoming.

However, opportunities may arise for the school to support a young person in coming out to parents. Some parents will be aware of what their child is facing and may welcome contact with their son or daughter's school, but few will have had any preparation for this responsibility (Smith 2008). Schools are uniquely placed to help them.

While many young people can and do keep their gender identity or sexuality issues secret, camp boys and butch girls are not in a position to hide (Crowley et al. 2001). It is important to be aware that they are not behaving in the ways that they do to annoy their teachers. Part of including the diversity of gender expressions and sexualities means accepting these young people as they are, and not pressurizing them to conform (Rogers 1994). A school's public recognition of a 'different' student, or its handling of a transition, can contribute to the normalization of gender identity and sexuality issues in school.

Young LGBT people need access to LGBT-specific information on local youth groups, websites and guidance on how to keep themselves safe (Douglas et al. 1997). This information could be made available on the school website so that young people and their parents can access it privately. LGBT young people with disabilities may require help in accessing the information they need. The firewalls in some schools prevent young people from accessing legitimate LGBT websites, and may need to be adjusted.

LGBT young people come from a range of cultures and religions, and will need access to information that meets their specific cultural and religious needs. Schools need to be aware of the extreme nature of the homophobia that exists in some communities and to be watchful of pupils who are vulnerable.

A significant number of gender-atypical or LGBT young people suffer from social isolation and ostracism. Some studies suggest that this is a more prevalent problem than homophobic bullying (Ellis and High 2004). Being without friends has profound effects on a young person's wellbeing and can affect mental health in later life. Sometimes young people withdraw from social contact when they realize they are different, or they fear exposure. A young person with gender identity or sexuality issues may find little in common with same-sex peers, or may not be accepted in the friendship groups they seek to join. Schools can tackle social isolation proactively in a number of ways. All adults can provide good role models of acceptance and friendliness. Teachers can use seating plans, move pupils around to sit with a range of different classmates, and provide plenty of pair-work and group-work in lessons. Schools can provide a diversity-friendly range of activities at lunchtimes and after school. Older students can be trained to act as befrienders.

Some situations pose particular difficulties. Areas such as toilets and changing rooms can feel unsafe to LGBT young people, and need good supervision. All schools need to be alert to difficulties that may be posed by residential school trips. Children with gender identity issues may be vulnerable for unexpected reasons, such as a boy who arrives with pink pyjamas. Many young LGBT people find sharing a bedroom challenging and may avoid going on trips for that reason. Schools can help by discussing arrangements in advance with students, or their parents, where this is appropriate.

Finally ...

This area of inclusion presents special challenges for schools and teachers, yet it is an area where comparatively small shifts in attitude and practice can bring about extraordinary benefits in the achievements and wellbeing of a significant number of individuals. Young people with gender identity and sexuality issues can be remarkably strong, articulate and resilient, but, time and again, we fail to realize how much they have to contend with. We need to let them know, in every way we can, that they are valued for who they are, and that they all matter.

Reflection on values and practice

You are walking into school one morning, unaware that a miracle has happened. The miracle is that, overnight, your school has become a world leader in including children and young people with gender identity and sexuality issues. Imagine the things you would notice that would tell you that the miracle has happened, and make a list (de Shazer 1994).

- Which of the things on your list could you achieve in your own classroom?
- Which would require a whole-school approach?

Notes

  1 'Transgender' is an umbrella term that covers a range of gender-related issues.
  2 Assuming Britain's LGB population is 5–7% (Stonewall, 2009) and the transgender population is about 1% (Reed *et al.*, 2009).

Resources

Families Together London: www.familiestogetherlondon.com
LGBT History Month: www.lgbthistorymonth.org.uk
Out for Our Children: www.outforourchildren.co.uk
School's Out: www.schools-out.org.uk
Stonewall: www.stonewall.org.uk
Terrence Higgins Trust: www.ygm.org.uk
No Outsiders Project Team (2010) *Undoing Homophobia*. Stoke on Trent: Trentham Books.

References

Airton, L. (2009) 'From sexuality (gender) to gender (sexuality): the aims of anti-homophobia education', *Sex Education*, 9(2): 129–39.

Atkinson, E. (2007) 'Speaking with small voices: voice, resistance and difference', M., DePalma, R. and Atkinson, E. (eds) *Marginality and Difference in Edu Beyond*, Stoke on Trent: Trentham Books.

Brill, S. and Pepper, R. (2008) *The Transgender Child: A Handbook for Families and Professionals*, San Francisco: Cleis Press.

Buston, K. and Hart, G. (2001) 'Heterosexism and homophobia in Scottish school sex education: exploring the nature of the problem', *Journal of Adolescence*, 24: 95–109.

Crowley, C., Hallam, S., Harre, R. and Lunt, I. (2001) 'Study support for young people with same-sex attraction – views and experiences from a pioneering support initiative in the north of England', *Educational and Child Psychology*, 18(1): 108–24.

DCSF (2008) *Homophobic Bullying. Safe to Learn: Embedding Anti-Bullying Work in Schools*, Nottingham: DCSF Publications.

DCSF (2010) *Guidance for Schools on Preventing and Responding to Sexist, Sexual and Transphobic Bullying, Safe to Learn: Embedding Anti-Bullying Work in Schools*, Nottingham: DCSF Publications.

DePalma, R. and Atkinson, E. (2009) 'Putting queer into practice: problems and possibilities', in DePalma, R. and Atkinson, E. (eds) *Interrogating Heteronormativity in Primary Schools: The Work of the 'No Outsiders' Project*, Stoke-on-Trent: Trentham Books.

DePalma, R. and Jennett, M. (2007) 'Deconstructing heteronormativity in primary schools in England: cultural approaches to a cultural phenomenon', in van Dijk, L. and van Driel, B. (eds) *Challenging Homophobia: Teaching about Sexual Diversity*, Stoke-on-Trent: Trentham Books.

DfES (2003) *Every Child Matters*, London: Department for Education and Skills.

DH (2007) *Reducing Health Inequalities for Lesbian, Gay, Bisexual and Trans People (Briefing Papers 1–13)*, London: Department of Health.

Douglas, N., Warwick, I., Kemp, S. and Whitty, G. (1997) *Playing it Safe: Responses of Secondary School Teachers to Lesbian, Gay and Bisexual Pupils, Bullying, HIV and Aids Education and Section 28*, London: Health and Education Research Unit, Institute of Education.

Ellis, V. with High, S. (2004) 'Something more to tell you: gay, lesbian or bisexual young people's experiences of secondary schooling', *British Educational Research Journal*, 30(2): 214–25.

Epstein, D. (1994) 'On the straight and narrow: the heterosexual presumption, homo-phobias and schools', in Epstein, D. (ed.) *Challenging Lesbian and Gay Inequalities in Education,* Buckingham: Open University Press.

Epstein, D., O'Flynn, S. and Telford, D. (2003) *Silenced Sexualities in Schools and Universities*, Stoke-on-Trent: Trentham Books.

Reed, B., Rhodes, S., Schofield, P. and Wylie, K. (2009) *Gender Variance in the UK: Prevalence, Incidence, Growth and Geographic Distribution*, London: Gender Identity Research and Education Society.

Rivers, I. (1995) 'The victimization of gay teenagers in schools: homophobia in education', *Pastoral Care*, March: 35–41.

——(2000) 'Social exclusion, absenteeism and sexual minority youth', *Support for Learning*, 15(1): 13–18.

Rogers, M. (1994) 'Growing up lesbian: the role of the school', in Epstein, D. (ed.) *Challenging Lesbian and Gay Inequalities in Education,* Buckingham: Open University Press.

de Shazer, S. (1994) *Putting Difference to Work*, Norton: New York.

Smith, M. (2008) 'Including lesbian and gay youth in school – parents find a voice', London: Institute of Education (unpublished dissertation).

Stonewall (2006) *The School Report: The Experiences of Young Gay People in Britain's Schools*, London: Stonewall.
—— (2008) *Love Thy Neighbour: What People of Faith Really Think about Homosexuality*, London: Stonewall.
——(2009) *The Teachers' Report: Homophobic Bullying in Britain's Schools*, London. Stonewall.
Wilson, G. and Rahman, Q. (2005) *Born Gay: The Psychobiology of Sex Orientation*, London: Peter Owen.
Yip, A. K. T. (2004) 'Negotiating space with family and kin in identity construction: the narratives of British non-heterosexual Muslims', *Sociological Review*, 52(3): 336–50.

Chapter 3

The role of the school in reducing bullying

Neil Duncan

What we know about bullying

What is known about bullying? Everything, it would seem. From the earliest times of public schooling, 'the bully' has been a recognizable figure in popular culture and common knowledge. However, until the late 1980s there were no books available in English with 'bullying' in the title – now there are literally hundreds. Unfortunately, mostly these books offer the same things: a mixture of knowledge based on narrow research mixed with folk wisdom. This chapter takes a very different approach to the topic of bullying for the needs of school teachers, and is intended to provoke consideration of alternative thinking to help professionals as they develop their inclusive practice, rather than offering a quick fix for bullying. So, what do we really know about bullying? Everything, possibly, apart from how to actually stop it.

We know that pupil-to-pupil aggression was common long before researchers started investigating the issue. *Tom Brown's Schooldays* (Hughes 1857 [1994]) and other literature about public schools in England featured bullies as typical characters. However, the original meaning of the word suggests someone to be admired for his (always a male) physical strength and fearless dominating behaviour. Shakespeare used the phrase 'I love the lovely bully' in *Henry V*, and the accompanying Arden notes interpret it as: 'bully – a fine fellow' (Craik 1995). These days, we might use the term 'alpha male' to the same effect, with a positive spin on qualities of informal leadership. The point of this digression into etymology is to underline that meanings and understandings are not set in stone – they vary over time and also shift between social groups and cultural settings. So if you hear someone state that a child is 'just a bully', think twice about their right to define the term.

I once carried out a bullying questionnaire survey in a high school, where I was shocked to see that one year 7 boy reported he was hit, kicked, pushed and spat upon on an almost daily basis. Despite having one of the highest frequencies of such aggressive acts against him, he ticked the 'I don't think I get bullied' box! I knew which boy had completed that questionnaire, and spoke to him in an attempt to help him. He was very matter of fact with me, and explained that the person doing all these things to him was his big brother, one of our year 10 boys. I asked him why he didn't feel bullied. He replied 'everyone gets it from their older brother, don't they? I do it to my little brother too.'

This young boy's toughness, and his idea of bullying, prevented him from thinking of himself as a victim. He didn't like the beatings, but accepted them as inevitable and not even unfair. On the other hand, in the same survey some pupils ticked none of the boxes for being attacked in any way, but then ticked the boxes that showed they worried all the time about being bullied, they changed their routes around school and avoided certain times and places in case they were attacked. Would you say these children suffered because of bullying even if it had not (yet) happened to them? If the presence and fear of bullying in their school made them permanently scared and miserable, couldn't they be called victims of bullying more than the boy that was beaten up but wasn't worried about it? All this is very complicated and depends more on social relationships and feelings rather than simple acts and behaviours.

While we do need a consensus understanding of the key terms used in bullying so that discussion is meaningful, we just need to avoid being too dogmatic that any single definition is correct. There is a variety of definitions of bullying, but no single definition gets it right in every case. One widely accepted example comes from pioneering work carried out in Sweden since the 1970s by Dan Olweus. Olweus (1993) states that bullying is an aggressive act with an imbalance of power, has some element of repetition, and can be physical or verbal, or indirect (for example, being sent hate texts, or socially shunned). One element often missed from formulations of bullying is the sense of intimate entrapment. There is something special about bullying that includes that element of being stuck in a relationship or situation with your aggressor or tormentor. This idea is very hard to include in a short definition, but one operational definition of bullying might be 'an interpersonal abuse of power'.

Prevalence of bullying in schools

However bullying is defined, all the statistics show a depressing picture of the extent and effects of bullying in schools. In terms of victimization, for example, the Tellus2 survey (Ofsted 2007) indicated that 17% of respondents claimed to have been bulllied that month. Research on children's perceptions about bullying for ChildLine and the Department for Education and Skills (DfES) found that just over half (54%) of both primary and secondary school children thought that bullying was 'a big/quite big problem' in their school. Distribution and frequency of bullying varies with school phase: 51% of year 5 students (aged 9–10) reported that they had been bullied during the preceding term compared with 28% of year 8 students (aged 12–13) (Oliver and Kandappa 2003). A quarter of children bullied by their peers reported that they suffered long-term harmful effects lasting into adulthood (Cawson *et al.* 2000: 30), with some especially tragic cases ending in suicide.

Smith and Shu (2000) found in their study of 2300 pupils aged 10–14 that 30% did not tell anyone when they had been bullied, the percentage for boys and older children being higher. Other studies (Katz *et al.* 2001) found that around a third of boys and a quarter of girls admitted they personally had bullied other children 'a little' and/or 'a lot' and 15% of primary school students and 12% of secondary school students said they had both bullied other children and been bullied themselves in the past year (Oliver and Kandappa 2003).

Characteristics of bullies

Most of us are capable of unfairly dominating other people, given the wrong circumstances, and we might have bullied other children, but then stopped under correction. Would we be happy with the label sticking? My preference is for the term 'aggressor' to replace bully, and 'target' instead of victim. But why bother changing words that we all know and are comfortable with? One reason is exactly that – we have become comfortable about using the concept of 'the bully', so we stop thinking carefully about how we use it. If we didn't reconsider and refresh our language, we'd still be using terms such as 'retard', 'lunatic', 'Negro' and 'fallen woman' without any sense of embarrassment. However, as the term is so prevalent, we must use it to discuss the work of other people.

Olweus (1997) believes that bullies are impulsive – they act without thinking too much about the consequences, and typically resort to violence to get what they want. Often they are more physically powerful than their peers, and have a greater mental toughness and lower empathy – in other words, they can hurt others without caring about their feelings. There are few surprises here – indeed, the surprise is that researchers have bothered to announce this as findings, when perhaps most teachers would give this description intuitively based on their own observations and experiences.

More significantly, it has been shown that bullies who engage in non-physical aggression have unusually high social intelligence (Sutton *et al.* 1999). They are experts in causing great pain and hurt in subtle ways, manipulating and entrapping their targets without guarding adults being aware of what is going on.

Characteristics of victims

Like the term 'bullies', the label 'victims' might raise the idea of a fixed, immutable condition – 'you can't help her, she's one of life's victims'. Often research will categorize these children as either passive or provocative. Passive victims may be viewed as displaying vulnerability that 'encourages' bullies to attack them. They put up no effective resistance and therefore bullies repeatedly abuse them without being punished. Provocative victims don't aggress others, but are thought to 'wind people up' by their words and actions, and their response to aggression is said to inflame that aggression even more. You need to make your own mind up as to whether that is just an excuse to hit someone who is irritating – we all encounter such people in life! While we might find them annoying, bullies respond to them with violence – 'he asked for it'.

An intriguing issue is raised by the question: if these categories were so simple, then why do so many children report being bullied in so many surveys: 69% in The National Bullying Survey (Bullying Online 2006). Applying this figure to the categories makes it sound like most of our children are either too provocative or too passive! This discrepancy suggests that what has been described by the researchers is too simplistic to give us the kind of understanding that would be helpful in dealing with the problems. If we recall a time when we were being bullied, would we be happy with that analysis – either we were too soft, or we wound the aggressor up?

Effects of bullying

One thing is certain about bullying – its effects can be long term, and in some cases deadly. Since the original suicides in Sweden that sparked off the scholarly research into bullying, many tragic cases have come to light. For every actual suicide caused by bullying, there might be 100 children who are driven to almost take their lives to free themselves from their persecution. The case of Laura Rhodes is relevant here. Laura was 13 years old and bullied about her sexuality. She took her own life in a suicide pact with her friend. Her friend survived the overdose, but only Laura's name remains in the public domain.

In addition to suicide, self-inflicted injury, and of course the direct damage of being physically abused, there are many lasting problems suffered by targets of bullying. These include loneliness, depression, panic attacks, anxiety, guilt, shame and low self-esteem (Schäfer et al. 2004). Less obvious perhaps, but just as important an effect of bullying, is truancy. It is impossible to know exactly how many school days are lost each year by pupils who are too frightened to come into school because their life has been made intolerable. The true figures of this effect are obscured by children's excuses, sometimes supported by unwitting parents telling the school that they are sick or otherwise unable to attend.

Alongside these outcomes, the way that bullying creates a general atmosphere in schools should not be underestimated. Unhappy or anxious children are not performing at their best academically. It is hard to concentrate on your studies if you are worried about being attacked or threatened at break-time or on the school bus. Children are reluctant to put a hand up or answer a teacher's question if they think they will be called a swot or worse and ridiculed by the rest of the class. If we want to establish an inclusive environment within our schools, we must meet create an ethos in which bullying has no place.

How schools deal with bullying

There is a plethora of different approaches to managing bullying, which may be categorized into pre-emptive or preventative, and responsive and remedial categories. Or put more simply: before and after measures. As a teacher, one can embed pre-emptive measures in the curriculum at any level of study, though it is less awkward to adapt the curriculum for the younger age range where the teaching is perhaps more child-centred than subject-centred. In PSHE, preventions include directly discussing bullying in the classroom, thereby promoting a 'telling school' to combat a culture of not 'grassing' or informing the authorities of wrongdoing.

You would need to use your own investigations and your own professional awareness of how realistic such a project for a 'telling school' is. A good number of professional anti-bullying experts are able to make suggestions from the position of never having been in a school, apart from to carry out their questionnaire surveys, and might not be the adults most in touch with children's culture. The culture of not grassing is a deeply embedded one, not just in schools, but also in communities and in children's families. This code extends from witnesses of murders denying any knowledge, even when it is a loved one that they have lost, right down to reception classes, where a pupil can be vilified for being the teacher's pet.

Teachers can inadvertently fuel anti-grassing behaviour by dismissing pupils' righteous but trivial indignation over rule-breaking with 'don't tell tales' or 'mind your own business'.

Another pre-emptive strategy used by some schools is a 'buddy' system to match up vulnerable pupils with older protectors. These older pupils monitor the safety of their younger partners and support them if there is a problem. This not only gives protection, but adds to the self esteem and social responsibility of the mentors in the partnership.

Apart from inter-year buddy work, some schools use a version of circle time where all the children in the same class are involved in formally organized social activities that raise empathy, improve pro-social behaviour and increase peer support (Smith 2004).

Responding to bullying incidents after they have happened depends to a great extent on the particular school's anti-bullying policy, and how assiduously the adults follows its guidance. If the perpetrators in a bullying incident are punished, it can range from a private apology and an undertaking not to repeat the offence, through to school exclusion or even criminal charges brought by the police.

Frequently, anti-bullying responses mirror the processes found in the courts of law. Unfortunately the investigative resources at schools' disposal are not of the quality or rigour required to serve such legalistic processes, and there is a natural tendency for people to lie over things they feel guilty about. This can lead to protracted denials and lack of conclusive evidence where all parties feel aggrieved and slighted. Where the burden of proof is only on probability, it can do serious damage to the children's sense of justice and their faith in the system.

Another unwanted outcome of trying to take a juridical line in bullying sanctions is the increased likelihood of retaliation by the accused or his/her friends against the complainant – a very real worry of many targets of bullying. The more severe the prospective punishment, the more hostile the accused is likely to become. Retaliation is a massive and realistic fear for many pupils who desperately want intervention to end their suffering, and this means that staff should be proactive but sensitive. Rather than interrogate the target of the bullying and elicit evidence from them against the perpetrator, it is safer to couch the accusations thus:

> 'I haven't spoken to Kim, but if you've been threatening her, you need to sort yourself out now before you get into real bother with me. I'll check up on this in a couple of days, and if I think you have been carrying it on, I'll be back to see you about it.'

By doing this, you are depersonalizing the spat between the pupils and taking the adult role on your own initiative.

Some schools reduce these problems by operating a 'no-blame' anti-bullying policy (Maines and Robinson 1992). In this seven-step programme, the adult concerns themselves with making the target feel better about things, and getting the perpetrators to stop their attacks and even to befriend or support the target. Anti-bullying initiatives across the world testify to the effectiveness of the strategy, and particularly appreciate the way it attempts to break the cycle of aggression and hurt that abides in bullying. However, as the no-blame approach takes more time and skill to apply than simple punishment, it can be unpopular because of resource costs as well as its non-punitive values.

Why bullying happens in schools

A view linked with the punitive approach is that some people bully because they are just horrible people. If that is really the case, one might expect that once the bullies have been kicked out of a school, then bullying in that school would cease.

We might also consider, if bullying is only the fault of a few nasty kids, then why do schools of similar size and intake report very different rates of bullying? Are there simply more nasty kids there, or is it something else? One clue to solving this puzzle comes from researchers Yoneyama and Naito (2003), who were struck by the powerful differences between school cultures in

Australia and their native Japan. In the western school systems, they noted that bullying tended to be one or two aggressive and violent pupils causing fear and harm to a larger group of pupils. In the Japanese school system, the situation was almost reversed, with the whole class picking on one child as a scapegoat and making their life unbearable.

Their analysis is worth reading in full, but suffice to say that their theory is that bullying is not just a personality flaw, but is conditioned by the way adults run schools and local cultures. Their message is clear: if you want to stop bullying, begin with how schools operate rather than blaming a few deviant pupils.

Bullying ethos in institutions

Although schools might seem principally to be about academic education, they are equally important in the social education of our children. Social education, or socialization, here refers to the inculcation of attitudes and behaviours acceptable to the majority of the community, or at least to satisfy those in charge of it. Schools train people in cultural norms to enable a life where that generation can get along with each other and enjoy what the community has to offer, as well as making a contribution to it. Usually we hear only about the first purpose of schooling – to educate – but schools are often criticized for not shaping pupils' behaviour effectively enough.

Some school rules need to be modelled rather than written, and how the staff do this, the nuanced way we interact and communicate our values to each other and to the pupils, creates an ethos peculiar to each individual school (see Rutter *et al.* 1979 for the enormous impact of ethos on school achievement, pupil behaviour and general quality of institution). These modelled behaviours reflect a power structure based on a hierarchy, a layered structure of the staff. At the top is the head teacher, then the senior management team. These are followed by middle management staff such as subject coordinators or heads of year. Beneath this rank are the teaching staff, followed by class-room assistants, mid-day supervisors and cleaning staff. Below this, at the bottom, are the pupils – even though they may be classified as being the school's *raison d'etre*.

Within the pupil culture, there are even more differentiated power levels, referred to by some as a 'pecking order'. These relations are driven by many factors – ability, strength, size, age, intelligence and popularity, among others. Pupils are influenced by what they see demonstrated by adult examples elsewhere in the school (and at home and in the community, as well as the ubiquitous influence of the mass media).

In some institutions, the official hierarchy is not as obvious as in others: the boundaries are blurred, or actors adopt more than one role. In some organizations, the strata are fewer and the difference between them is less important. In other cases, the power is much more evident and is zealously defended by those who have it. In order to assert their dominance over other workers in the institution, they may demand that they are referred to by title rather than name, or they may have a special parking space, a grander office, and a demeanour that warns you not to take liberties with their authority without penalty.

In schools where the ethos is one of deference to superior rank rather than warm human relationships, and where personal feelings come second to achieving goals, bullying among pupils is more likely to thrive. These signs of the cultural values of the leadership are very difficult for staff to challenge – they can be subtle and seemingly innocuous or natural. This illustrates to us as professionals involved in anti-bullying just how tough the task is to get children to confront, resist or avoid being bullied if we ourselves find it a problem to be treated fairly and respectfully.

How schools can bully children

This section aims to challenge your assumptions as professional educators about the universal benefits of schooling. We are brought up to believe that schools are wholly benign institutions, designed with pupil welfare at the centre, and with the aim of providing enjoyable learning experiences for all. This ideal is not shared by everyone. Many people look back on their schooldays with a shudder at the unpleasant experiences they had, and think of schools as places where they were humiliated and disempowered. As a teacher, you are unlikely to be such a person. Most people who go into the teaching profession have had a good quality of experience – they were rule-abiding, friendly, popular and successful with their peers, and schools fitted their needs very well. But for those who struggled socially, who were disempowered and marginalized by a system that figured them to be less desirable, school might have been viewed through a very different lens.

Compulsory schooling for some children often means being deprived of liberties that adults take for granted. We demand they attend the institution for six hours a day, five days a week. There they are worked in minute detail for no extrinsic reward, or even for realistic future gains – deferred gratification does not work for them. The micro-control extends to speaking only with permission; performing activities they have no interest in; and being harassed for not trying hard enough. It also entails being measured and set against their peers as competitors. It includes the control of their appearance in clothing, hair and jewellery, when to eat and where to drink. It extends so far as controlling their visits to the toilet. In schools where such conditions exist in an oppressive ethos, bullying can become a real problem among pupils.

Everyone needs some control over basic areas of their lives or else they maladapt in different ways. Some children do this by seeking unfair and cruel control over their peers. They bully.

The way schools go about their functions, even though those functions are predetermined, can make a big difference to the quality of relationships in them. Some schools have much higher rates of bullying than others, despite having strong similarities otherwise (Xin Ma et al. 2001; Roland and Galloway 2004). It is highly improbable that that those schools have a higher number of naughtier and nastier kids, and high exclusion rates in those schools do not appear to improve the problem either (Ball and Hartley 2003). While we should accept that schools have to maintain discipline, and all schools need some form of hierarchy in order to run smoothly, we must take care to be fair and humane in the eyes of the children.

Most children are happy within a hierarchical structure as long as they perceive it to be safe and fair, but if they are abused, ridiculed in public, shouted at, punished as a group, or treated with sarcasm and disdain, they resent it (Ross-Epp 1996). In the 11-year-long competition that is compulsory schooling, there are winners and losers. Some children rarely succeed in that competition, and so bossing someone else about can be the release they crave from failure. Their predicament is described, in studies of oppressed groups in other situations, as 'horizontal violence' (Freire 1972; Leymann 1996).

Most teachers are caring and intelligent people doing a difficult and demanding job. There are times when they are less than perfect, and this can only be expected. When such lapses in their high professional standards prove effective − if they achieve the right results in the wrong way − others might emulate the same undesirable behaviours. Effectively, they may be bullying to enforce discipline. I confess to such lapses myself, having used them to great effect over a period of years when I was praised for getting good behavioural results from very difficult students. It was only when I witnessed one of my younger staff copying my approach that I realized the harm that I might be doing.

So what advice would be helpful to new teachers in managing discipline in schools? One strategy I came up with was to imagine in every exchange with students that their parents were present while you were dealing with them. Can you justify your words, your tone and your body language? If so, then you can be pretty sure that you are not bullying them. If we preach the values of fairness and decency to students, then we ourselves should not be sarcastic or mean. We must retain a professional level of dignifying children equivalent to that which we would use when dealing with parents and other adults. In my practice in secondary schools, pupils were quick to complain (when they felt safe to do so) about what they perceived as double standards. The teachers who ate or drank in their classrooms while confiscating pupils' snacks, or arrived late to lessons but meted out detentions for the same crime, were disliked and resented. Power without justice was always noted, such as a whole class being punished for the misdemeanours of one pupil.

Although these may seem petty injustices, to some pupils they signal a strong message of 'might is right': if you are powerful enough, you can get away with anything, and staff behaviour was seen as a hypocritical working model for children to bully others.

Summary

Bullying is often seen as the fault of particular children who are labelled as 'bullies'. I would argue that such labels are not helpful as they prevent us from looking at what we as adults could and should change (our relationships with children, the professional standards we consider important, and the unnecessary or punitive rules we set in our classrooms). This would have a greater impact than focusing on things we are unlikely to be able to change, such as a child's personality, where bullying is a response to their individual situation. Interventions to reduce bullying should be preceded by discussion on how the school can improve its ethos and culture. While it may well be more comfortable and acceptable to consider bullying in school to be purely a pupil problem, any attempt to make a lasting impact will be unsuccessful until the adults engage with their own role in creating and maintaining a pro-social and non-oppressive, inclusive environment.

Reflection on values and practice

Defining bullying

Instead of using common definitions of bullying, listen to the range of things that pupils do to other pupils that they say they don't like. What really bothers them? What can you do to address this and to increase an inclusive ethos in your classroom?

Developing fairness and justice

If you have a pupil who is involved in bullying others, how can you encourage them to rethink occasions when they were treated unfairly, drawing out a sense of empathy from this experience and a recognition that they are emulating the unfair person? How could this practice be incorporated into your teaching and learning practice?

The acid test

You are a role model to the children in your class. Reflect on your own interpersonal exchanges with pupils. Think back to an incident when you were disciplining a pupil. How would you feel if you had to watch a video of this with the child's parents? If you would not feel comfortable, then consider how you should conduct yourself. Many pupils' behaviour does change when they realize you are treating them with dignity and professionalism.

References

Ball, C. and Hartley, M. (2003) *Zero Tolerance to Bullying*, Alberta: Mentone Education Centre.

Bullying Online (2006) *National Survey Report*, www.bullying.co.uk/index.php/young-people/the-national-survey

Cawson, P., Wattam, C., Brooker, S. and Kelly, G. (2000) *Child Maltreatment in the United Kingdom: A Study of the Prevalence of Child Abuse and Neglect*, London: NSPCC.

Craik, T. (ed.) (1995) Henry V, by William Shakespeare, London: Routledge.

Freire, P. (1972) *Pedagogy of the Oppressed*, London: Penguin.

Hughes, T. (1857 [1994]) *Tom Brown's Schooldays*, London: Penguin.

Katz, A., Buchanan, A. and Bream, V. (2001) Bullying in Britain: Testimonies from Teenagers, East Molesey, UK: Young Voice.

Leymann, H. (1996) 'Psychological terrorization – the problem of the terminology', in *The Mobbing Encyclopaedia*, www.leymann.se/English/11130E.HTM

Maines, B. and Robinson, G. (1992) *Michael's Story*, video cassette recording, Bristol: Lucky Duck Publishing.

Ofsted (2007) *2007 TellUs2: Children and Young People Survey: Technical Report*, www.ofsted.gov. uk/Ofsted-home/Publications-and-research/Browse-all-by/Documents-by-type/Statistics/Other-statistics/TellUs2-children-and-young-people-survey

Oliver, C. and Kandappa, M. (2003) *Tackling Bullying: Listening to the Views of Children and Young People. Summary Report*, London: DfES and ChildLine.

Olweus, D. (1993) *Bullying at School. What We Know and What We Can Do*, Oxford: Blackwell.

——(1997) 'Bully/victim problems in school: facts and intervention', *European Journal of Psychology of Education*, 12: 495–510.

Roland, E. and Galloway, D. (2004) 'Professional cultures in schools with high and low rates of bullying', *School Effectiveness and School Improvement*, 15(3): 241–60.

Ross-Epp, J. (1996) 'Schools, complicity and sources of violence', in Ross-Epp, J. and Watkinson, A. (eds) *Systemic Violence: How Schools Hurt Children,* London: Falmer Press.

Rutter, M., Maughan, B., Mortimore, P. and Ousten, J. (1979) *15000 Hours: Secondary Schools and their Effects on Children*, London: Open Books.

Schäfer, M., Korn, S., Smith, P. K., Hunter, S. C., Mora-Merchán, J. A., Singer, M. M. and Van der Meulen, K. (2004) 'Lonely in the crowd: recollections of bullying', *British Journal of Developmental Psychology*, 22(3): 379–94.

Smith, C. (2004) *Circle Time for Adolescents: A Seven Session Programme for 14 to 16 year olds*, London: Paul Chapman/Sage.

Smith, P. and Shu, S. (2000) 'What good schools can do about bullying: findings from a survey in English schools after a decade of research and action', *Childhood*, 7(2): 193–212.

Sutton, J., Smith, P. K. and Swettenham, J. (1999) 'Social cognition and bullying: social inadequacy or skilled manipulation?', *British Journal of Developmental Psychology*, 17: 435–50.

Xin Ma, Stewin, L. L. and Mah, D. L. (2001) 'Bullying in school: nature, effects and remedies', *Research Papers in Education*, 16(3): 247–70.

Yoneyama, S. and Naito, A. (2003) 'Problems with the paradigm: the school as a factor in understanding bullying (with special reference to Japan)', *British Journal of Sociology*, 24(3): 315–30.

Chapter 4

Supporting Gypsy, Roma and Traveller pupils

Chris Derrington

Introduction

Gypsy, Roma and Traveller children attend every type of school and early years' setting throughout the UK. They are all different and individual, but it is recognised officially that, as a group, they are the most 'at risk' in the education system in terms of their attendance, engagement and attainment (Ofsted 1999a: 7). National attainment data show that, while attainment levels for most groups of pupils in our schools have improved over the past few years, in the case of Gypsy, Roma and Traveller pupils these levels have actually deteriorated (DCSF 2009b). So who are these children, and why are they underperforming so dramatically in our schools?

The government's education department uses the generic term 'Gypsy, Roma and Traveller' (GRT) to embrace a number of different communities. Some families from these communities no longer travel and have settled permanently in one place; others maintain a nomadic lifestyle and travel almost continuously or on a seasonal basis between different parts of the country. Children from the most highly mobile communities (for example, those who move around frequently because they have no legal place to stay) typically experience a fragmented education which, not surprisingly, has a negative impact on their attendance and attainment at school. They might attend many different schools, each for a short period of time, provided there are places available. Others might spend considerable periods (months or even years) out of school altogether. Children who travel on a seasonal basis due to their parents' work patterns (for example, Fairground families) are often enrolled at a 'base' school all year round, even though they only attend physically during the winter months. Some of these children then continue to receive their education when they are travelling by means of distance-learning materials provided by their base school.

However, most Gypsy, Roma and Traveller families these days live permanently on authorised sites or in houses, either by choice, or because there is no other legal option available to them. This may surprise you. Some people assume, wrongly, that you can't be a Traveller if you live in a house.

Furthermore, if the majority of Gypsy, Roma and Traveller children now live in housing or on a permanent site, then why should they have the lowest attainment at all Key Stages, and why is the gap getting wider instead of narrower?

This chapter aims to help you understand and address the particular needs of this diverse group of children and young people.

Who are Gypsies, Roma and Travellers?

The term GRT represents a diverse collection of communities, including Romany Gypsies, Travellers of Irish heritage, European Roma, Fairground and Circus showmen and New Travellers. While it is fair to say that these communities have some shared cultural characteristics, there are also some important distinctions to make. The main one is that some, but not all, are recognised in law as constituting a minority ethnic group. In considering whether a community is an ethnic group (as opposed to a social group), a number of criteria must be met. Two essential characteristics are:

- ancestry and a long shared history of which the group is conscious as distinguishing it from other groups, and the memory of which it keeps alive
- a distinct cultural tradition including social customs and manners, often but not necessarily associated with religious observance.

Let's explore this further by looking at the various communities included under the generic term 'Gypsy, Roma and Traveller'. The first three groups described below are recognised in law as having a distinct ethnicity.

Romany Gypsies

The largest group of Travellers in the UK is often referred to in the literature as Romany Gypsy, although other terms such as Gypsy Traveller, English or Scottish Gypsy, Romany and Romanichal may also be applied. Increasingly, the term Roma (see below) is adopted. It should be recognised that people have the freedom to describe themselves in whatever way they wish, and teachers should take the lead from parents and pupils rather than making assumptions about 'correct' terminology.

Regardless of the preferred term, this community is believed to have descended from north-west India. Around 1000 years ago, groups of nomadic migrants fled the Indian subcontinent during clashes between invading warriors and settled in almost every region from Persia to the Balkan states, eventually arriving in the UK in the fifteenth century. With their dark skin, it was assumed that they were pilgrims from Egypt, so they were called Egyptians (from which the word 'Gypsy' is derived). Linguistic evidence, however, supports the theory of their Indian origins and, although it is not widely known, Romany Gypsies have retained elements of a language known as Romanes or Romani, which has its roots in ancient Sanskrit (the language used in northern India around the ninth century). A hybrid version of this language is commonly spoken by Romany families, and a number of words have been incorporated into common English usage (for example, cushti, bloke, pal, gaff).

Many Romany Gypsies today live in houses; others might live in trailers (caravans) or mobile homes. Regardless of where they live, they are Romany Gypsies by birthright and are therefore recognised in law as being a legitimate ethnic group, protected by race relations legislation.

Travellers of Irish heritage

The next largest group in the UK are Travellers of Irish heritage. As the name suggests, these Travellers are indigenous to Ireland and are believed to be descendents of travelling entertainers, itinerant craftsmen and metal workers. The derogatory term 'tinker' refers to the traditional occupational status of tinsmith. Travellers of Irish heritage have retained aspects of a Celtic language which has its roots in Gaelic. Although their historical roots are different, their customs and traditions have similarities with those of Romany Gypsies, partly for pragmatic reasons associated with a nomadic way of life, and partly due to intermarriage between the communities.

Roma

Roma are European Gypsies. This diverse subgroup, believed to number around ten million globally, also constitute a minority ethnic group in the UK. The largest numbers continue to live in Eastern Europe, particularly in Romania, Bulgaria and Hungary. However, after the demise of the communist regime, standards of healthcare, access to education and opportunities for employment were largely denied to these communities, and racial attacks led to a wave of asylum-seekers entering Western Europe. Each Roma group has its own national identity and language, and families will often identify themselves first in national terms and then as Roma, for example 'Czech Roma'.

It is important that teachers and schools understand that all the groups described above are legitimate minority ethnic communities and are therefore protected under Race Relations legislation. Statutory ethnic monitoring of Gypsy, Roma and Traveller pupils in schools has been in place only since 2003, when 'Gypsy/Roma' and 'Travellers of Irish heritage' were included for the first time as two distinct ethnicity group categories within the School Census. Consequently, all maintained schools are now required to include these categories as part of the data collection reported in PLASC returns.[1] Unfortunately, many Traveller parents and children choose not to disclose their identity for fear of bullying and prejudice. This has a significant impact on the accuracy of statistical data available, and led to government guidance for schools to encourage wider practice in self-ascription (Ivatts 2006; DCSF 2008a).

The School Census does not explicitly identify pupils from Fairground or Circus (showmen) communities, 'New Travellers', or those dwelling on the waterways, unless they also belong to one of the above groups. These communities are recognised as Occupational Travellers or social groups, as opposed to minority ethnic groups. However, it is very important to mention these other Traveller groups within this chapter, as they experience many of the same educational challenges.

Fairground showmen

Fairground communities have a distinctive culture and lifestyle that stretches back many centuries. Their ancestral links date back to the travelling merchants and entertainers of the Charter Fairs in the Middle Ages, and possibly beyond that to pagan times, when seasonal gatherings were held for trade and festivity. Today, Fairground showman families tend to own or rent land, which serves as their base during the winter months, but spend the majority of the year following a circuit of meticulously planned events both in the UK and, increasingly, on the continent. Children from these communities tend to be enrolled at a base school near their winter quarters, and in many cases these schools are involved in the development of distance-learning packs, which are sent to the pupils on a regular basis while they are travelling with the fair. It is estimated that over 1000 children from Fairground families now access this type of flexible, personalised education (Marks and Wood 2008), which also helps to strengthen and maintain home–school relationships (Wilkin et al. 2009b).

Circus communities

Like Fairground showmen, Circus communities may describe themselves as Occupational Travellers, although some performers may also be Gypsies. Circus groups are usually diverse, typically comprising a troupe of international performers, some of whom will have children. The frequency of movement between venues can make access to school difficult for them, and although some benefit from distance-learning programmes organised by their base school, other circuses employ tutors who travel and live as part of the community.

New Travellers

New Travellers (commonly referred to in the past as 'New Age Travellers') are, by definition, a more recent cultural phenomenon. Groups of younger people (known as 'hippies') opted for a nomadic lifestyle during the 1960s, but the phenomenon grew during the 1970s and 1980s with the emergence of the free festival movement, as more young people bought large vehicles to transport themselves and their possessions between the summer festivals. In the late 1980s, cutbacks in social security and housing benefits, made by the Thatcher government, had a particular impact on young people between the ages of 16 and 25, leading to a surge in youth homelessness and in young economic refugees taking to the road and an alternative travelling lifestyle (Martin 1998).

Key considerations for teaching and learning

Having provided a brief overview of the various Traveller communities in the UK, let's now consider the key implications for teachers and schools. National initiatives aimed at narrowing the achievement gap have been targeted at these groups because there has been so little progress recorded over recent years. If anything, the gap is getting wider rather than narrower (DCSF 2009b). In the past, the educational underachievement of Gypsy, Roma and Traveller pupils was associated with problems around practical access to school due to a mobile lifestyle. Later, as planning law became more restrictive, and families began to settle on permanent sites or into housing, cultural influences were assumed to be largely responsible for non-registration, poor attendance and progress. More recent research, however, identifies 'push' factors as well as 'pull' factors that can impact on Gypsy Roma and Traveller pupils' attendance and engagement in school (Derrington 2007). Push factors can be either subtle or overt school-based effects, which deter some Traveller pupils from achieving their educational potential. In order to help address this inequality, teachers and schools need to:

- be alert to and challenge racism
- be aware of and respect cultural influences
- maintain and communicate high expectations.

Racism

Children from Gypsy, Roma and Traveller families have exactly the same rights to education as any other child, and it is unlawful for schools to discriminate on the grounds of lifestyle, culture or ethnicity. Under the Race Relations Amendment Act (2000), schools have a general duty to promote equality of opportunity, eliminate racial discrimination and promote good relationships between people from different racial backgrounds. They are also charged with specific duties such as preparing a written statement of policy for promoting race equality. This applies to all schools, regardless of whether there are pupils from different ethnic groups on roll. It is important that all schools remember to include Gypsy, Roma and Traveller communities in their work on inclusion and diversity in order to challenge the negative stereotypes that abound in the media.

People and groups that do not conform to, or fit neatly into, our own perception of 'normality' tend to be stigmatised and rejected, and it is often said that Gypsies, Roma and Travellers are the only minority ethnic groups about whom it is still socially acceptable to be racist (CRE 2005). Some people have a mental image of a 'true' Gypsy: the exotic and romanticised version, which is deemed more acceptable than the alternative, criminalised Gypsy, associated with theft, deception and mess. Both of these are unhelpful stereotypes generated and fuelled by reports and images in the media and consolidated through a lack of awareness. Travellers are as diverse as any other group of people and, if left unchallenged, such stereotyped attitudes will affect our behaviour towards and expectations of Traveller children in our schools, resulting in unprofessional practice.

Gypsy, Roma and Traveller pupils probably endure more racist name-calling than most teachers realise. A growing number of research studies reveal that this is a very common problem, which can discourage these children from attending school regularly (Lloyd et al. 1999; Reynolds et al. 2003; STEP 2003; Bowers 2004; Warrington 2006). In one study (Derrington and Kendall 2004), it was observed that around one in three Traveller students dealt with racist name-calling by retaliating physically, often with the encouragement of their parents. Unfortunately, this way of coping attracted negative attention from teachers. What's more, it was found that teachers were likely to attribute the retaliating behaviour to cultural traits rather than emotionally fuelled responses to racial harassment. Teachers were also inclined to believe that Gypsy, Roma and Traveller pupils were the initiators of conflict between peers (Wilkin et al. 2009a).

Awareness of Traveller culture

Although it can be detrimental to generalise cultural characteristics (particularly as these communities are diverse), some insight can help teachers to gain a better understanding of Gypsy, Roma or Traveller pupils and their families. It is important to appreciate, for example, that Traveller parents do tend to be very child-centred and highly protective, and it may take time and effort for a trusting relationship to develop between home and school. It is important to remember that Gypsies and Travellers have endured a long history of persecution and rejection by the settled community, and many parents continue to express anxiety about the physical, moral and psychological welfare of their children in school (Kiddle 1999, Parker-Jenkins and Hartas 2002; Ofsted 2003; Bowers 2004; Derrington and Kendall 2004; Padfield 2005). Older siblings and cousins may be under strict instructions from home to look out for and protect younger ones in the playground, and there may be reluctance from parents to allow their children to take part in school trips and extracurricular activities. Not all Traveller parents will have attended school as children themselves. Those parents may not be able to read and write well, or may be confused by educational jargon used in school. Some Traveller parents may have had unhappy personal experiences of school, making them wary of, or intimidated by, the school environment. Events such as pupil progress consultations, review meetings and curriculum information evenings may be avoided by anxious parents, perhaps giving teachers the impression that they are unsupportive or uninterested in their child's education (Derrington and Kendall 2004).

Traveller parents' anxiety about secondary school (in particular) is sometimes driven by the generalised belief that non-Traveller society is corrupt and lacking in moral standards. Strict moral codes are generally upheld in the community, and consequently, Travellers tend to marry at a young age. Widely publicised reports in the media of mainstream social problems related to drugs, alcohol and promiscuity are often cited by young Travellers and their parents in discussions about secondary education (Derrington 2007). These also feature strongly among the concerns that Traveller parents articulate when opting for Elective Home Education. Consequently, Traveller parents are likely to be attracted by the prospect of small schools, culturally diverse schools, single-sex secondary schools, faith schools, and those that are genuinely 'welcoming', where staff are perceived as having knowledge of, and respect for, Traveller culture, and where they believe their children will be safe (Parker-Jenkins and Hartas 2002; Wilkin et al. 2009b). This said, opposing concepts of safety and danger are socially constructed, and there may be cultural differences that are difficult for schools to understand. As mentioned previously, young Travellers are usually afforded a high level of protection by their families, and it is not uncommon for them to be forbidden to go on residential trips, parties or school discos for their own safety. Young children tend to be perceived and treated as 'babies' for several years, and it can be difficult to persuade some parents of the benefits of early years provision. However, paradoxically, once they reach middle childhood, Traveller children tend to assume adult responsibilities such as taking care of domestic and childcare duties, gaining financial independence, using tools and learning to drive. Most Traveller children are therefore quite used to working and socialising alongside adults, and tend to display a level of maturity that sets them apart from peers. They are often confident communicators, and their conversational style with adults can be direct and may even be perceived in school as outspokenness (Lloyd et al. 1999; MacNamara 2001).

Traditional gender roles are also promoted in some Traveller families, and girls may be discouraged from pursuing further education and a career. Another potential source of frustration for teachers is that strongly upheld values linked to family and community loyalty can take priority over education. This is gradually changing, as more parents realise the impact of irregular school attendance on academic progress, but opportunities for gatherings to celebrate birthdays, anniversaries and traditional horse fairs may still take precedence over anything that is happening at school.

Traveller pupils should be encouraged to be proud of their culture, and it is important that it is recognised within the curriculum. In schools where there is a lack of recognition, or denial of cultural difference, it can perpetuate 'the continuing ignorance of individual teachers' (Lloyd and McCluskey 2008: 10). There is a wealth of culturally relevant resources available for schools from the National Association of Teachers of Travellers + Other Professionals (www.NATT.org.uk), and most local authorities have staff with expertise in supporting the achievement of Gypsy, Roma and Traveller pupils.

An enhanced awareness of some of these cultural influences should enable teachers and schools to respond more empathically and flexibly to the needs of Traveller pupils and their families. However, maintaining high expectations and providing consistent messages to *all* pupils in terms of their behaviour, attendance, effort and attainment is fundamental.

Maintaining high expectations

Low expectations are often manifestations of generalised, stereotyped beliefs, and we develop them when we are unwilling or unable to obtain all the information we would need to make fair judgements about people or situations. These generalised beliefs may have their roots in our own limited experiences ('I got tricked once by a Gypsy') or those that have been relayed to us by relatives, friends or colleagues ('I had his brother in my class last year – good luck!'). They are also generated from stories we read in newspapers or what we see on TV and film and, as already mentioned, these are likely to be less than positive. Teachers' expectations of their pupils therefore tend to be based on limited evidence gleaned before they have even met the pupil(s) in question. Teachers' expectations (whether high or low) also tend to be self-fulfilling.

A number of studies have noted that teachers' expectations in relation to Gypsy Traveller pupils can be unreasonably low (Kiddle 1999; Ofsted 1999a,b; Bhopal et al. 2000; Derrington and Kendall 2007). Low teacher expectations may be expressed in conscious or unconscious, overt or subtle ways in the classroom, and they may even be well intentioned. Consider the following examples.

- A reception class teacher removes a shared reading record card from a Gypsy pupil's book bag because she has been told that the parents are illiterate.
- A Traveller pupil new to the school is placed in the lowest literacy and numeracy groups because it is assumed that he will have gaps in his learning.
- A pupil tells the teacher that her parents won't allow her to transfer to secondary school because 'Gypsy girls don't go to high school'. When no transfer form is returned, the school makes little attempt to follow this up.
- A Traveller pupil is absent from school most Fridays and this is marked in the register with the code T.[2]

- A fight breaks out in the playground and it is assumed that the Traveller boys started it.
- A part-time vocational course aimed especially at Traveller students is set up at the local college.

Even though some of these actions might have been implemented with the best interest of the child and his/her family at heart, what message might each one convey? The chances are, even the most subtle expression of low expectation will be internalised by pupils and their parents. For example, if absence from school is not followed up rigorously in the same way that it is for other pupils, this may be interpreted as an act of passive condoning that encourages further disengagement (self-fulfilling prophecy).

Conclusions

Despite official guidance aimed at raising outcomes for Gypsy, Roma and Traveller pupils over the past 15 years or so (Ofsted 1996, 1999a,b, 2003; Bhopal *et al.* 2000; DfES 2003; DCSF 2008a,b), the achievement of these groups remains unacceptably low. Some commentators argue that the predominant data-driven approach to raising educational standards has failed to take account of the complex and holistic needs of individual Gypsy, Roma and Traveller pupils (Foster and Walker 2009). A recent systematic review of the literature (Wilkin *et al.* 2009a) concludes that a history of low expectations and negative attitudes (on the part of teachers, parents and pupils), a lack of cultural awareness in schools, racist bullying, and discriminatory policies and practices have collectively been associated with the long-standing record of poor educational outcomes for these pupils.

In an effort to address this inequality, the former government stepped up its response by introducing a national targeted intervention programme to enhance the quality of educational provision, improve rates of attendance, reduce exclusions and raise attainment. This programme, part of the then government's Ethnicity, Social Class and Gender Achievement Plan, is known as the Gypsy, Roma and Traveller Achievement Programme (GRTAP). A number of participating primary and secondary schools across the UK worked closely with advisory teachers and National Strategy advisers to develop practice, build capacity and improve pupil outcomes. The key priorities of the programme were more effective use of data to track pupil progress, literacy interventions, parent partnership, early years education, better preparation and support for transfers and transition, the raising of ascription levels, and improvements in behaviour and attendance.

A significant outcome of the GRTAP is a set of four interrelated booklets entitled *Moving Forward Together: Raising Gypsy, Roma and Traveller Achievement* (DCSF 2009b). This set of materials (also available online) provides advice and information on a range of issues such as learning and teaching approaches, conditions for learning, the promotion of cultural diversity, challenging racism, and working effectively in partnership with families and communities.

Secondly, the Gypsy Roma Traveller History Month (GRTHM, www. grthm.co.uk), first launched in June 2008, aims to raise the profile and celebrate the culture and history of various Traveller communities. Like Black History month, this annual event takes place at the same time all over the country, and is marked by community-led activities to raise awareness of Gypsy, Roma and Traveller contributions to society. Schools are supported by the government's education department, and schools are encouraged to participate, regardless of whether or not they have Gypsy, Roma and Traveller pupils on roll.

Finally, a longitudinal research project into the underachievement of these groups was commissioned by the former government's education department (Wilkin et al. 2009b). This study identified a number of interwoven conditions that have a positive impact on educational outcomes for these groups of learners. These include the establishment of parental trust in the school as a perceived place of safety, evidence of mutual respect between pupils and staff and between parents/carers and staff, flexibility of school and teacher responses to cater for individual needs, and the communication of consistently high expectations for GRT pupils.

Every teacher has a professional duty to help close the attainment gap for all groups of pupils. The provision of high-quality teaching, underpinned by a commitment to inclusive education and equality issues, is likely to benefit all pupils including those from Gypsy, Roma and Traveller backgrounds. Furthermore, it has been suggested that the experiences and achievements of Gypsy, Roma and Traveller pupils in the classroom can be said to represent the 'litmus test' of inclusive education (Foster and Walker 2009).

Reflection on values and practice

- A Gypsy Roma Traveller pupil in your class is reported for fighting in the playground. He defends his actions by saying he was called 'Gyppo'.
  What would your response be in the immediate term, and as a follow-up to the incident?
- You have never had an opportunity to talk with the parents of a Traveller child in your class. They sit in the family vehicle rather than waiting at the school gate with other parents, and they have never been to a parents' evening.
  How do you interpret this behaviour? What could you do to encourage dialogue and build a relationship?

Notes

1 Pupil Level Annual School Census. Once a year, all maintained schools must provide the Department for Education with detailed information about each pupil, including

their ethnicity in order to monitor, among other things, whether certain groups of pupils are under-achieving disproportionately in relation to others.

2 The 'T' code denotes periods of travelling.

Resources

National Association of Teachers of Travellers + Other Professionals (NATT+): www. NATT.org.uk

Bhopal, K. and Myers, M. (2009) Gypsy, Roma and Traveller pupils in schools in the UK: inclusion and 'good practice', *International Journal of Inclusive Education* 13(3): 219–314.

O'Hanlon, C. and Holmes, P. (2004) *The Education of Gypsy and Traveller Children: Towards Inclusion and Educational Achievement,* Stoke on Trent: Trentham Books.

Tyler, C. (ed.) (2005) *Traveller Education: Accounts of Good Practice,* Stoke-on-Trent: Trentham Books.

References

Bhopal, K. with Gundara, J., Jones, C. and Owen, C. (2000) *Working Towards Inclusive Education for Gypsy Traveller Pupils* (RR 238), London: Department for Education and Employment.

Bowers, J. (2004) *Prejudice & Pride: The Experience of Young Travellers,* Ipswich: Ormiston Children & Families Trust.

CRE (2005) *Gypsies and Travellers: Strategy Plan 2004–7,* London: Commission for Racial Equality.

DCSF (2008a) *The Inclusion of Gypsy, Roma and Traveller Children and Young People,* London: Department for Children, Schools and Families.

——(2008b) *Raising the Achievement of Gypsy, Roma and Traveller Pupils,* London: Department for Children, Schools and Families.

——(2009a) *Schools, Pupils and their Characteristics,* SFR08/2009, London: Department for Children, Schools and Families.

——(2009b) *Moving Forward Together: Raising Gypsy, Roma and Traveller Achievement,* London: Department for Children, Schools and Families, http://nationalstrategies.standards. dcsf.gov.uk/node/248709

Derrington, C. (2007) 'Fight, flight and playing white: an examination of coping strategies adopted by Gypsy Traveller adolescents in English secondary schools', *International Journal of Educational Research,* 46(6): 357–67.

Derrington, C. and Kendall, S. (2004) *Gypsy Traveller Students in Secondary Schools: Culture, Identity and Achievement,* Stoke-on-Trent: Trentham Books.

——(2007). 'Challenges and barriers to secondary education: the experiences of young Gypsy Traveller students in English secondary schools', *Social Policy and Society,* 7(1): 1–10.

DfES (2003) *Aiming High: Raising the Achievement of Gypsy Traveller Pupils: A Guide to Good Practice,* London: Department for Education and Skills.

Foster, B. and Walker, A. (2009) *Traveller Education in the Mainstream: The Litmus Test,* Corsham: Hopscotch Educational Publishing.

Ivatts, A. (2006) *The Situation Regarding the Current Policy, Provision and Practice in Elective Home Education (EHE) for Gypsy, Roma and Traveller children,* London: Department for Education and Skills.

Kiddle, C. (1999) *Traveller Children: A Voice for Themselves*, London: Jessica Kingsley.

Lloyd, G. and McCluskey, G. (2008) 'Education and Gypsies/Travellers: "contradictions and significant silences"', *International Journal of Inclusive Education*, 12(4): 331–45.

Lloyd, G., Stead, J., Jordan, E. and Norris, C. (1999) 'Teachers and Gypsy Travellers', *Scottish Educational Review*, 31(1): 48–65.

MacNamara, Y. (2001) 'Education on the move', *ACE Bulletin*, 104 (December): 13.

Ofsted (1996) *The Education of Travelling Children*, London: Office for Standards in Education.

——(1999a) *Raising the Attainment of Minority Ethnic Pupils*, London: Office for Standards in Education.

——(1999b) *Raising the Attainment of Minority Ethnic Pupils: School and LEA Responses*, London: Office for Standards in Education.

——(2003) *Provision and Support for Traveller Pupils*, London: Office for Standards in Education.

Marks, K. and Wood, M. (2008) 'Supporting Traveller children', in Richards, G. and Armstrong, F. (eds) *Key Issues for Teaching Assistants: Working in Diverse and Inclusive Classrooms*, Abingdon: Routledge.

Martin, G. (1998) 'Generational differences amongst New Age Travellers', *Sociological Review*, 46(4): 735–56.

Padfield, P. (2005) 'Inclusive educational approaches for Gypsy/Traveller pupils and their families: an "urgent need for progress?" ' *Scottish Educational Review*, 37(2): 127–44.

Parker-Jenkins, M. and Hartas, D. (2002) 'Social inclusion: the case of Travellers' children', *Education 3–13*, 30(2): 39–42.

Reynolds, M., McCartan, D. and Knipe, D. (2003) 'Traveller culture and lifestyle as factors influencing children's integration into mainstream secondary schools in West Belfast', *International Journal of Inclusive Education*, 7(4): 403–14.

STEP (2003) *Inclusive Educational Approaches for Gypsies and Travellers within the Context of Interrupted Learning: Guidance for Local Authorities and Schools*, Glasgow: Learning and Teaching Scotland/Scottish Executive, Scottish Traveller Education Programme.

Warrington, C. (2006) *Children's Voices: Changing Future – The Views and Experiences of Young Gypsies and Travellers*, Ipswich: Ormiston Children & Families Trust.

Wilkin, A., Derrington, C. and Foster, B. (2009a) *Improving Outcomes for Gypsy, Roma and Traveller Pupils: A Literature Review*, London: Department for Children, Schools and Families.

Wilkin, A., Derrington, C., Foster, B., White, R. and Martin, K. (2009b) *Improving Outcomes for Gypsy, Roma and Traveller Pupils: What works? Contextual Influences and Constructive Conditions*, London: Department for Children, Schools and Families.

Chapter 5

The influence of gender in the classroom

How boys and girls learn

Steve Bartlett and Diana Burton

Introduction

All of us are affected in some way by issues of social class, ethnicity and gender. In this chapter we look specifically at the influence of gender on the achievement of pupils in our education system to raise the implications for inclusive ways of working. We consider how, for much of the twentieth century, research concentrated on the inequality of opportunity for girls and the social changes that have attempted to rectify this. We then look at the current debates surrounding the now apparently poor achievement of boys and the culture of underperformance accompanying this. We conclude by suggesting that any examination of the self-perception, motivation and achievement of children and young people needs to include a consideration of social class and ethnicity as well as gender. It is only by being aware of such factors that policies promoting social inclusion can have any hope of success. All teachers need to understand these significant forces in pupils' lives in order to make their practice more effective.

Sex and gender

Before we consider the impact of gender on pupil achievement, it is important to examine the terminology that is used in such debates. The term 'sex' is usually used when referring to our biological make-up. It identifies us as male or female. Biological differences include chromosomes, hormones, and physical sexual characteristics such as sexual organs, body hair and physique. The term 'gender' refers to the social construction of masculine and feminine. It is what we expect males and females to be like in terms of behaviour, appearance, beliefs and attitudes. There is a continuing debate as to how much of our maleness and femaleness is biologically determined and how much is socially constructed.

A biological determinist position holds that our biological sex is significant in determining us as individuals. Our biological make-up plays the major part in deciding how we behave. Thus mothering and caring are presented as female traits, while aggression and protecting are male. This biological base can be seen as underpinning many explanations for the structure of families and the conjugal roles within them. An alternative view is that, although there are certain biological differences between males and females, it is society and the culture that we live in that creates the notions of masculinity and femininity.

Early feminist writers such as Oakley (1975) wished to highlight the significance of cultural as opposed to biological factors in explaining the ongoing socially inferior position of women in society. Their argument was that it was the social constructions of gender and sexuality that led to the oppression of women. The biological accounts were seen as part of male social control that perpetuated the myth of male superiority. The whole notion of masculinity and femininity from this perspective was socially determined.

There are physical differences between males and females, and these become more obvious as we grow up and move through adolescence and into adulthood. However, there is a wide variation both within and across the genders in terms of individual physical characteristics. What is deemed as attractive to the opposite sex is different from society to society, and changes over time with fashion. Clothing, diet and body-building/-reducing exercises to change our appearance are all used, and with advances in medical science people can radically alter their physical characteristics and even biological sex. In modern societies, and across a range of cultures, any presentation of a clear, uncomplicated sexual divide is rather an oversimplification.

Masculinities and femininities

As teenagers strive to be independent from their elders, they are also subject to strong peer pressures. Gender characteristics that stereotype appropriate physical appearance and behaviour can cause pressure to conform, particularly on young people who are coming to terms with themselves as they develop. To be identified as different or 'other' can have a significant effect on the self-image of young people. Pupils' interactions and perceptions are significant in the 'othering' process. Labels become attached to pupils, and some are more difficult to resist or counter than others. Language plays a very powerful part in this process, and use of sexual insults such as 'gay', 'queer' or 'slag' may have lasting repercussions for the identity, future interactions and sexual behaviour of the young people involved (Vicars 2006).

Stereotypical images of boys in school include loud, boisterous behaviour, lack of interest in studying, and generally taking a rushed and untidy approach to work. Images of stereotypical girl behaviour include being quiet, hardworking, neat and careful in appearance. If we look at real groups of young people and consider the broad range that exists in terms of behaviour, beliefs, values and appearance, we see how inappropriate it is to use such stereotypes. One should beware of using too rigid a definition of what constitutes female or male behaviour of young people. Some writers, such as Mac an Ghaill (1994), Swain (2004) and Connell (2006) speak of a range of masculinities and femininities, thus allowing for greater variation.

Paechter (2006) suggests that as children grow older, they move through successive overlapping communities as they develop their understanding of what it means to be an adult man or woman. Swain (2004) says that pupils live within the context of their own communities, and that these wider contexts influence individual school policies and cultures. Thus schools are influenced by local employment opportunities, housing type, and the religious and ethnic mix of the area. Within this, Swain says that each school also has its own *gender regime*. This 'consists of ... individual personnel expectations, rules, routines and a hierarchical ordering of particular practices' (*ibid.*: 182).

It is worth considering the integral part that gender relationships play in school life and how these vary depending upon the ethos of the school (Liu 2006; Mellor and Epstein 2006). School uniform, lining up in the playground or outside the classroom, class lists that separate boys and girls, and how pupils and teachers are addressed are all instances where gender may or may nor be highlighted in formal school procedures. Gender is also part of informal school processes, for example, the arrangement of each individual classroom and where pupils sit, who children play with at break times and what they play, the number of pupils choosing different subjects at secondary school, and the number of male and female adults employed by the school and their positions of responsibility. Since schools are a key part of the wider socialisation process, they both influence and are influenced by gender relationships.

A historical view of recent developments in gender relations in Britain

How the roles of men and women and their relationships to each other vary over time can be illustrated by considering the period from Victorian England to the present day. In the early 1800s, Britain was very much a patriarchal society. Women were not able to vote, own property or obtain a divorce. Within the middle classes, women were effectively under the control of either their father or their husband. It was men who governed the empire and the society, ran businesses and supported the family. Women did not work, and were confined to a life that revolved around the home. Boys from the more affluent classes would be educated at public and grammar schools, but the education of girls would be primarily left to governesses and conducted in the home, based on the knowledge deemed suitable for a lady. For the working classes, life was much harder and both men and women worked, although women did the more menial factory work and were paid less than men. In the early educational provision for the working classes, girls were able to attend school as well as boys, although both were taught appropriately to the social expectations of the time.

It has taken many years of political and social pressure for women to achieve legal equality with men. They gained the right to divorce, they won the vote, and the Sex Discrimination Act 1975 outlawed discrimination on the grounds of gender. From this date women, legally at least, had equality with men. However, there were still economic and social differences that were strongly influenced by gender. In employment terms, women remained underrepresented in many, usually more highly paid, professions, and the average earnings of women remained well below those of men. It has actually proved very difficult for women to 'break into' male-dominated areas such as medicine, law and engineering. At the time of the Sex Discrimination Act, it was still widely accepted that a woman's place remained in the home and that the man was the main breadwinner. Women's employment was largely seen as temporary before starting a family, or as a way of supplementing the family income when the children were older. Changes in attitude have continued to take place, and over the years women have increasingly taken up careers in many areas in which previously they had not.

Education reflects social and political attitudes. State education has been provided throughout the twentieth century to all pupils, regardless of gender. In the early part of the 1900s, the elementary schools were co-educational. While primary schools have always been co-educational, the introduction of a selective secondary system saw the development of single-sex secondary schools. It was the development of new, large comprehensive schools from the 1960s onwards that saw boys and girls taught together in their secondary education. From this time, it could be argued that there was gender equality in state education.

Gender and achievement

Being taught in the same school did not remove the impact of gender on pupils' experiences. In the 1970s and 1980s, much feminist research in education was concerned with the perceived underachievement of girls, and how the education process worked to maintain this through discrimination and marginalisation (Oakley 1975; Sharpe 1976; Spender 1982; Whyte 1983). Gender differences were maintained and highlighted through the processes of schooling, which involved the separation of the genders through school uniforms, differential expectations of behaviour, and a gender-specific curriculum (for example, needlework and typing for girls; metalwork and technical drawing for boys). This was further enforced through the attitudes of teachers, peers, parents, and later (usually male) employers. Thus the ambitions of female students remained low, and they were discouraged in a variety of ways from choosing the 'hard' mathematical and scientific subjects so important to future employment prospects in favour of the more 'feminine' arts and humanities.

Curriculum strategies

In the 1970s and 1980s, strategies were developed to make the curriculum more girl-friendly, and a number of initiatives were designed to improve the achievement of girls by raising awareness, altering attitudes and increasing ambition. Consideration was given to the curriculum and teaching methods. For example, The Girls into Science and Technology Project investigated the reasons for girls' underachievement in science and technology, and encouraged teachers to develop classroom strategies to change this (Smail 2000). Similarly, Genderwatch was a practical evaluation pack that promoted an action research approach, enabling teachers to monitor gender in all areas of the daily life of their schools. Teachers were able to analyse curriculum content, their teaching practices, and how pupils were treated in all aspects of their school experience. The pack was designed to raise awareness and encourage the adoption of positive antidiscriminatory action (Myers 1987). An updated version, *Genderwatch – Still Watching*, has also been published (Myers *et al.* 2007).

Raising girls' achievement

While the raising of awareness and the development work that accompanied it were all based on a belief in the underachievement of girls relative to boys, the reality was not that straightforward. Even in the 1970s, girls were out-performing boys in English and modern foreign languages. Also, more girls were achieving five or more O-level passes (equivalent to A*–C, GCSE) than boys. However, because these included subjects that were seen as low status, such as home economics, and because boys were doing better at maths and sciences, regarded as 'hard' subjects of high status, girls were perceived as underachieving (Francis 2000). Also, the selective system of grammar and secondary modern schools, in operation before the development of the comprehensive system, had favoured boys due to the larger number of places available in boys' grammar schools as opposed to those admitting girls. Thus boys did not need to score as highly as girls in the 11+ to secure a grammar school education. It was not the case, then, that girls were necessarily under-achieving, but their success was not being recognised and they were not offered the same opportunities or encouragement as boys in order to pursue the more rewarding economic options. Girls' futures were still being perceived as domestically based.

The introduction of the national curriculum in 1988 unwittingly had what is now often regarded as a significant impact on the achievements of girls (*ibid.*). From its inception, all pupils were required to study the national curriculum. Thus it was no longer possible for boys or girls to drop some subjects in favour of others. Along with the new curriculum, a system of national assessment for all pupils at different stages in their education was introduced. It was now possible to produce league tables based on these Key Stage tests, and also GCSE and A-level results. These were, and are, used to judge overall school performance, making the achievements of boys and girls more transparent than ever. They show how the performance of both boys and girls has steadily improved. What has caught the public attention, though, is that the improvement in the results of girls has been greater than that of boys. While continuing to outperform boys in language subjects, girls have caught up with boys in maths and the sciences. Concern now became focused on the performance of boys.

Current performance of boys and girls

We need to be very cautious when interpreting statistics on gender and examination performance. Looking at national curriculum assessment, the picture is of a general trend towards increasing achievement of all pupils since national testing began. There appears to be little significant difference in achievement between boys and girls in maths and science, although girls continue to perform better than boys in English. (Data and analysis of national curriculum assessments can be found on the government's education website.)

In terms of GCSE performance, DCFS statistics (www.dcfs.gov) show that over the past decade the percentage of all pupils gaining five or more GCSE grades at A*–C has steadily increased. Girls continue to attain a higher percentage of five or more passes at A*–C and to perform better than boys in English, although there is little statistical difference in the area of maths and science.

It is important for teachers to realise that the difference in performance between boys and girls is not that great, with high percentages of boys continuing to perform well. Also, there is a wide range of achievement both among boys and among girls, with many young people continuing to experience academic and behavioural difficulties at school. It is these pupils who need the support of education professionals.

Explanations for boys' underachievement

Recent industrial and economic changes have meant that the male is now no longer the only, or even the major, 'breadwinner' in the family. Thus the traditional masculine image in working-class communities is not as applicable as it was even 20 years ago, and it is suggested that many working-class boys see no particular role for themselves. They see no need to work hard at school, as it will make little difference to their future. At the same time, these boys emphasise and play out their masculinity at school, where it is important to be seen as 'hard' and 'cool', not a 'poof' or a 'swot' (Smith, 2003). Elwood

(2005: 337) notes that over the past 20 years, the debate has thus shifted from being about the creation of equal opportunities and improving the educational experiences of girls to concerns about male underachievement and disadvantage.

Connolly (2004) suggests that the panic surrounding the underachievement of boys has been rather an overreaction. The media have portrayed boys as falling behind, and have homed in on an apparent growth of a 'laddish' culture among teenage boys that is anti-study, against school values, and leads to underachievement. Calls for developing strategies that focus on the motivations, attitudes and performance of boys have resulted. The DCSF (2009a) publication *Gender Issues in Schools* points out that to see all boys as underachieving is misleading, as some groups of boys do achieve highly while some groups of girls do not. It can of course be argued that as working-class boys could always get masculine jobs in the past, they have never really had reason to work hard at school. Arnot and Miles (2005) suggest that the increasing emphasis on a performative school system has led to greater resistance from working-class boys who have a history of low achievement. This, they say, is being misinterpreted as a new development, termed 'laddishness'. Significantly, Connolly (2006: 15) says that masculinities and femininities are not just about gender alone, but must be seen as combining with social class and ethnicity to 'produce differing and enduring forms of identity'. It is this complex mix that teachers need to be aware of.

It is important to consider some of the explanations for the achievement of both boys and girls, if only to 'identify and dispel some of the current and unhelpful myths about gender and education' (DCSF 2009a).

Explanations involving genetic differences

A biologically determinist view may look for mental differences between males and females to help explain any subject preferences or differences in achievement. However, there is little neurological evidence to suggest that boys have different cognitive ability or ways of learning than girls (*ibid.*), and while we become more sceptical of the whole concept of learning styles (Coffield *et al.* 2004; Burton 2007), there is no clear evidence that any such styles could be gender-specific. In fact, DCSF (2009a) suggests that any learning practices or preferences that are gendered are likely to be due to social rather than biological pressures. Feminist analysts would suggest that the 'moral panic' that has accompanied this perceived failure of boys and the demand to rectify the situation is a reflection of fear within the male-dominated political establishment.

Explanations involving school culture

It is suggested that schools have become more female-oriented in recent decades, and that school culture now works in favour of girls and against the achievement of boys (Noble *et al.* 2001 and Smith 2003 discuss these arguments). It has been assumed that the assessment regimes have developed to favour girls, with more emphasis on coursework rather than final exams. However, this trend in assessment has reversed in recent years with no significant falling back of girls' performance. Girls appear to do well in examinations as well as coursework assignments (Elwood 2005).

The curriculum is said by some to favour girls, with little to excite boys. This point does ignore the many areas of the curriculum where the content has been specifically chosen to attract boys. DCSF (2009a) suggests that there is no evidence that the content of the secondary curriculum reflects particularly gendered interests, though it does warn that girls still remain underrepresented in science, technology and maths subjects at university, and that the introduction of vocational diplomas at 14–19 may encourage many boys and girls to opt for traditional gendered routes from 14.

Jones and Myhill (2004) note how beliefs about identity can inform teachers' perceptions, resulting in a tendency to associate boys with underachievement and girls with high achievement. Elwood (2005) says that for many teachers and policy makers, boys are now seen as 'poor boys', or that 'boys will be boys', or as 'problem' boys. This labelling process may contribute to the low expectations of boys, thus creating a self-fulfilling prophecy. It is these expectations that are perhaps part of the problem. Proposed solutions to low achievement emanating from these stereotypes involve shifting classroom practices in order to engage boys' interests. However, as noted above, there is no evidence to suggest that the curriculum as in any way 'anti-boy' (DCSF 2009a). Changing the curriculum to make it boy-friendly appears to have little affect on boys' achievements; in fact, such changes may involve gender stereotyping that could actually limit the choices that boys and girls make (Keddie and Mills 2008).

It is also a myth that boys prefer a competitive environment. In fact, if they are not succeeding, an emphasis on competition may actually be counterproductive. It also appears to be a fallacy that introducing single-sex classes is a way to improve achievement in secondary schools. While, in some cases, single-sex classes may benefit girls, the evidence for boys is much more mixed.

Strategies for raising achievement

As pupils' achievement is based on a number of interrelated factors, it would be expected that strategies to raise attainment would not just focus on gender. Both boys and girls want teachers who are able to motivate through exciting and challenging lessons, regardless of whether they are male or female. The overall quality of the curriculum is more significant than whether some parts are gender biased. DCSF (2009b) has produced guidance for teachers seeking to improve boys' and girls' achievement. It suggests that tackling gender differences that have a negative impact on achievement should be done at a whole-school level. The guidance borrows a number of key components from Warrington *et al.* (2006), and suggests that the following contribute to the establishment of an inclusive school ethos:

- high expectations of behaviour from all pupils, with emphasis on the development of self-discipline
- valuing diversity in all areas of school life; intolerance and discrimination are challenged
- encouraging pupils to have a pride in their work and achievements
- enabling pupils to become fully involved in the life of the school
- continually emphasising the values of inclusion and opportunity as an integral part of school life.(Adapted from Warrington *et al.* 2006.)

DCSF (2009b) suggests a number of gender-related strategies that can be used when developing an equitable and inclusive school ethos. These include:

- creating a gender-equitable school culture by tackling gender stereotypes in behaviour
- deconstructing and challenging stereotypes in the content of the curriculum
- applying expectations of high achievement for all pupils.

Each of these strategies involves a process of reviewing current positions, deciding appropriate actions and monitoring changes. They will involve teachers, other adults working in the school, and also pupils.

Conclusions

In summarising the arguments concerning gender and achievement, we can say that the performance of boys and girls overall has improved throughout the 1990s and the 2000s, that girls have been improving faster than boys, and that they are now performing at least equally to boys in all subjects and outperforming them in some. However, to portray girls as achieving and boys as underachieving is too simplistic a view (Arnot and Miles 2005; Elwood 2005; Gipps 2006). It should be noted that the differences in overall performance of boys and girls are not that great. It is the improvement in performance of girls from the more middle-class backgrounds in all subjects that has caused the rise in girls' performance overall. Boys from middle-class backgrounds continue generally to perform well. Boys and girls from the lower socio-economic groups continue to underperform when compared with their more affluent peers. Thus, as Connolly (2006) points out, while gender does exert an influence on attainment, this may be overshadowed by the effects of social class and ethnicity. Effective teachers must take account of these factors while endeavouring to treat pupils as the individuals they are. We should not focus on gender alone. Good teaching aims to empower all pupils.

Reflection on values and practice

• Draw an organisational chart for your school. Identify whether each position is occupied by a male or female. Compare your results with colleagues working in other schools. What conclusions can you draw from the results of this exercise in terms of gender and employment in schools? Do your findings have any policy implications?

• Conduct a gender audit of one area of the curriculum. Consider content, teaching approaches, and resources used such as worksheets and text books. What conclusions do you draw about the gendered nature of the curriculum? Do you need to make changes or not? What can you do to develop and improve this curriculum for all pupils?

• Observe pupils working in class. Consider how different groups and individuals work differently over a period of time. Look particularly at the characteristics of the groups – how long is spent on each task, cooperative behaviour, and quality of work produced. Is gender a factor in any of the variations you notice? How might you intervene to change things?

Resources

DCSF (2009a, 2009b): these two short booklets are available on the teachernet website (www.teachernet.gov.uk). They are clearly written, explain the current position, provide many current academic sources and give practical advice. They should be read together.

Oakley (1975): though now rather old, this is still a classic feminist text on gender relationships in society. A very interesting account that encourages the reader to reflect on how things have changed, or not, since its publication.

Skelton et al. (2006): this edited text provides a comprehensive overview of different theoretical positions on gender issues from early years to higher education.

References

Arnot, M. and Miles, P. (2005) 'A reconstruction of the gender agenda: the contradictory gender dimensions in New Labour's educational and economic policy', Oxford Review of Education, 31(1): 173–89.

Burton, D. (2007) 'Psychopedagogy and personalised learning', Journal of Education for Teaching, 33(1): 5–17.

Coffield, F., Moseley, D. and Hall, E. (2004) Should We Be Using Learning Styles? What Research Has To Say To Practice, London: Learning and Skills Research Centre.

Connell, R.W. (2006) 'Understanding men: gender sociology and the new international research on masculinities', in Skelton, C., Francis, B. and Smulyan, L. (eds) The Sage Handbook of Gender and Education, London: Sage.

Connolly, P. (2004) Boys and Schooling in the Early Years, London: RoutledgeFalmer.

——(2006) 'The effects of social class and ethnicity on gender differences in GCSE attainment: a secondary analysis of the Youth Cohort Study of England and Wales 1997–2001', British Educational Research Journal, 32(1): 3–21.

DCSF (2009a) *Gender and Education – Mythbusters. Addressing Gender and Achievement: Myths and Realities*, London: Department for Children, Schools and Families.

——(2009b) *Gender Issues in School – What Works to Improve Achievement for Boys and Girls*, London: Department for Children, Schools and Families.

Elwood, J. (2005) 'Gender and achievement: what have exams got to do with it?', *Oxford Review of Education*, 31(3): 373–393.

Francis, B. (2000) *Boys, Girls and Achievement. Addressing the Classroom Issues*, London: Routledge.

Gipps, C. (2006) 'Gender, performance and learning style', public lecture, University of Wolverhampton, 10 May 2006.

Jones, S. and Myhill, D. (2004) ' "Troublesome boys" and "compliant girls": gender identity and perceptions of achievement and underachievement', *British Journal of Sociology of Education*, 25(5): 547–61.

Keddie, A. and Mills, M. (2008) *Teaching Boys*, Crows Nest, NSW: Allen and Unwin.

Liu, F. (2006) 'School culture and gender', in Skelton, C., Francis, B. and Smulyan, L. (eds) *The Sage Handbook of Gender and Education*, London: Sage.

Mac an Ghaill, M. (1994) *The Making of Men: Masculinities, Sexuality and Schooling*, Buckingham: Open University Press.

Mellor, D. and Epstein, D. (2006) 'Appropriate behaviour? Sexualities, schooling and hetero-gender', in Skelton, C., Francis, B. and Smulyan, L. (eds) *The Sage Handbook of Gender and Education*, London: Sage.

Myers, K. (1987) *Genderwatch: Self-Assessment Schedules for Use in Schools*, London: Schools Curriculum Development Council.

Myers, K., Taylor, H. with Adler, S. and Leonard, D. (eds) (2007) *Genderwatch – Still Watching*, Stoke-on-Trent: Trentham.

Noble, C., Brown, J. and Murphy, J. (2001) *How to Raise Boys' Achievement*, London: David Fulton.

Oakley, A. (1975) *Sex, Gender and Society*, London: Temple Smith.

Paechter, C. (2006) 'Constructing femininity/constructing femininities', in Skelton, C., Francis, B. and Smulyan, L. (eds) *The Sage Handbook of Gender and Education*, London: Sage.

Sharpe, S. (1976) *Just Like a Girl: How Girls Learn to be Women*, Harmondsworth: Penguin.

Skelton, C., Francis, B. and Smulyan, L. (eds) (2006) *The Sage Handbook of Gender and Education*, London: Sage.

Smail, B. (2000) 'Has the mountain moved? The Girls Into Science and Technology Project 1979–83', in Myers, K. (ed.) *Whatever Happened to Equal Opportunities in Schools? Gender Equality Initiatives in Education*, Buckingham: Open University Press.

Smith, E. (2003) 'Failing boys and moral panics: perspectives on the underachievement debate', *British Journal of Educational Studies*, 51(3): 282–95.

Spender, D (1982) *Invisible Women: The Schooling Scandal*, London: Writers and Readers.

Swain, J. (2004) 'The resources and strategies that 10–11-year-old boys use to construct masculinities in the school setting', *British Educational Research Journal*, 30(1): 167–85.

Vicars, M. (2006) 'Who are you calling queer? Sticks and stones can break my bones but names will always hurt me', *British Educational Research Journal*, 32(3): 347–61.

Warrington, M., Younger, M. and Bearne, E. (2006) *Raising Boys' Achievement in Primary Schools: Towards a Holistic Approach*, Maidenhead: Open University Press/McGraw Hill.

Whyte, J. (1983) *Beyond the Wendy House: Sex-Role Stereotyping in Primary Schools*, York: Longman.

Chapter 6

Not in my image

Personalisation and ethnic diversity in the classroom

Raphael Richards

Typically, the ethnic diversity context of UK maintained schools includes some or all of the following:

- increasing numbers of pupils from black and minority ethnic (BME) groups, with five of every 30 pupils in a secondary school, and six of every 30 in a primary school, being of BME heritage
- a significant proportion of BME pupils having English as an additional language (EAL)
- fewer than one in 15 core subject lessons being taught by a teacher of BME heritage
- boys of BME heritage being disproportionately excluded from classroom learning environments covering the core curriculum.

Introduction

Do you remember the times when, as a student or teacher, you longed for some support, needed advice and someone to reflect on an issue with you? Now, imagine spending five to six hours each day in lessons doing History, Geography, Science and English, without seeing or hearing from adults who look like you or reflect you as a Black, Asian or Muslim young person. When we reflect on our schooling experience, there are often two or three people who stand out, mostly because they took an interest in our learning. They may have helped us to develop a sense of who we were, or believed we were talented and capable of achieving in their classroom and beyond.

In this chapter I want to explore the varied characteristics that make up the diversity of our classrooms, with a focus on BME children and young people, and link them to the personalisation agenda. By highlighting some of the key issues around education in an ethnically diverse classroom, and how personalisation can help respond to these issues, it is hoped that teachers and other education professionals will reflect on their own development and practices in our increasingly ethnically diverse classrooms. As we explore 'Not in my image', you will see that the debate is increasingly about us as individuals and the relationships we are able to build with children and young people, their parents and our understanding of the families we serve and their communities. Finally, I aim to leave readers with a basis from which to expand their role in raising the achievement of BME children and young people.

In schools across the country, the ethnic diversity of the classroom will vary widely depending on where you are in the country and in the city in which you live. Even within many cities, the ethnic diversity of neighbouring schools can be very different. In 2006, the minority ethnic population in schools nationally stood at 18.5%. The (then) Department for Education and Skills predicted that by 2010 over 20% of pupils would be of minority ethnic heritage in maintained schools (DfES 2006). In 2010 the Department for Education reported that 6% of teachers in maintained schools were from ethnic minority communities (DfE 2010).

The key tenor of this chapter is that for 'personalisation' to be successful, teachers and other educators must consider what knowledge and experience they bring to the classroom, and how that influences children's and young people's culture, language and social development. A targeted approach to supporting individual BME pupils and groups, which is designed to raise their achievement and improve their progress and educational experience, will enhance our collective success and wellbeing in schools and local authorities. However, for us to be successful, each and every pupil needs detailed personal attention from teachers who understand their life experiences.

Ethnicity and diversity in schools

The National Census provides the official ethnographic data for the UK. In the 1951 Census, the ethnographic measures were 'White' and 'Non-White' (the latter of which were reportedly fewer than 1%) (Peach 1996). Over time, the ethnographic categories have expanded to reflect the changing population of Britain. In the main, schools today are educating second- or third-generation British-born children, whose heritage is from the West Indies, India, Pakistan, Somalia or Poland, and who between them speak over 300 languages. Some examples of key events that have contributed to the rich ethnic diversity of schools today are described below.

- During the Second World War, over 100,000 refugees entered Britain from Norway, Denmark, Holland, Belgium and France after the fall of their countries to Hitler; these included around 25,000 Austrian and German Jews, who had previously fled to those countries (Refugee Council 1998).
- The 1948 Commonwealth Act granted Commonwealth subjects the statutory right of entry to the UK; large groups came from the Caribbean islands

and the Indian subcontinent to work in the British service industries (Kitchen 1996).

- The *Empire Windrush* docked in Tilbury, Essex on 28 June 1948 with 492 Caribbean men and women, signalling a new wave of immigration from Britain's former colonies (Mead 2009).
- In 1972, Asians in Uganda were ordered to leave the country. Half those leaving held British passports and had the right of entry to resettle in the UK.
- Since 2004, there have been more than one million EU migrant workers from EU accession countries entering the UK to work (www.researchasylum.org.uk).

The schools' population is measured yearly through the Pupil Level Annual School Census (PLASC). The Schools Census, as it is now commonly known, captures information about children, provided by their parents. When a child enters a school, his or her parents or legal carers complete a form declaring the child's ethnicity, first language and other information. While most BME populations can be found in the urban areas of England, few schools have no BME or EAL pupils. Most BME pupils are born in the UK and are of second or third generation.

Within the context of ethnicity and diversity, teachers often ask for clarification of terms used to describe groups. It is important to be explicit and clear about what one means when using such terms; it is common to use these very loosely. Below I set out a working definition of key terms used; however, it is important that readers review and contextualise diversity, ethnicity, race and home language within their school and local community.

- **Culture** encompasses the learned traditions and aspects of lifestyle that are shared by members of a society or community, including their habitual ways of thinking, feeling and behaving. The use of this term is often based on an assumption that there is cultural cohesion and homogeneity in the society or community (Fredrickson and Cline 2002).
- **Ethnicity** is a label that reflects perceived membership of, and a sense of belonging to, a distinctive social group. The crucial distinguishing features of an ethnic group vary between different contexts, and change over time. They may include physical appearances, first language, religious belief and practices, national allegiance, family structure and occupation (Phinney 1990). Ethnicity may be self-defined, or assigned by how others categorise individuals or groups.
- **Race** was originally a concept categorising a group of people who are connected by common descent or origin and have some common physical features. However, there is no single characteristic, trait or gene that distinguishes all members of one 'race' from all members of another. Race is a construct created by society to describe people according to their outward

appearance. Race is a powerful marker that has often been used for monitoring purposes.

- **BME** (Black and minority ethnic) refers to all people in the UK who are not White British. These include people of mixed parentage where one parent is white, and now, people from other predominantly non-white countries. Categories include Black, Pakistani, Gypsy Traveller, and Mixed Black African. These selections can vary from official form to form; however, all will either contract or expand the 19 choices available in the 2001 National Census.
- **EAL** (English as an additional language) refers to the teaching of English to speakers of other languages. Current statistics indicate that significant numbers of pupils in maintained schools are learning English as a second, third, or indeed fourth language.

The terms and concepts that are used to describe society's diversity are relevant in our schools as they are micro-reflections of local communities (Corbett *et al.* 1998; Ryan 1999). In many cities, the minority ethnic school population is greater than 30% (for example, London, Birmingham, Leeds and Manchester). In other areas, such as Cumbria, Norwich and Plymouth, the minority ethnic school population is less than 6%. Regardless of the setting, the support needs of minority ethnic pupils must be met (DfES 2004; Knowles and Ridley 2006). At some point in their careers, the majority of teachers and teaching assistants across Britain are likely to work with minority ethnic pupils.

Minority ethnic attainment characteristics

A key purpose of Children's Services is to implement the 'Every Child Matters' agenda. This may suggest that the need for focusing on ethnic diversity has become redundant, particularly when schools are being encouraged to focus on the needs of the whole child, using a personalised approach. I would argue that ethnicity is an integral part of individual pupils, and that to varying degrees it has an impact on how they view their environment. More importantly, pupils react to the way teachers and other adults in school interact with them on a range of levels, including verbal, non-verbal, active and inactive. Many teachers talk about not 'seeing' colour; others see cultures and social class as barriers to BME pupils achieving. These views are often manifested in the way teachers interact with BME pupils.

There are high achievers in all minority ethnic groups, with Chinese and Indian pupils generally outperforming all groups at all Key Stages. In my experience, high-achieving pupils regularly cite supportive teachers, parents or other significant adults, including mentors. They tell of people inspiring them and believing they would achieve, and also talk about wanting to attain a particular goal. Some talk about overcoming adversity and defying teachers and other adults who told them they would not achieve. Successful BME children and young people usually have an understanding of the academic challenges, are aspirational, and have their pastoral needs met at school and at home. They are also often part of a supportive community of self-sufficient, informed and engaged, high-achieving young people.

One of the major features of minority ethnic pupils' underachievement is 'low expectation' stemming from teachers and sometimes from parents. Recent research in the UK has found that (after controlling for all other factors) for every three White British pupils entered for the higher-tier examinations, only two Black Caribbean pupils are entered (Strand 2008), and black students are more likely to be placed in lower-ability groupings than their white peers (GLA 2006; Gillborn and Youdell 2009). Educators commonly agree that the stigma of underachievement needs to be removed from all groups. This means tackling low expectation, creating an inclusive environment, and responding to individual needs (Green 2000).

The Every Child Matters agenda combined with its 'five outcomes' helps us to look at the individual child's experience. That said, group data provide useful indicators in schools as to how specific groups fare in the classroom and in the wider school community. By looking at trends over time, we can see if specific groups are underachieving or consistently failing to make progress. The government's education department now reports yearly on ethnicity and education for maintained schools nationally.

Since ethnicity data have become more readily available throughout schools, they have highlighted the reality of BME pupils' progression and outcomes in maintained schools: while some minority ethnic groups are out performing their white counterparts, others, including Caribbean, Pakistani and Bangladeshi pupils, are significantly underperforming. National ethnicity data show that regional and local outcomes vary significantly. For example, Caribbean pupils do well at GCSE in a few cities, while in others their progress is slow throughout secondary schooling (DfES 2006). However, the topical attainment debate in 2007 focused on white working class boys' progress in secondary schools compared with minority ethnic pupils' progress. This reflected the complex interconnectedness of issues of attainment and progression when comparing and reviewing groups by either class or ethnicity.

English as an additional language

English as an Additional Language (EAL) is the expression used in the UK to refer to the teaching of English to speakers of other languages. Current statistics indicate that almost 10 per cent of pupils in maintained schools are learning English as a second, third, or indeed fourth, language, in addition to the language spoken in their families and homes. Over 300 languages are spoken by pupils in UK schools.

(Multiverse 2009)

In some ethnic groups, the majority of pupils are registered as EAL pupils: over 90% of Bangladeshi and Pakistani pupils are registered as EAL, 82% of Indian, 75% of Chinese and 65% of Black African. This compares with fewer than 2% of White pupils and fewer than 7% of Black Caribbean pupils.

The objectives of teachers are to help EAL pupils beyond being able to communicate fluently in English, and to help them acquire sound academic language as appropriate to their curriculum levels. As with all learners, pupils learning EAL should be encouraged to become increasingly independent in their learning. If a pupil appears fluent in social English, it is still important to plan carefully for language development so the pupil can manage the literacy demands of curriculum subjects. Bearing this in mind, English language teaching (ELT) is vital to an inclusive curriculum; it is essential that teachers in schools with a high percentage of bilingual pupils develop their ELT skills and utilise the number of existing specialist roles to support EAL, among them Specialist Language Support Teachers, Bilingual Teaching Assistants, Higher Level Teaching Assistants, EAL Coordinators and EAL Champions.

For teachers and teaching assistants, the challenge is to identify how their individual actions and continued professional development can be shaped to have a positive impact on the underachievement of individuals and groups in their classroom, particularly those from minority ethnic communities. According to the GTC:

> Teachers believe that for pupils, the most important issues to address are social class, race/ethnicity and gender. Asked what is needed to tackle underachievement, the overwhelming majority of teachers believe that 'the achievement of each individual child needs to be maximised'. They identify a mix of measures to help, including raising parental and school expectations of the child.
>
> (GTC 2006)

Personalisation and ethnic diversity

Like all significant debates, it is difficult to pinpoint the exact starting point. David Miliband, Schools Standards Minister in 2003, was clear about what personalisation entailed: 'fitting the "learning styles, motivations and needs" of individuals, empowering young people to become self-starters and ready to add to their learning. Not letting pupils do what they liked, which would simply trap children in their own low aspirations'. David Hopkins, who was a Chief Advisor to UK Ministers of Education in 2004, identified the foundations of personalisation as reflecting people's aspirations and their growing appetite for learning. He particularly stressed the *moral purpose* that drives personalisation: teachers matching teaching to the individual learner, and teachers as a profession working together to equip learners with the proficiency and confidence to pursue understanding for themselves.

The Canadian example of personalisation put forward by Hébert and Hartley (2006: 498) is that change (to personalisation) will occur through societies shaped by moral, socio-economic, political and legal influences. They consider that these sociological and historical perspectives are important in relation to the personalisation agenda. What counts as "personal" is not fixed but highly bound by cultural and historical factors. Therefore educators are called upon to see beyond broad social representations of children and young people so as to support their strengths, legitimacy, diversity and vitality. In structuring personalised learning, a crucial element must be to ensure that those in greatest need, and often those with low attainment or attendance, are targeted and then offered support, such as personal timetables, additional lessons and extended school activities.

Personalisation begins with the teacher and his or her aspirations for individual pupils. Gary Howard, in his book *We Can't Teach What We Don't Know* (Howard 1999), suggests that teachers need to know themselves very well in order to take on knowing others in an open and respectful way. He advocates teachers spending time getting to know the backgrounds of children they are teaching, a journey he highly recommends. When we explore ethnic diversity, we are mostly talking about people with origins in lifestyles and cultural experiences significantly different from ours. Research shows that as significant adults in the classroom (teachers or teaching assistants), we rarely explore who we are and how we come to believe the things we take for granted, and use this to inform our assumptions, intuitions and decisions.

The *2020 Vision* report (DfES 2006) considers ways to improve and sustain the rate of pupils' progress, strategies to enhance teachers' skills and share best practice, and means of engaging pupils and parents in the learning process. The document also looks at ways in which flexibilities within the curriculum might support personalised learning, and how to establish a better system of innovation in teaching and learning in schools. Other research findings suggest the classroom curriculum was closely connected to the pedagogical content knowledge base, and that teachers' curricular decisions regarding content inclusion/exclusion may be based primarily on their perceptions of students' learning abilities. Chen and Ennis (1995) suggest that this may imply that enhancement of prospective teachers' pedagogical content knowledge should be emphasised in teachers' preparation programmes, serving as a bridge linking subject content knowledge with the curriculum delivered in classrooms.

The curriculum and ethnic diversity

In the *Diversity and Citizenship Curriculum Review*, Sir Keith Ajegbo (2007) identified that schools, through their ethos, through their curriculum, and through work with their communities, can make a difference to the way children and young people experience learning. However he, like others, identified persistent barriers: for example, not all school leaders have bought in fully to the imperative of education for diversity for all schools, and its priority is too low to be effective; there is insufficient clarity about the flexibility within the curriculum and how links to education for diversity can be made; some teachers lack confidence in engaging with diversity issues and lack the training opportunities to improve in this area; and the notion of racial hierarchies has not altogether disappeared – stereotypes still abound in society.

The importance of getting our approaches right is not new, and over the past ten years we have been reminded by reports and legislation that the needs of all children and young people must be met. The most prominent of these are the Aimhigher Report on Raising Black Pupils' Achievement (Morris and Golden 2005), the Race Relations (Amendment) Act 2000, the Education and Inspections Act 2006 which places a new duty on schools to promote community cohesion, the New Ofsted Framework, and the Narrowing the Gap (NtG) agenda.

Often, when I raise with head teachers the prospect of having to have a positive impact on BME teaching and learning, I am challenged and directed to 'quality-first teaching'. As new teachers, high-quality teaching must be your priority – and yes, in an ideal world, all pupils in lessons delivered to a quality-first standard would benefit. The reality, however, is different. We can see that the curriculum has different impacts on BME pupils. Strand (2008) argues that when all the allowances for deprivation and socio-economic standing are controlled, certain groups benefit less than their peers. The schools' self-evaluation form and the Ofsted framework for inspection of maintained schools are key drivers in helping us to think about how the curriculum is meeting the needs of groups of children.

Quality-first teaching must respond to the make-up of the classroom, and be aware of pupils' learning preferences. The curriculum is now viewed as flexible and dynamic enough for teachers to bring in cultures, textures and histories from local, national and international perspectives. The National Curriculum inclusion statement outlines how teachers can modify, as necessary, the Curriculum's programmes of study to provide all pupils with relevant and appropriately challenging work at each Key Stage. It sets out three principles that are essential to developing a more inclusive curriculum by:

- setting suitable learning challenges
- responding to diverse learning needs and overcoming potential barriers to learning
- assessment for individuals and groups of children.

Taking positive action to identify role models that reflect the diversity of your city, and choosing people who are relevant, can inspire children and young people. When developing an inclusive curriculum, it is really important to make choices that reflect pupils' own experiences, where they can see something of their identity and culture reflected in what they are being taught. It is equally important to give key roles – for example, director, narrator, main character – to pupils who are not necessarily in the highest literacy groups, in order to develop their self-esteem as writers and performers. Further examples of this could include:

- 'culture and identity' incorporated into geographical teaching and learning – ideas around culture and identity can be incorporated into studies that cover the full range and content, and support the diverse 'Curriculum Opportunities' and 'Key Processes' of the new Geography Programme of Study
- mathematics taught as a universal human language, used in different cultures and societies
- African and Asian number systems explored, including historical references, such as the Islamic contribution to mathematics in Europe
- all tasks, problems, materials and activities reflect the multi-ethnic nature of modern societies.

Conclusion

With the changing demography of the pupil population, it is vital that all staff in schools feel confident about working in a culturally and ethnically diverse school environment. The classroom must be an inclusive environment, where difference does not displace or undermine each individual's sense of self. Significant adults within the classroom have a duty to ensure equality of opportunity and outcome for all pupils, regardless of race, gender, ethnicity, ability or sexual orientation.

Knowing what we bring to the classroom helps us to shape pupils' experiences. The debate today is not limited to individual or institutional racism; it is more focused on our level of self-awareness and our ability to take ownership and responsibility for our day-to-day engagement with our environment (Hooks 1989; Delgado and Stefancic 2000). This should lead to us never making assumptions, instead treating each student first and foremost as an individual, and personalising our response to maximise their progress and outcomes. Pupils who are enthusiastic and engaged with and through the curriculum are more likely to become confident, independent learners who are able to articulate what they are learning.

Given the growing opportunities for teachers to engage with increasing numbers of minority ethnic groups of pupils, their training and continuing professional development must include greater emphasis on what can be done to maximise the outcomes for minority ethnic children and young people in the school environment. Constructing personalised learning plans provides a greater opportunity for teachers to get to know individual children. There are extended networks available to them in the local community, and nationally, that can be called on for support.

The personalisation agenda is very much about how we contribute individually to collective networks that will help individual children to stay safe, and to enjoy, achieve and maximise their life chances. There are many opportunities now available to teachers to review and undertake small research projects, and to acquire the knowledge and experiences necessary to meet the needs of BME children and young people coming into the classroom.

Reflection on values and practice

- Often we achieve success with children through building an effective rapport, and just getting on well with them. Reflect on what helps you to make such relationships with *all* children.
- What would it mean to challenge yourself to overcome any barriers to building good relationships with, and enhancing teaching and learning for, minority ethnic students?
- Take time to find out about the ethnic diversity of your school and how it has changed over the past five years.

Resources

Equality and Human Rights Commission (EHRC): www.equalityhumanrights.com
Ethnic Minority Achievement Unit: www.standards.dfes.gov.uk/ethnicminorities
National Association for Language Development in the Curriculum (NALDIC): www.naldic.org.uk
Runneymede Trust: www.runnymedetrust.org
Teachernet – English as an Additional Language: www.teachernet.gov.uk/teachingandlearning/library/EALteaching

References

Ajegbo, K. (2007) *Diversity and Citizenship Curriculum Review*, Nottingham: Department for Education and Skills.
Chen, A. and Ennis, C. (1995) 'Content knowledge transformation: an examination of the relationship between content knowledge and curricula', *Teaching and Teacher Education*, 11(4): 389–401.
Corbett, N.L., Kilgore, K.L. and Sindelar, P.T. (1998) 'Making sense of a collaborative teacher education program', *Teacher Education and Special Education*, 21(4): 293–305.
Delgado, R. and Stefancic, J. (2000) *Critical Race Theory*, Philadelphia: Temple University Press.
DfE (2010) *Statistical First Release. School Workforce in England*, SFR 11/2010, London: Department for Education.
DfES (2004) *Ethnicity and Education: The Evidence of Minority Ethnic Pupils age 5–16*, Nottingham: Department for Education and Skills.
——(2006) *2020 Vision: Report of the Teaching and Learning in 2020 Review Group*, Nottingham: Department for Education and Skills.

Fredrickson, N. and Cline, T. (2002) *Special Educational Needs, Inclusion and Diversity*, Buckingham: Open University Press.

GTC (2006) *Survey of Teachers*, Birmingham and London: General Teaching Council.

Gillborn, D. and Youdell, D. (2009) 'Critical perspectives on race and schooling', in Banks. J.A. (ed.) The Routledge International Companion to Multicultural Education, New York: Routledge.

GLA (2006) *Black Teachers in London*, London: Greater London Authority.

Green, P. (2000) *DIECEC Raising the Standards – A Practical Guide to Raising Ethnic Minority and Bilingual Pupils' Achievement*, Stoke-on-Trent: Trentham Books.

Hébert, Y. and Hartley, W.J. (2006) 'Personalised learning and changing conceptions of childhood and youth', *Canadian Journal of Education*, 29(2): 497–520.

Hooks, B. (1989) *Talking Back: Thinking Feminist, Thinking Black*, Toronto: Between the Lines.

Howard, G. (1999) *We Can't Teach What We Don't Know – White Teachers, Multicultural Schools*, New York: Teachers College Press.

Kitchen, M. (1996) *The British Empire and Commonwealth: A Short History*, Basingstoke: Macmillan.

Knowles, E. and Ridley, W. (2006) *Another Spanner in the Works – Challenging Prejudice and Racism in Mainly White Schools*, Stoke-on-Trent: Trentham Books.

Mead, M. (2009) 'Empire Windrush: the cultural memory of an imaginary arrival', *Journal of Postcolonial Writing*, 45(2): 137–49.

Morris, M. and Golden, S. (2005) *Evaluation of AimHigher: Excellence Challenge Interim Report 2005*, Nottingham: Department for Education and Skills.

Multiverse (2009) *English as an Additional Language (EAL)*, www.multiverse.ac.uk

Peach, C. (ed.) (1996) *Ethnicity in the 1991 Census: Volume Two: The Ethnic Minority Populations of Great Britain*, London: HMSO.

Phinney, J.S. (1990) 'Ethnic identity in adolescents and adults: review of research', *Psychological Bulletin*, 108(3): 499–514.

Refugee Council (1998) *A Resource Book for Primary Schools*, London: Refugee Council.

Ryan, J. (1999) *Race and Ethnicity in Multi-ethnic Schools*, North York, Canada: Multilingual Matters Ltd.

Strand, S. (2007) *Minority Ethnic Pupils in the Longitudinal Study of Young People in England*, Department for Education and Skills Research Report RR-002, London: Department for Children, Families and Schools.

——(2008) *Minority Ethnic Pupils in the Longitudinal Study of Young People in England. Extension Report on Performance in Public Examinations at 16*, Nottingham: Department for Children, Families and Schools.

Chapter 7

Invisibility and Otherness

Asylum-seeking and refugee students in the classroom

Mano Candappa

This chapter is about asylum-seeking and refugee[1] children and their experiences in British schools. The refugee experience makes these children resilient, but they are among the most marginalized in our society, and the Other among their peers. Paradoxically, these students are often 'invisible' within schools, yet they desperately need the school's support to help them get on with their lives, and the challenge for schools is how best to support them while not taking agency away from them. The chapter argues that the inclusive school is the most supportive environment for asylum-seeking and refugee students. I use the term 'inclusive' to mean including the child with his/her own culture and values in the school, within a culture that celebrates diversity (Corbett 1999; Armstrong 2008). In this model, the school adapts to respond to the needs of its students, as against the integrationist model, where the student has to fit into the school. It is the right of asylum-seeking and refugee children to be supported to enjoy their right to education under the UN Convention on the Rights of the Child (UNCRC; United Nations 1989).

Background

A sharp rise in asylum applications in the UK since the 1990s[2] led to perceptions in many quarters of an 'asylum crisis', with applications reaching a peak of 103,000 (including dependants) in 2002. The political sensitivity of this issue gave rise to five major parliamentary acts since 1990, which saw a progressive reduction in financial and material assistance to people seeking asylum and their marginalization from mainstream support services. Key among these for schools was the Asylum and Immigration Act 1999, which witnessed the compulsory dispersal of adults and families seeking asylum away from traditional areas of settlement in London and south-east England to predominantly White areas, mainly in northern England, Scotland and the Midlands. Many asylum-seeking families were housed in areas where accommodation was available, in many cases in socially and economically deprived areas. Many schools in dispersal areas had little experience of multi-ethnic communities, and were ill-prepared to receive children with English as an additional language and for diverse religious traditions.

While the UK has a long history of providing asylum and refuge, in the past this had mainly been for White populations, such as Jews facing persecution and dissidents from former Soviet-bloc countries. Today's asylum-seeking and refugee communities, by contrast, originate largely from Africa, Asia and the Middle East. Thus in the past decade the main countries of origin of people seeking asylum in the UK were (in order of significance) Somalia, Iraq, Sri Lanka, Former Republic of Yugoslavia, Afghanistan, Turkey, Pakistan, China, India and Iran (Castles *et al.* 2003). These are more visible populations, bringing with them different languages, religions, customs and traditions, and their presence significantly increased the UK's Black and minority ethnic (BME) population.[3]

Their highly visible presence and aspects of 'difference' that single them out as the Other[4] have been factors in the politics of 'race' being heavily implicated in the country's response to asylum-seeking and refugee communities. They are pathologized in political and media discourses, associated with criminal activity, a drain on the nation's resources, and more recently, even with terrorism. The challenge for schools is how to address these negative images and encourage their students to celebrate the diversity these students' presence brings.

Rights of the child

Asylum-seeking and refugee children, as children, are protected by international rights under the UNCRC, to which the UK is a signatory.[5] They are entitled to the same rights as other children; and as children seeking refugee status or considered refugees, these children are given additional protection under Article 22, which states that they should receive 'appropriate protection and humanitarian assistance' in the enjoyment of Convention rights.

The UNCRC gives children protection, provision and participation rights based on four general principles, concerning –

- the child's right to life, including the development of the child 'to the maximum extent possible'
- the best interests of the child
- respecting the views of the child
- that no child should suffer discrimination, stipulating equality of rights for all children (Hammarberg 1995).

Additionally, specific articles *inter alia* give children the right to education: Article 28 recognizes the child's right to education on the basis of equal opportunity; Article 29 states, among other things, that the child's education shall be directed to the 'development of the child's personality, talents and mental and physical abilities to their fullest potential'. Furthermore under Article 19, schools need to take appropriate action to protect children from all forms of violence, which includes bullying. Asylum-seeking and refugee children are therefore entitled to a learning environment where their abilities can be nurtured and developed to the fullest without fear of being subjected to violence. These rights are all the more precious to them because the school as a universalist service might be the only statutory agency from which they derive support (Candappa and Egharevba 2000), and, as Elbedour *et al.* (1993) indicate, for many children 'the school serves as a second security base outside the home, or perhaps their only security base'.

Asylum-seeking and refugee children are also entitled to protection under UK law, in particular the Children Acts 1989 and 2004, which are underpinned by the UNCRC. Within the framework of the Green Paper *Every Child Matters* (legislative proposals given effect in the Children Act 2004), every child, from birth to age 19, whatever their background or their circumstances, should have the supports they need to be healthy, stay safe, enjoy and achieve, make a positive contribution, and achieve economic wellbeing. The Children Act 2004 also places a duty on local authorities to promote cooperation between agencies to improve children's wellbeing, and a duty for key agencies (including education departments and schools) to safeguard and protect the welfare of children.

It is to be hoped that with their rights under the UNCRC, the provisions of the Children Acts and the *Every Child Matters* agenda, asylum-seeking and refugee children's educational needs would be supported so they achieve their full potential, but as we shall see, various factors operate to make this goal more challenging. But let us first consider what these children have had to endure, using evidence from the author's recent research.

The child as refugee

Many asylum-seeking and refugee children have had extraordinary childhoods (see Melzak 1997; Bolloten and Spafford 1998; Candappa and Egharevba 2000; Stanley 2002; Chase *et al.* 2008). For some children, such as Sheik[6] (a Somali boy from the minority Brava community) who survived war and an ensuing breakdown of law and order, this involved, at age 10, putting his own life at risk to save his neighbours:

> I was playing outside when somebody [thugs] came and tell me, 'Go and knock at your neighbours' door and speak Bravanese. Tell them to open the door or I am going to shoot you.' And then I went to knock. (They told me 'Go and knock at that door' because they can't speak my language.) I said, 'Don't open it, there are some robbers here.' And they [thugs] thought that I said, 'Open the door.' They didn't open the door. And I say [to the thugs], 'They don't want to open it.'
>
> The robbers say, 'Tell those people to open it.' And I say to my neighbours, 'Don't open the door because they are still here. They kill

people.' They [thugs] say to me, 'You lie to us.' They hit me with a gun! The gun never had any bullets, they just use it to hit my legs. Now I've a problem with my legs. They give me pain.

(Candappa and Egharevba 2002: 158)

For Bazi, another Somali Brava boy aged 11 at the time, trying to reach safety resulted in losing a cousin at sea while they fled, and then his grandmother at a refugee camp:

One day we leave by boat ... but the boat broken in the middle of Somalia and Kenya and some of our family fell in the water and drowned – our cousin. And we just prayed to God, and God pushed us through the sea to the land ... It was very deep in the middle of the sea ... It was night and everybody was praying. The boat was slowly going down to the sand, until it got to the sand. In the sand there was nobody and one day we slept on the sand. And another day, we were scared, some people came ... by small boats and they came to collect us and they took us to their island. We was very hungry that day. They gave us food ... And then we stayed for week ... After two weeks, some people say that our family sent small ship from Mombasa to that small island ... and they took us and then we got to Kenya ...

We stayed in place for refugees [refugee camp] ... There was bad disease in there. My Grandma, she died from malaria ...

(*ibid.*: 158)

Other asylum-seeking and refugee children have lived through dangers and trauma of war, persecution and flight to safety, or lived for periods in refugee camps; some have been at the mercy of unscrupulous agents, some have fled alone, some have had to support emotionally absent parents. Their resilience is remarkable.

Once they reach a safe country such as the UK, these children's troubles are far from over. Starting a new life as an 'asylum-seeker' is hard. They face dismal poverty living on state benefits, which since 1999 have been equivalent to 70% of income support, and since 2002 their parents do not have the right to work while their claim is under consideration. Additional to the poverty of their existence is the insecurity of not knowing if their claim for asylum will be successful. Families have to get on with rebuilding their lives in the new country, not knowing whether the next day, the next week, the next month, or some day in the future they will be asked to leave, putting them under great emotional stress with implications for their physical and mental health and general wellbeing.

Families who have been compulsorily dispersed to predominantly White areas can feel even more vulnerable and unsafe because of their visibility among the local, often hostile population. Here a 10-year-old boy and a

10-year-old girl living in a new dispersal area in Scotland talk of their fears and worries:

> We live in a bad neighbourhood and there are a lot of bad young people hanging around. We are not allowed to go out without supervision. We only go out with my dad. [translation]

> There's no homework club in school – we are allowed to use help at the library, but it is too far. I can't stay because of drunks around. They shout, come and talk with you – I feel scared …
>
> (Candappa *et al.* 2007: 25)

Their visibility makes asylum-seeking children particularly vulnerable to racism, reported by many interviewees in that city. The oppression and powerlessness such racism causes are here captured in the testimony of an unaccompanied minor youth:

> They call me [racist] names … I do not respond. Sometimes I feel no freedom because people abusing us
>
> (*ibid.*: 27)

As Arshad *et al.* (1999: 16) point out, to be abused in a country where one has sought refuge from abuse seems 'a double injustice and particularly cruel'.

'Invisible' students and visible Otherness

Asylum-seeking and refugee children are often 'invisible' in schools[7] (Arshad *et al.* 1999; Pinson *et al.* 2010). Students are not required to reveal their immigration status to the school, and schools, unless officially provided this information as part of a dispersal programme, for instance, do not see it as their business to be involved with immigration issues. In multicultural schools, therefore, asylum-seeking and refugee students could blend in with the school population; in more monocultural areas their ethnicity would make them visible. In either school setting, they might come to the attention of the average teacher only as a new arrival, a bilingual learner, or a migrant child new to the British education system. Sometimes, after trust has been established, some students or their parents might tell their stories to a sympathetic teacher, but they might also choose not to talk about their experiences to anyone at the school. Research suggests that teachers who work most closely with asylum-seeking and refugee students respect this silence and the student's choice of if and when to disclose their experiences (Pinson *et al.* 2010). However, at times trying to cope with memories and effects of past traumas as well as the stresses of their new life might manifest in unruly or disruptive behaviours in the school. The following account from Kasim (a Somali boy who arrived in Britain as an unaccompanied minor) demonstrates the types of behaviour that have sometimes been misinterpreted because teachers have not been sensitized to the experiences and needs of refugee students:

> I come to this country in 1994 [and]. I was a bit upset because of my Mum. I didn't see her ... for seven years ...
> Still worried about my Mum. Can't do my homework ... can't do nothing because I'm worried. When I walk [down] the street, I think about my Mum. Sometimes I cry, you know that? ... Last week at school I was thinking about my Mum and I was crying in my head. And one boy hit my head. I was so angry I got him back. That's how I almost get expelled.
> (Candappa 2002: 232)

Too often, their silence and invisibility or stereotyping have led to asylum-seeking and refugee students being penalized rather than provided the supports they need (*ibid.*).

The decision not to disclose their refugee experiences is sometimes a coping strategy, a way of putting the past behind and getting on with their lives. More often, asylum-seeking and refugee students are aware, from the press and media, from community experiences and from playground talk, of negative images of asylum-seekers and refugees, and for this reason – for self-preservation – they do not wish to reveal their past (Pinson *et al.* 2010). Christopoulou *et al.* (2004) suggest that silence is one of the mechanisms these young people use to handle trauma, exclusion and discrimination in their present lives. But even through this silence, their peers can still identify them as the Other – the outsider, whose lack of competency in English and lack of understanding of local youth cultures and modes of dress makes their Otherness visible and excludes them from membership of the peer group until they have negotiated this painful rite of passage (Candappa and Egharevba 2002; Pinson *et al.* 2010). This often takes the form of general low-level bullying and harassment directed at all newcomers (Pinson *et al.* 2010), but for an anxious asylum-seeking or refugee student, such behaviour could be experienced as hostility, non-acceptance and exclusion. If they are non-English speakers these students are highly visible and particularly vulnerable, as the accounts of Rathika and Serpil, two refugee girls, demonstrate:

> That first day, they don't sit with us. They like to feel that we are separate, us two. They don't talk to us, no-one. My sister and me were just talking our language. (.) There was one girl, she taking us to the coat room where we had to leave our coats. ... She said, like, 'You can't talk English'. ... She was like ... kicking us.
> (Candappa 2002: 231)

> I had two Turkish friends, but not that close. Sometimes they helped me but most of the time they didn't.... When they translated anything,

I think they were, like, embarrassed. They didn't want to talk to me. They were embarrassed that other kids will say, 'Oh, don't talk to that girl, she doesn't speak English' ...

(Candappa and Egharevba 2002: 165)

It is significant that in both cases the girls were rejected by students from their own culture, those they and the school might have expected to help them. While it reveals the low status of non-English-speakers within peer cultures, it also points to complexities within peer group relations that have an impact on developing and sustaining an inclusive school ethos.

Building inclusivity

As we have seen, under the UNCRC and British law, asylum-seeking and refugee children have a right to an education where they can flourish and develop to their fullest potential, and under Convention rights they should be protected and supported in the enjoyment of this right. Three other pieces of legislation, the Race Relations (Amendment) Act 2000, the Education Act 2002, and Education and Inspections Act 2006, place a related statutory duty upon schools,[8] and together the Convention and these acts carry the message of respecting difference and of inclusion.

The inclusive message has special resonance for asylum-seeking and refugee children. The trauma of war, forced migration and loss, together with anxieties about trying to settle in a new country, could affect their ability to enjoy their right to education. Children from families seeking asylum have the added worry and uncertainty of awaiting a decision on their asylum claim. If their claim is unsuccessful, families have to return to their home country, sometimes being forcibly removed from their homes in dawn raids. If this were to happen to someone in their community, other families fear their turn, and this could affect the children. Mary Campbell, a teacher in a dispersal area in Scotland (interviewed for Candappa *et al.* 2007), here describes the trauma for her school when a family is removed:

Those periods when families are sent back are very difficult for us in trying to support the children. The children are very apprehensive about what lies ahead, and it manifests itself in school, their progress becomes slightly retarded on occasions ... You can find behaviour difficulties, emotional difficulties

(Pinson *et al.* 2010: 283)

The added protection that UNCRC Article 22 bestows is therefore an entitlement asylum-seeking and refugee students often badly need. And the school can play a pivotal role in helping to rebuild their lives: a restoration of normality and order through schooling can in itself act as a healing agent (Bolloten and Spafford 1998).

The most supportive environment for asylum-seeking and refugee children is a school that respects its students as individuals, tries to empathize with their experiences and needs, and responds to these, showing a willingness to put themselves 'in someone else's shoes' – in other words, an inclusive school. For asylum-seeking and refugee students, this would mean seeking not just to respond to immediate needs, but to situate these needs in the context of their previous experiences. But as we have seen, these students can be 'invisible' in classrooms, and the question about how to support invisible students might seem contradictory. But if a school were to provide a safe environment that seeks to address the needs of all students, identifying individual needs without resorting to stereotypes and assumptions, then many of the needs of asylum-seeking and refugee students, too, would be met. Indeed, as Arshad *et al.*'s research indicates, being inclusive means 'not being picked out as different or special, even in positive ways' (Arshad *et al.* 1999: 20). It means feeling included in the normal learning environment of a caring school.

To sustain an inclusive ethos a school will need to develop specific structures and practices. These could include a celebration of diversity and difference; exploration and debate around social justice and humanitarian issues within the curriculum; and robust equal opportunities, anti-racist and anti-bullying policies which are rigorously implemented. It could also involve seeking ways of including parents of asylum-seeking and refugee students within the school community.[9] Specific curricular and pastoral supports that could be responsive to the needs of asylum-seeking and refugee students, even without disclosure, would also need to be developed. Key among these is support for language and accessing the curriculum, fostering friendships, and supporting emotional needs.

Language and curricular supports

While some asylum-seeking and refugee children may have enjoyed uninterrupted education, for many the war situations in their home countries could mean they have had little formal schooling or their education had been disrupted. Some could find UK schools significantly different from schools in the home country in terms of pedagogical practice and discipline; for others, the school they join in the UK might be the first they have attended. Research suggests that young people's early school experiences in this country are central to how well and how quickly they adjust to their new lives. Many require help in schools for an extended time thereafter.

Acquiring competence in English is a key factor in asylum-seeking and refugee students' new lives, crucial both for accessing the curriculum and for developing self-confidence and aiding social interaction (Candappa and

Egharevba 2000). Many asylum-seeking and refugee students are new to English on joining school in the UK, and in some education authorities intensive language support is provided at the outset, with English language acquisition seen as a basic survival need (Candappa *et al.* 2007). Many schools provide English training in separate classes or with special support in mainstream classes, and the question of the relative merits of withdrawal as against mainstreaming are often debated. It has been suggested that withdrawal allows the teacher to give individual attention to the student, who could work at his/her own pace. However this approach, especially if prolonged, could be stigmatizing and inhibit building friendships with the wider peer group. Indeed, parents in Candappa *et al.*'s (2007) study queried whether, if withdrawal was necessary, it could be done in a way that did not suggest a student's difficulties with language are synonymous with academic failure. Some education authorities and schools have therefore sought ways to effectively support asylum-seeking and refugee students' language needs without the need for withdrawal. Below are two possible approaches.

School A: dispersal area, Scotland

School A is located in a city that had little experience of responding to the needs of asylum-seeking and refugee students prior to dispersal policies. (The authority's minority ethnic population is also lower than the UK average.) The school had been asked by the education authority to place students from asylum-seeking families on class registers, though in reality they would work in a bilingual unit providing students with intensive English language support. The school had been multi-ethnic prior to dispersal, and found this approach contrary to its usual way of working, as the headteacher explained:

> ... we very quickly moved away from that and began to refine our thinking – we asked, what can children do that the class was doing, e.g., expressive art, environmental studies, behind that maths, then language. We've got to get teachers and children to seek ways around that. And we also began to get peer support ...
>
> Now ... we work on a completely different basis ... the two refugee support teachers with the EAL[10] teachers work in classrooms across the school, mainly at language times. Teachers work with groups of children, which include asylum-seekers and refugees, local bilingual and monolingual pupils ... We feel that all children benefit from this ...
>
> We had a debate within the school about 'withdrawal' ... for limited times in corners ... With joint planning with the class teacher and the support teacher ... , where the support teacher takes the group becomes irrelevant.

> (Candappa *et al.* 2007: 41)

School B: London borough

School B is located in a borough that has a long tradition of providing for the needs of a diverse student community, with a non-White population well above the UK average. At the time of Candappa et al.'s (2007) study, asylum-seeking and refugee students in the borough's schools represented 16.9% of the student population. To respond to the needs of these students, the LEA had a Refugee Education Service, which had a range of guidance and resources for schools. School B exemplified the LEA's approach to inclusion within the classroom, as described by the EAL Coordinator:

> We have admissions day every Monday afternoon ... very rarely a week passes when we didn't have a new child ... Children move straightaway into [mainstream] classes ... Assessment is carried out within the first two weeks of admission – short and sharp sessions are found to work better ...
>
> (*ibid.*: 41)

In these two examples, any stigma that could attach to withdrawal is absent, and children spend class time with their peers in a situation that is more conducive to forming friendships and socializing.

Pastoral care and fostering friendships

As we have seen above, the experiences of many asylum-seeking and refugee students are certainly extraordinary, especially so when compared with normative notions of childhood in the UK. While these young people's strength and resilience through such experiences should be valued, it is important for schools and teachers to remember that these students may also carry scars from their experiences, and could need sensitive pastoral care to support their rehabilitation. Many examples of compassionate support provided to asylum-seeking and refugee students can be found within inclusive schools, such as teachers going out of their way to provide academic and cultural support underpinned by a deep level of care, and keeping watch over them at a very personal level (Pinson et al. 2010). The best supports are directed to the needs of the whole child, offering students the chance to gain confidence, self-esteem and a sense of agency in taking control of their future world, such as reported by Lena, a Year 11 girl from Nigeria:

> The Learning Support staff's brilliant, they're really helpful ... taught me to be more independent than always get help ... They kind of like, when they give you work, they make you try and do it without asking for help all the time. Like, so you can depend more on yourself than other people to help you all the time
>
> (Pinson *et al.*: 205)

Most inclusive schools also recognize the importance of friendships in children's lives, and have schemes such as 'buddying' or 'class friends' to ease new students into the life of the school, and various clubs and extracurricular activities to encourage socializing, sometimes leading to lasting friendships. However, a tension can exist between an inclusionary school ethos and exclusionary practices within peer cultures towards newcomers: as research has shown (Candappa and Egharevba 2002; Pinson *et al.* 2010), youth cultures can exclude asylum-seeking and refugee students even within inclusive schools. A challenge for schools is how to educate young British students to learn how to cope and befriend strangers, to reduce xenophobia and racial prejudice while encouraging compassion for those who have suffered persecution. The Citizenship Education curriculum might afford teachers an opportunity to confront these issues, and to develop appropriate materials, topics and activities to link refugee issues to the promotion of democracy, social justice and human rights.

Reflections on values and practice

I have contended in this chapter that the inclusive school is the most supportive for needs of asylum-seeking and refugee students. There are concerns however, that current initiatives such as the creation of free schools may adversely affect the education of already marginalized groups (Shepherd and Vasgar 2010). Late arrivals such as many asylum-seeking and refugee students might have difficulty accessing school under the new system; it may also prove more difficult to support them without an appropriate local authority infrastructure. However, these students' right to education under the UNCRC will continue, and there have not been fundamental changes to schools' statutory duties either. In order to fulfil schools' responsibilities towards these students therefore it might be the time, as Cruddas argues, to re-open a debate on how we might 'move from a competitive system to a collaborative one, reconnecting teaching with pedagogy...' (Runnymede 2010).

New teachers might consider:

- Are issues of asylum and refuge given adequate place in the curriculum, and how can teachers foster compassion for the suffering of others among students?
- How can teachers' pedagogical practice support asylum-seeking and refugee children effectively without the need for disclosure?

Notes

1 **Asylum seeker**: a person who has left their country of origin and formally applied for asylum in another country, but whose application has not yet been decided. **Refugee**: someone whose asylum application has been successful, and who is allowed to stay in another country having proved they would face persecution back home. (www.refugeecouncil.org.uk/practice/basics/truth.htm)

2 This reflects a growth in numbers of refugees worldwide, linked to the end of Cold War politics plus ethnic conflicts in many parts of the world towards the end of the twentieth century.

3 At the 2001 Census, the BME population stood at an average of 7.9% of the total, found clustered mainly in metropolitan areas; so that in a London borough one might find the BME population comprising 34% of the total, while in a county in the east of England they could comprise just 2.9%.

4 Otherness is defined by difference, marked by outward signs such as 'race', and often associated with marginalized people living outside the dominant social group (Onbelet, 2010).

5 In September 2008 the UK government withdrew the discriminatory reservation on immigration it had entered when ratifying the UNCRC, whereby it reserved the right to apply legislation as it deemed necessary in relation to entry into, stay in, and departure from the UK and to the acquisition and possession of citizenship. Asylum-seeking and refugee children are now entitled to the same rights under the UNCRC as other children in the UK.

6 Pseudonyms have been used for research participants throughout this chapter.

7 There are no accurate demographic data on the number of asylum-seeking and refugee children in UK schools, and known cases might be less than total numbers present. Rutter (2006) estimates that there are at least 60,000 asylum-seeking and refugee children of compulsory school age currently residing in the UK.

8 Under the Race Relations (Amendment) Act 2000, a duty is placed on schools to eliminate racial discrimination and to promote equality of opportunity and good relations between people of different groups; under section 78 of the Education Act 2002 the curriculum for all maintained schools should promote the spiritual, moral, cultural, mental and physical development of pupils at the school and of society; and the Education and Inspections Act 2006 places a new duty on schools to promote community cohesion.

9 Possible initiatives for supporting parents can be found in Ofsted (2003).

10 English as an additional language.

Resources

Beard, J. and Bradley, N. (2001) 'Raising the barriers: meeting the needs of refugee pupils and families in a North London borough', *Multicultural Teaching* 19(3): 26–29.

Bolloten, B. (ed.) (2004) *Home from Home: A Guidance and Resource Pack for the Welcome and Inclusion of Refugee Children and Families In School*. London: Save the Children. www.savethechildren.org.uk/en/54_2330.htm

Closs, A., Stead, J. and Arshad, R. (2001) 'The education of asylum-seeker and refugee children', *Multicultural Teaching* 20(1): 29–33.

Rutter, J. (2003) *Supporting Refugee Children in the 21st Century – A Compendium of Essential Information*, Stoke-on-Trent: Trentham Books.

Rutter, J. and Candappa, M. (1998) *'Why do they have to fight?' Refugee Children's Stories from Bosnia, Kurdistan, Somalia and Sri Lanka*, London: Refugee Council.

References

Armstrong, F. (2008) 'Inclusive education', in Richards, G. and Armstrong, F. (eds) *Key Issues for Teaching Assistants: Working in Diverse and Inclusive Classrooms*, Abingdon and New York: Routledge.

Arshad, R., Closs, A. and Stead, J. (1999) *Doing Our Best: Scottish School Education, Refugee Pupils and Parents – A Strategy for Social Inclusion*, Edinburgh: Centre for Education for Racial Equality in Scotland.

Bolloten, B. and Spafford, T. (1998) 'Supporting refugee children in East London primary schools', in Rutter, J. and Jones, C. (eds) *Refugee Education: Mapping the Field*, Stoke-on-Trent: Trentham Books.

Candappa, M. (2002) 'Human rights and refugee children in the UK', in Franklin, B (ed.) *The New Handbook of Children's Rights: Comparative Policy and Practice*, London: Routledge.

Candappa, M. and Egharevba, I. (2000) *"Extraordinary Childhoods": The Social Lives of Refugee Children*, Children 5–16 Research Briefing No. 5, Swindon: Economic and Social Research Council.

——(2002) 'Negotiating boundaries: tensions within home and school life for refugee children', in Edwards, R. (ed.) *Children, Home and School*, London: RoutledgeFalmer.

Candappa, M., Ahmad, M., Balata, B., Dekhinet, R. and Gocmen, D. (2007). *Education and Schooling for Asylum-Seeking and Refugee Students in Scotland: An Exploratory Study*, Scottish Government Social Research 2007, Edinburgh: Scottish Government.

Castles, S., Miller, M.J. and Ammendola, G. (2003) *The Age of Migration: International Population Movements in the Modern World*, New York: Guilford Press.

Chase, E., Knight, A. and Statham, J. (2008) *The Emotional Well-Being of Unaccompanied Young People Seeking Asylum in the UK*, London: British Association for Adoption and Fostering.

Christopoulou, N., Rydin, I., Buckingham, D. and de Block, L. (2004) *Children's Social Relations in Peer Groups: Inclusion, Exclusion and Friendship*, London: Children in Communication about Migration (CHICAM) project, European Commission.

Corbett, J. (1999) 'Inclusive education and school culture', *International Journal of Inclusive Education*, 3(1): 53–61.

Elbedour, S., ten Bensel, R. and Bastien, D.T. (1993) 'Ecological integrated model of children of war: individual and social psychology', *Child Abuse & Neglect*, 17: 805–19.

Hammarberg, T. (1995) 'Preface', in Franklin, B. (ed.) *The Handbook of Children's Rights: Comparative Policy and Practice*, London: Routledge, ix–xiii.

Melzak, S. (1997) 'Meeting the Needs of Refugee Children', unpublished training material, London: Medical Foundation for the Care of Victims of Torture.

Pinson, H., Arnot, M. and Candappa, M. (2010) *Education, Asylum and the 'Non-Citizen' Child: The Politics of Compassion and Belonging*, London: Palgrave Macmillan.

Ofsted (2003) *The Education of Asylum-seeker Pupils*, London: Ofsted.

Onbelet, L. (2010) 'Imagining the other: the use of narrative as an empowering practice', *McMaster Journal of Theology and Ministry*, www.mcmaster.ca/mjtm/3-1d.htm

Runnymede (2010) 'Vox Pop' *Runnymede Bulletin*, Issue 361, Spring.

Rutter, J. (2006) *Refugee Children in the UK*, Buckingham: Open University Press.

Shepherd, J. and Vasagar, J. (2010) 'Swedish-style free schools may increase social divide-study', *guardion.co.uk*, 21 July.

Stanley, K. (2002) *Cold Comfort: The Lottery of Care for Young Separated Refugees in England*, London: Save the Children.

Stead, J., Closs, A. and Arshad, R. (2002) 'Invisible pupils: the experience of refugee pupils in Scottish schools', *Education and Social Justice*, 4(1): 49–55.

United Nations (1989) *UN Convention on the Rights of the Child*. New York: United Nations.

Chapter 8

I feel confident about teaching, but 'SEN' scares me

Moving from anxiety to confidence

Gill Richards

Introduction

> At the end of the third year I was confident about teaching, but SEN scared me.

These words, spoken by a student teacher nearing the end of her course, reflect the concerns of many new teachers. Indeed, they may also reflect the views of more experienced teachers as they respond to national developments and the challenges of inclusive education. As mainstream schools increasingly include numbers of pupils identified as having special educational needs, what is being done to increase teachers' confidence and skills?

Initial teacher education (ITE) programmes follow a national curriculum linked to regulated standards for the award of qualified teacher status. These standards have increasingly been influenced by the national strategy 'Removing Barriers to Achievement' (DfES 2004), which held the expectation that all teachers would teach children identified as having special educational needs. ITE programmes are now expected to cover 'inclusion of pupils with SEN, behaviour management, assessment for learning and specialist support, all within the core knowledge and understanding of teaching' (*ibid*.: 57). So, does this make a difference?

Evidence, including that from government agencies, seems to imply that more still needs to be done. The Office for Standards in Education (Ofsted) report *How Well New Teachers are Prepared to Teach Pupils with Learning Difficulties and/or Disabilities* (Ofsted 2008: 5) identified variable experience within ITE programmes, a heavy reliance on schools to provide most of the training on special educational needs, and a weakness in monitoring this. As a result, many new teachers have completed their programmes lacking confidence and feeling unprepared for teaching children seen as having 'additional' or 'special' learning needs. Similar evidence can be found in the Training and Development Agency for Schools' *Newly Qualified Teacher Survey* (TDA 2007) and Moran's (2007) research with head teachers, suggesting the need for a different approach to this part of the ITE curriculum so that all new teachers can approach their classes confidently.

What are special educational needs?

The concept of special educational needs came from the Warnock Report (DES 1978), replacing categories from the 1944 Education Act previously used to classify children with labels such as 'maladjusted', 'delicate' and 'educationally subnormal'. With this new concept came the role of the special educational needs coordinator – the SENCO – who became the lead teacher in supporting children identified with special educational needs though the formal 'statementing' process. From this, a team of professionals grew to support this work; educational psychologists were required for assessing special educational needs, teaching assistants to support identified pupils and trainers started to offer focused staff development courses – arguably creating a 'special needs industry'.

Subsequent legislation, policy and initiatives embedded the concept of special educational needs and focused on developing teachers' practice (Special Educational Needs and Disability Act 2001 (SENDA); DfES 2004; House of Commons 2006). Over time, government agencies' terminology changed variously to include special needs and disabilities, disabled children, learning difficulties and disabilities, but the group of children given these labels remained those originally highlighted by Warnock and set out in the 1996 Education Act – those who have a learning difficulty that calls for some kind of special educational provision to be made (Education Act 1996, Section 312). This deceptively simple definition may be the cornerstone of conflicting perspectives about pupils seen as 'special' and subsequent expectations of teachers.

When one group of learners is perceived as special, it implies that they are different from other 'ordinary' pupils. This can translate into teachers expecting special provision to be made through additional resources and special skills needed to deliver these, a view further compounded by other terminology commonly heard in schools, which describes such pupils as having 'additional' needs. The danger of this is clear: if 'special' children are conceptualised as needing a specialised education, how then will 'ordinary' teachers see their duty towards them? Dividing pupils in this way may lead teachers to question whether they feel competent enough to meet some children's needs, and whether someone else, such as a teaching assistant, or somewhere else, such as a special school, could do this better. Even more confident teachers may balk at what they see as extra demands being made on them.

So, 'special educational needs', a label that was originally intended to move away from negative categorisation in the past, now raises further issues for teachers to consider. Hall's (1997) challenging perspective of a 'Special Land' to which pupils with special educational needs can be consigned after rejection from mainstream activities draws attention to some of the complexities found within school provision. He asks us to reflect on the actual words 'special' and 'needs' and the effect of the concepts implicit within them. He reminds us that 'special' is something usually wanted by society, for example, special offers or special events, but within the educational context, a special need is not one to which pupils generally aspire; instead it is often seen by teachers as a euphemism for 'problem'. Similarly, he contests the word 'need', suggesting that this implies neediness and a want, rather than a learning requirement, which implies a right to schools providing for this.

Other concerns about labelling are identified in the House of Commons *Special Educational Needs* report (House of Commons 2006: 16). This describes the separation of learners with and without special educational needs as fundamentally flawed, arguing that children do not fit into neat categories, but exist on a broad continuum of needs which are often influenced by social disadvantage. It suggests that, as many conditions that pupils have may be syndromes with different characteristics or linked with other impairments and issues, 'diagnosis' becomes complex. Within this context, the report suggests that the use of simplistic categories can lead to false classifications and intervention strategies that do not address individuals' unique learning requirements. Further concerns are highlighted through past studies showing that teachers' expectations of pupils can differ in relation to the labels allocated to them (Rosenthal and Jacobson 1968; Norwich 1999). These concerns are also raised by more current writers (for example, Rix *et al.* 2004; Thomas and Vaughan 2004; Ainscow 2007; Wearmouth 2009), who reflect on the power of labels in creating teachers' perceptions and subsequent behaviour towards children. Linked to this are issues of professionals' use of power that enables them to impose particular identities (and labels) upon pupils and make subjective decisions on definitions of 'normal' or 'ordinary' (Frederickson and Cline 2009), thereby separating groups of learners within schools.

Although this consideration of language and labels may seem overstated, the impact on teachers' thinking cannot be underestimated. School staffroom discussions about pupils described as 'the SENs', and SENCOs being seen as totally responsible for 'SEN pupils', are not uncommon, and serve to distance teachers from some children. The special educational needs label also identifies the problem as being located within the child – that they have the learning difficulty and so own the problem. This does not encourage consideration of other contextual issues, such as teaching styles, classroom structures and access to appropriate resources. All this can reinforce an uncritical acceptance that *special* children need to go to *special* places for a *special* education.

Moving beyond a label

So, if we look beyond special educational needs towards an inclusive education system that values diversity, where does that leave us? Clearly, there are pupils who have conditions and impairments that affect the way they learn, so teachers need to become familiar with these to ensure their teaching is effective. However, from my experience, while there are benefits in attending courses and reading about specific conditions, a focus on individual children and how they learn in *your* classroom is much more helpful.

Often it is argued that a label is needed to ensure the right teaching strategies and resources are provided (Lauchlan and Boyle 2007). We might like to consider why this is thought to be the case. If we reflect upon the Audit Commission's view that the statutory assessment and statementing procedure, which identifies learners' special educational needs and creates such labels, is 'a costly, bureaucratic and unresponsive process ... which may add little value in helping meet a child's needs' (Audit Commission 2002: 14–17), we might question the validity of this view. Similarly, Ofsted (2006: 17) states that statements of special educational needs were overly cumbersome and bureaucratic and did not ensure quality of provision; and the British Psychological Society (2005: 4) suggests that a statement of SEN can become a barrier to inclusion that creates dependency on 'specialist' resources. So, how can we move beyond a reliance on labels? How do we create a situation where teachers' judgements are valued and access is routinely provided to required resources? How can teachers feel confident in their own ability to design learning activities from which all pupils can benefit?.

I would like to suggest that, although there will always be children whose learning requirements are outside our experience, and for whom we will need to seek advice from others, maintaining a focus on the process of learning is particularly helpful. Accepting that *all* pupils' participation in tasks is affected by the demands of different classroom activities, rather than solely by some perceived innate ability, could further clarify the teacher's role. If we return to the expectation from *Removing Barriers to Achievement* (DfES 2004) that all teachers are teachers of pupils with special educational needs, then a focus on what and how pupils need to learn becomes more important than a label. This isn't to argue that all pupils should be taught without regard for any specified learning requirements, but that designing activities for the diversity found within any classroom becomes integral to teachers' planning. This can help teachers view their class as a community of learners, rather than as separated into those with and without special educational needs – or any other perceived difference – for which one activity is organised for most of the class and something separate provided for those seen as 'special'.

The Disability Discrimination Act 2005 requires schools to increase access to the curriculum and make adjustments to physical features, eliminate discrimination and promote equality for disabled children. Many were slow to respond to this statutory requirement, and the early focus was on physical changes to buildings rather than accessibility related to attitudes and classroom management. This could be considered an interesting response by schools, for changes to buildings can be financially costly, whereas changes to behaviour may involve a more personal 'cost'. Perhaps this reflects some underlying concerns. Could it be that, despite a growing acceptance of barriers to learning not being located 'within the child', and some external (physical) barriers therefore being recognised, acceptance of the role of individual teachers in creating and breaking down barriers is more challenging to address?

So, what is being done to prepare new teachers for the diversity they face within their classrooms, and what can be done to increase their confidence and professional skills further?

Preparing for a community of learners

Over the past 30 years, there have been many developments in special and inclusive education. The concept of integration as introduced by Warnock (DES 1978) intimated that pupils should be assimilated into mainstream classrooms. Later, this view was challenged by the 'social model of disability', inspired by disabled people who argued that it was schools and teachers who should change to accommodate the true diversity of learners. The focus then became centred on the barriers to learning constructed by school environments, rather than a child's individual condition or impairment and whether s/he could fit into a mainstream school environment. Alongside this, national policy and legislation developed, producing key initiatives such as the Special Educational Needs and Disability Act 2001, *Removing Barriers to Achievement* (DfES 2004), the Disability Discrimination Act and the Inclusion Development Programme.

During this time, ITE struggled to keep pace with these developments, despite recommendations for all programmes to contain a core element of 'SEN curriculum' (House of Commons 2006). Student teachers received information of variable quality (Winter 2006; Hodkinson 2009), leading many to feel that they lacked confidence and were unprepared for teaching children with special educational needs (Ofsted 2008). New teachers also reported that although they were mainly satisfied with the theoretical knowledge they had received, they would have benefited from more practical experience (DRC 2006). Concern was also expressed by tutors, who suggested that the increasing focus on meeting specific standards to achieve Qualified Teacher Status encouraged student teachers and ITE providers to adopt a 'technician approach' (Pearson 2007), concentrating on auditable skills rather than underpinning pedagogical issues (Hodkinson 2009). This concern had previously been acknowledged by the Audit Commission (2002: 51), who had observed that the 'standards fall short in their failure to reflect the wider policy context of inclusion'.

Changes occurred as the TDA started to work with ITE providers to develop and pilot new initiatives arising from *Removing Barriers to Achievement* (DfES 2004). These included the design of new resource materials for tutors and their students on ITE programmes and 'specialised placements' in special schools or units. After evaluation, the TDA provided ITE tutors with an *SEN and/or Disabilities Training Toolkit* for Primary teaching programmes, followed by another version in 2009 for Secondary programmes. These toolkits contained off-the-shelf teaching sessions with supplementary resources, primarily for tutors with only a 'general knowledge and understanding of SEN and disability issues' (TDA 2009: Introduction). Additional professional development opportunities for student teachers included 'specialised placements' in special schools or additionally resourced units; resources on autism, dyslexia, language and communication needs; and web-based training materials. Funding was made available for ITE tutors to pilot these initiatives and conduct small-scale research projects so that feedback could be used to further inform teacher education programmes.

Feedback on student teachers' experiences of these pilot initiatives has been positive. My own university was involved with a research project focusing on specialised placement. Although the TDA originally intended this placement to be in special schools, we received agreement to offer an alternative setting. Two cohorts were provided with different experiences to compare the impact on their professional development. Both cohorts undertook the placement in addition to their ITE programme, so it was voluntary and not assessed. The first cohort was given a two-week placement in a special school, followed by a two-week placement in a mainstream school that was recognised as having excellent practice in inclusive education. The intention of this pilot was for student teachers to reflect on transferability of knowledge and skills from special school to mainstream settings. The second cohort was given a two-week placement in either a special or a mainstream school, and provided with additional resources about inclusive practice. Both cohorts were set the same activities to complete, including a focus on children's own voices about their experiences and social inclusion. Student teachers were asked to reflect on their learning from the experience and how they had applied this to their professional practice.

The students from both cohorts universally commended the opportunity to take part in a specialised placement. They stated that it had significantly increased their skills and confidence, with one commenting that:

> Knowing what I do now, and feeling as confident as I do now, will undoubtedly make me a much more informed and inclusive teacher. People I know on the BA course have the same 'awkwardness' as I felt before about special needs, but because they haven't done these placements, they will probably still feel like that when they begin teaching their own class.

Some spoke of their initial anxieties, for example:

> It was a very new experience for me and at the start I was anxious and thought 'I can't do it'. But my confidence grew and I saw how to make adaptations and that it only had to be small things.
>
> It's about confidence – I could talk and communicate better. ... Now if I see a child struggling I have the confidence to adapt the teaching or

change the resource, looking at what they were doing instead of just working with the better ones to push them on.

When describing the effect the placement had on their professional development, students from both cohorts identified similar key learning experiences from working with teachers skilled in inclusive education:

> Before I did the placements I didn't think about it; some [teachers] kept children separate from other children with a teaching assistant, but they have got so much to share – to give everyone else.

> You can't identify children with SEN by looks or behaviour. You have to get to know children.

> I really enjoyed my placement. Very positive outlook on the part of the staff, they didn't make a 'big deal' out of a child's learning difficulty. They didn't tend to label children. All the children benefited from the strategies put in place for SEN.

One student teacher powerfully described how the placement had changed her:

> The placement has really changed me as a teacher. It has afforded me the confidence to work, teach and plan with children who have complex needs, alongside giving me more confidence when teaching all children. I am now more imaginative with my planning and willing to take risks with both my planning and teaching ... it has prepared me for a life of teaching, where anything could happen.

Where the two cohorts did differ was in relation to the way that they spoke about the children. While the language of both groups of student teachers suggested that the concept of special educational needs as a specific group was already deeply ingrained, those who had experienced 'excellent' practice of including children with this label indicated a growing awareness of issues of labelling and separating some learners from their peers. This led them to question the need for special schools, why teaching assistants withdrew children from classes, and why ability grouping was so popular, when they had seen alternatives work so successfully. They started to think about their own practice and the impact this had on pupils' learning, although from their comments it was clear that this was just the start of a change of mindset, and that more consolidation would be needed. In comparison, student teachers who had only experienced a special school placement did not question the impact of labels or whether pupils could have been alternatively accommodated in a mainstream school.

Whatever the length or setting of the placement, both cohorts concluded that all student teachers should have this experience. To return to the student teacher's comment at the start of this chapter, the reason for this is clear:

At the end of the third year I was confident about teaching, but SEN scared me. Without the experience of the placement I would have been thinking, 'How will I cope with my own class and SEN?' Now I am more confident and think why should a child suffer while a teacher learns what to do ... I can now see that SEN is an integral part of teaching.

Some also argued strongly that the placement should not be assessed because this allowed them to experiment without any feeling of 'failure'. As one student stated:

On a voluntary placement, I felt that I could make mistakes and ask questions when I wasn't feeling confident, without people judging me. It was like being in the first year again and that was good.

These experiences raise some important questions for tutors and student teachers. Clearly, the new TDA initiatives have a place in preparing new teachers for the diversity they will face in their classrooms. However, the success, or otherwise, for individual new teachers may well depend on the quality of the practice they are exposed to, and what the tutors themselves bring to the delivery of this part of the ITE curriculum. The reality for many ITE programmes is that there may not be large enough numbers of schools with excellent inclusive practice in which to place all student teachers: if their only placement is in special schools, or they do not have access to excellent inclusive role models, this may reinforce the whole notion of pupils identified as having special educational needs needing special education. In addition, there may not be enough tutors experienced in, and committed to, inclusion available to deliver the taught component. This may create an overdependence on off-the-shelf resources such as the *SEN and/or Disabilities Training Toolkit*, raising the issue of tutor confidence in dealing with more challenging considerations such as those of personal values and attitudes, and teachers' roles in affecting the inclusion and exclusion of children.

So, despite the apparent advantages of these pilot developments within ITE, the route to making them available to all student teachers in the future is far less clear. This leaves new teachers still in a situation where many feel anxious about working with children identified as having special educational needs, seeing them as a separate group of learners. Moving from this perspective to a confident acceptance of individual learners bringing valued diversity into the classroom is a key challenge for teachers' development.

Professional responsibilities for all learners

In this final section, I would like to return to my suggestion of classrooms having a community of learners. In such a community, individuality is recognised and teaching is planned to take account of this as a core part of planning, rather than an add-on for different groups of (labelled) children. The Audit Commission (2002) made several observations concerning special educational needs that may still provide a useful starting point for teachers as they consider a community of learners approach.

- Despite duties set out in the Special Educational Needs and Disability Act 2001 to increase accessibility (in its widest sense) and not to treat disabled children less favourably than their peers, there is great variability of practice in schools (p. 11). Factors such as gender, ethnicity, family and locality circumstances can affect how learners' needs are identified and supported; barriers to learning are created through inaccessible environments, unwelcoming attitudes and shortfalls in specialist support (p. 51).
- When a child is identified as having special educational needs, the processes that follow can induce 'separateness', despite providing the advantages of additional resources. This can mean, for example, that a teacher will spend less time with a child because of the presence of a teaching assistant, or that 'the interests of children with SEN may remain peripheral in mainstream policymaking' (p. 51).
- Diversity should become an embedded concept, moving teachers from separating learners into groups identified by labels such as 'SEN', 'gifted', 'EAL' and 'working-class boys' to focusing on individuals' learning and how they can be helped to progress (p. 52).
- An attitudinal shift is required. This, linked with sustained investment in school facilities and staff development, will enable children to be genuinely included (p. 52).

These observations suggest that pupils have different experiences, based on a range of external factors. While teachers may not be able to do anything about some of these, they can certainly affect change in relation to inaccessible environments and unwelcoming attitudes. From my experience, people often focus only on expensive adaptations such as ramps and lifts when inaccessible environments are discussed, when often really small things can make a significant difference. This is where a can-do, flexible attitude is important, linked to a willingness to learn from others. Seeking support from colleagues should be seen as a strength; effective teams are built on interdependence, where skills and knowledge are shared. Parents with whom I work particularly mention that it is the welcome their child receives and the teacher's willingness to learn about him/her as an individual that is the most important factor for successful inclusion. This is something that all teachers can achieve.

Teachers can also ensure that pupils who have been identified as having special educational needs still receive equitable amounts of their time, rather than expecting a teaching assistant to provide this. This would help to avoid situations where learners become separated from their peers through well intended support structures, leaving them socially and educationally isolated

(Anderson *et al.* 2003). A further way to support school-wide development includes teachers examining how policies and practices contribute to the inclusion or otherwise of particular learners. Many schools, for example, have a Special Needs Policy, but how are these learners accounted for within other school policies? Teachers may increase their confidence through taking up staff development opportunities. While this may involve useful strategies and tips for teaching, these alone may not bring about the attitudinal shift that comes from reflecting on personal values and challenging ideological positions.

Understanding differing perspectives, particularly those of people who have experienced living with labels imposed upon them, can provide teachers with a strong professional foundation for the way in which they view and respond to all learners. Listening to a range of people's views helps teachers to make balanced judgements about how they work with learners. It can be tempting to listen only to those seen as experts, rather than others such as parents and the children themselves, but all have a valuable contribution to make so that you receive the whole picture. Clearly, there is much to be gained from the experience of your SENCO and external advisers, but an overdependence on specialists can make you feel deskilled (Goodley 2009). Much advice that is offered relies on good teaching and learning techniques, which can be practised by all teachers.

Within this wider picture of teaching and learning lie more specific strategies for new teachers to engage with. Mixed-ability groupings, balanced groups, cooperative groups and differentiation are all strategies that work successfully (Gillies 2003; Boaler 2007; Cole 2008). Teachers can also benefit from observing each other's practice, team teaching, and national initiatives such as the Inclusion Development Programme. Key to all of these is the belief in all children's ability to learn and progress. Cole (2008) and others (Hart *et al.* 2004) refer to this as 'learning without limits'; their challenge to any group being seen as of 'fixed ability' or placed within a 'no-hope' category centres on the belief that teachers are fundamental in transforming pupils' learning capacity.

Conclusion

The Lamb Inquiry Report on *Inspection, Accountability and School Improvement* (DCSF 2009) focused on securing accountability within schools for the quality of the learning experience provided to pupils identified as having special educational needs. Teachers' responsibility within this is clear: they will be expected to have high aspirations for pupils with special educational needs, just as they have for all other pupils. Support to achieve these aspirations must be organised in a way that enables every pupil to have a high-quality learning experience. For teachers committed to inclusive education, this will involve a shared learning experience, rather than one where different groups identified by one of their characteristics spend significant time away from the rest of the class.

Teachers' attitudes towards diversity within their classrooms will be a key component in setting the context for the quality of pupils' learning experiences. How they think about individual learners, and the way they engage with them, will be important. Teachers are role models: children observe closely how their teachers treat other children and note the language they use. References to the 'SEN group' and problematising changes needed to facilitate particular children can be picked up and replicated by pupils. A welcoming attitude and commitment to solving difficulties encountered can become a positive class ethos.

Many of us become anxious when faced with new situations for which we feel unskilled, but if we focus on how these link to situations in which we do feel confident, then solutions are more easily identified. This does not mean that we ignore individual differences, just that we do not get sidetracked by the many labels children are given within our education system. If we focus on teaching and learning, this is what teachers are trained for, and should continue to develop skills in, throughout their career. New teachers will take time to learn the skills that will enable them to work confidently with all learners in their classrooms. Removing labels from the context in which they work will enable them to focus on what is important – the learners themselves.

Reflection on values and practice

Think about the children who you know have been identified as having special educational needs.

- What has been written and said about them by others? How much of this presents a positive perspective, and how much seems negative? What impact has this had on your own views?
- What is their classroom experience? Do they receive a similar amount of time with teachers to other pupils? Do they routinely work with their peers, or does their support system replace this?
- How can you explicitly demonstrate a commitment to valuing diversity in your classroom? What welcome do you give to learners?

Resources

Inclusion Now – The Magazine of the Inclusion Movement in the UK: ww.allfie.org.uk
TTRB (Teacher Training Resource Bank) Special Educational Needs: www.sen.ttrb.ac.uk
Mason, M. (2005) *Incurably Human*, 2nd edn, London: Working Press.

References

Ainscow, M. (2007) 'Taking an inclusive turn', *Journal of Research in Special Educational Needs*, 7(1): 3–7.

Anderson, V., Faraday, S., Prowse, S., Richards, G. and Swindells, D. (2003) *Count Me in FE*, London: Learning and Skills Development Agency.

Audit Commission (2002) *Statutory Assessment and Statements of SEN: In Need of a Review?*, Policy Focus, London: Audit Commission.

Boaler, J. (2007) 'Promoting "relational equity" and high maths achievement through an innovative mixed ability approach', *British Educational Research Journal*, 34(2): 167–94.

British Psychological Society (2005) Submission to House of Commons Select Committee Inquiry (5.4: 4).

Cole, M. (2008) 'Learning without limits: a Marxist assessment', *Policy Futures in Education*, 6(4): 453–63.

DCSF (2009) *Inspection, Accountability and School Improvement*, www.dcsf.gov.uk/lambinquiry

DES (1978) *Special Educational Needs. Report of the Committee of Enquiry into the Education of Handicapped Children and Young People*, London: HMSO.

DfES (2004) *Removing Barriers to Achievement: The Government's Strategy for SEN*, Nottingham: Department for Education and Skills.

DRC (2006) *Supporting New Teachers – Early Professional Development including Induction*, London: Disability Rights Commission.

Frederickson, N. and Cline, T. (2009) *Special Educational Needs, Inclusion and Diversity*, Maidenhead: Open University Press.

Gillies, R. (2003) 'Structuring cooperative group work in classrooms', *International Journal of Educational Research*, 39: 35–49.

Goodley, C. (2009) 'Include me out: a vision for 21st century schools?', *Inclusion Now*, 22: 5.

Hall, J. (1997) *Social Devaluation and Special Education. The Right to Full Mainstream Inclusion and an Honest Statement*, London: Jessica Kingsley.

Hart, S., Dixon, A., Drummond, M.J. and McIntyre, D. (2004) *Learning without Limits*, Maidenhead: Open University Press.

Hodkinson, A. (2009) 'Pre-service teacher training and special educational needs in England 1970–2008: is government learning the lessons of the past or is it experiencing a groundhog day?', *European Journal of Special Needs Education*, 24(3): 277–89.

House of Commons (2006) *Special Educational Needs. Third Report of Sessions 2005–6.* Vol.1, London: The Stationery Office.

Lauchlan, F. and Boyle, C. (2007) 'Is the use of labels in special education helpful?', *Support for Learning*, 22: 36–42.

Moran, A. (2007) 'Embracing inclusive teacher education', *European Journal of Teacher Education*, 30(2): 119–34.

Norwich, B. (1999) 'The connotation of special education labels for professionals in the field', *British Journal of Special Education*, 26(4): 179–83.

Ofsted (2006) *Inclusion: Does it Matter Where Pupils are Taught?*, London: HMSO.

——(2008) *How Well New Teachers are Prepared to Teach Pupils with Learning Difficulties and/or Disabilities*, London: HMSO.

Pearson, S. (2007) 'Exploring inclusive education: early steps for prospective secondary school teachers', *British Journal of Special Education*, 34(1): 25–32.

Rix, J., Sheehy, K., Simmons, K. and Nind, M. (2004) *Starting Out*, Milton Keynes: Open University Press.

Rosenthal, R. and Jacobson, L. (1968) *Pygmalion in the Classroom*, New York: Holt, Rinehart and Winston.

TDA (2007) *Results of the Newly Qualified Teacher Survey*, London: Training and Development Agency for Schools.

——(2009) *Initial Teacher Training Toolkit for SEN/LD& D*, London: Training and Development Agency for Schools.

Thomas, G. and Vaughan, M. (2004) *Inclusive Education. Readings and Reflections*, Maidenhead: Open University Press.

Wearmouth, J. (2009) *A Beginning Teacher's Guide to Special Educational Needs*, Maidenhead: Open University Press.

Winter, E. (2006) 'Preparing new teachers for inclusive schools and classrooms', *Support for Learning* 21(2): 85–91.

Chapter 9

Inclusive education and gifted and talented provision

Roger Moltzen

Introduction

The notion that learners who are gifted and talented can legitimately be considered to have special educational needs has been slow to gain general acceptance. This is particularly true in countries where egalitarian ideals have traditionally dominated decision-making on social policy. Such ideals have tended to focus on equality or sameness of provision, rather than on equity or fairness of provision. More recently, as many countries have become much more sensitive to the needs of diverse groups, treating people equitably has become much more common than treating them the same. Gifted and talented learners have definitely benefited from this shift, and there is a much wider acceptance among educators and educational policy-makers that these learners have needs that often require differentiated provisions. The view that this is blatant elitism appears to be much less prevalent nowadays. As a result, in a number of countries there has been a greater attention to policy development in gifted and talented education.

Another factor that has increased awareness of the needs of this group has been what is sometimes referred to as 'parent power'. Educational reforms over the past 20 years, in western countries at least, have tended to elevate the role of parents in school governance. Research undertaken in the early 1990s in New Zealand, where some of the most radical reforms in educational administration were introduced, found that as parents were given a greater voice in educational matters, advocacy for the needs of gifted and talented students also increased (Moltzen 1992).

This increased attention to the nature and the needs of gifted and talented learners has brought to the forefront issues concerning how these needs can most appropriately be met. In some educational jurisdictions, this decision is largely taken away from schools. However, in most instances individual schools enjoy a level of autonomy in deciding the most appropriate educational provisions for these young people. In virtually all countries of the world, the majority of our most able learners spend the majority of their time at school in regular classrooms alongside their same-age peers. Experts, advocates and parents have lamented this 'default' environment for decades as an intellectual wasteland for gifted and talented learning. The reason for such disillusionment with the inclusive classroom is easy to understand. Within this environment, the needs of these students were more often overlooked, and probably continue to be so in many such classrooms. The reasons for this neglect are easily identified by those with an understanding of the needs of gifted and talented learners. First, there is frequently a lack of professional knowledge of the needs of learners with exceptional ability. Often these students do not present overtly as having special needs. Many may have switched off, some passively and others expressing their frustration through non-compliant behaviour. Some teachers may acknowledge these students' needs, but lack the professional knowledge to respond appropriately to them. Learners identified as gifted and talented are far from a homogeneous group of students. The regular teacher will likely rely on some widely held stereotypes and remain ignorant of behavioural indicators of exceptionality that fall outside this concept. Second, there is a widely held misconception that these students have the ability to 'make it on their own' and thus have much less need for support than most other students. In a classroom replete with competing demands, the needs of these learners can fall well down the busy teacher's priority list of what can be achieved in any single day. Unfortunately, without appropriate support some of these young people do not 'make it', and the impact of repeated neglect can have consequences well beyond their time at school. Third, rigid adherence to a set curriculum, designed for the majority and delivered in a lock-step manner, sees many of those with gifts and talents being asked to engage with ideas and activities that they may have mastered some years previously.

It is important to point out that any oversight of gifted and talented students in regular or inclusive classrooms has been more the result of teachers' ignorance than teachers' arrogance. Such a situation is unsurprising, given the widespread omission of attention to this area in both pre-service and in-service teacher education. On the other hand, some teachers with little specific knowledge of gifted and talented are skilled at providing for exceptional ability and nurturing the talents of these young people. These are teachers who respond to the needs of learners as individuals in their classrooms. They get to know the needs, strengths and interests of each class member and structure the learning in response to this. Of course, these teachers' practice would be further enhanced with greater knowledge of the specific nature and needs of gifted and talented students, and of research and effective practice in gifted and talented education. However, appropriate provisions for this group are not inconsistent with the broader principles of effective pedagogy.

While there is a greater awareness now of the special needs of gifted and talented students, the response of schools to addressing these has tended to be conservative. The spectre of elitism raises its head when alternatives to the regular classroom are tabled for consideration by schools and teachers. In contrast, many experts in gifted and talented education, and advocates for gifted and talented students, maintain that the inclusive classroom represents the most, not the least restrictive environment for this group. However, in an educational era that has moved philosophically and practically from exclusion to inclusion, the argument that gifted and talented learners should be an exception can elicit fierce debate. Nonetheless, ideological arguments can be sustained only where it can be demonstrated that people will benefit from the practices associated with this way of thinking. In the minds of many people, inclusion is totally antithetical to the needs of gifted and talented students.

Considering the options

Most experts on the education of young people with special abilities would maintain that a singular approach to addressing their needs is not defensible. To some extent, then, discussing these as mutually exclusive alternatives is artificial and does not represent the reality of decision-making and practice. However, most schools have a primary or first-level approach on which other provisions are built or of which they are an extension. This generally reflects a particular view of gifted and talented education and the most appropriate way of responding to educational and personal needs. The options here can be broadly described as acceleration, segregation and inclusion.

Acceleration

To many people, acceleration is synonymous with year-level advancement – commonly referred to as grade-skipping. However, acceleration is much more than this, and the following definition captures this broader interpretation of the approach. 'Accelerated learning, or acceleration, refers to instruction which matches the readiness and needs of the gifted child more closely with the curriculum ... In essence, acceleration occurs when children are exposed to new content at an earlier age than other children or when they cover the same content in less time. Acceleration is sometimes referred to as vertical development, as distinct from lateral development, in that students are developing "upwards" (Townsend 2004: 290). There is little dispute that acceleration, as defined by Townsend, should characterise all forms of provision. It is when it is interpreted as advanced placement or grade-skipping that the issue becomes contentious.

A recent review of the research on acceleration was undertaken by a group of recognised experts in this field. Their findings are tabled in the publication *A Nation Deceived: How Schools Hold Back America's Brightest Students* (Colangelo *et al.* 2004). The title gives a clear indication of the conclusion at which the authors arrived after reviewing available research on the practice. They are unequivocal and emphatic in declaring that acceleration is the easiest and most effective way to help highly capable students.

The authors acknowledge that acceleration can take many forms, and in fact identify 18 different types of acceleration. However, implicit in this publication is the view that it is virtually impossible to do this without placing a gifted and talented student at a higher year level, either part- or full-time. Holding children back is regarded as potentially more damaging academically and socially than moving them ahead. The authors discuss other educational approaches, acknowledging that these have a place, but they are insistent that, individually or in tandem, these do not come close to matching the positive outcomes associated with acceleration.

On the basis of this report, one could easily conclude that acceleration is the only ethical response to the educational and social needs of gifted and talented students, and that the arguments that have characterised the resistance to this practice are flawed. However, a number of issues remain unresolved and should be considered before embracing acceleration as the provision of choice. In this chapter, only two of these are discussed.

First, almost all the research that the authors reviewed was undertaken in the United States. The authors have acknowledged this limitation, and latterly have broadened the research base to include other countries. The problem here is that robust research on acceleration undertaken outside the United States is minimal. In the United Kingdom, arguably the most significant research in this field is Freeman's (1991, 2001) longitudinal study. While not a study on acceleration, many of her participants had been accelerated in the form of year-level advancement. Most interestingly, her findings are in completely the opposite direction to those reported in *A Nation Deceived*. Moltzen (2005), in an investigation into the life stories of gifted New Zealand adults, found that, like the participants in Freeman's study, most of his group that had been advanced a year or more at school were cynical of the practice.

Second, the research findings and the conclusions drawn by the reviewers seem based on classroom practices that are more traditional and may be more of a feature of schools in the United States than some other countries. In these classrooms there is a rather rigid adherence to a tightly prescribed grade-level curriculum, and differentiation to meet the needs of individual students is minimal. Many of those advocating for acceleration hold the view that, even where regular class teachers are disposed towards accommodating different needs, the task is humanly impossible and an unrealistic expectation to place on them. In contrast, educators in many countries would argue that curriculum differentiation is an essential ingredient of effective teaching, and this view is consistent with recent initiatives designed to further personalise teaching and learning. An example of this can be found in the recent English publication *Personalised Learning – A Practical Guide* (DCSF 2008).

Segregation

In a similar vein to the proponents of acceleration, those arguing for segregated provisions for gifted and talented learners maintain that the inclusive classroom sees these students' abilities unrealised and can place them at risk of underachieving. The arguments here are compelling, and there is certainly some evidence to support this contention (Delcourt *et al.* 1994; Kulik 2003). Grouping students together on the basis of ability can take many forms and includes separate schools, separate classes, streaming or grouping, withdrawal or pullout programmes, ability grouping (across classes or within class), and cluster grouping. Unfortunately, the research into these options varies greatly in quality, and the findings, although generally suggesting that homogeneous grouping carries some academic and social benefit, are far from conclusive. A salient question here is whether or not these gains are as much, or more, to do with teacher effect than with grouping students together on the basis of ability. It is reasonable to expect that teachers assigned to work with gifted and talented students are carefully selected, and that some thought has been given to matching their attitudes, knowledge and abilities with those of the group. It is equally reasonable to expect that such teachers either have undertaken, or will have opportunities to undertake, professional learning related to teaching such students.

Inclusion

Those who argue that the inclusive classroom has the potential to be a rich and rewarding setting for gifted and talented students are often accused of being politically correct and educationally naïve. Yet many supporters of the regular classroom approach, such as this author, can cite innumerable examples of teachers effectively catering for more able students in this environment. More than this, the inclusive classroom, rather than a default option, carries the following advantages over acceleration and/or segregation.

- **Most gifted and talented students are, and will continue to be, educated in inclusive classrooms.** At this point in time, most gifted and talented students in most countries of the world will spend all, or nearly all, their schooling in inclusive classrooms. Those vehemently opposed to this approach must accept that it is unrealistic to expect the situation to change any time in the foreseeable future. Even if there was a more widespread acceptance of alternatives, it is unlikely that the impact would see more than a very small proportion of gifted and talented students affected. Quite simply, policies or initiatives that bypass the regular class teacher bypass the majority of our gifted and talented students.
- **The inclusive classroom approach is potentially a more equitable approach.** Around the world, children from economically disadvantaged backgrounds and children from ethnic minorities are underrepresented among those identified as gifted and talented. There are a number of reasons for this situation, but probably the most influential is the widely held misconception that the potential for outstanding achievement is much more prevalent among some groups than it is others. Targeted provisions beyond

the inclusive environment frequently perpetuate, often quite unin-
tentionally, this way of thinking.

- **The inclusive classroom future-proofs provisions for gifted and
talented students.** Dedicated provisions for this group are among the most
tenuous and vulnerable to change of all educational initiatives. They are
often described as 'the last to arrive and the first to leave'. Recent events in
England and New Zealand reflect this syndrome. Both countries have a
rather inglorious history of support for their most able young people. In
stark contrast to this historical neglect, in the past decade a raft of initiatives
was introduced in both, and almost overnight the situation changed for the
better. In the past year, the two countries have experienced significant
cutbacks, and what promised to be the beginning of a new era of hope for
gifted and talented students appears to be under threat. Once again, provisions for them appear to be considered an optional extra and something that
can be culled when money is tight or where political whim sees a shift
in priorities. Building the capacity of inclusive class teachers through dedicated professional development and support will help insulate gifted and
talented learners from the impact of 'external' provisions that are 'here
today and gone tomorrow'.

- **The inclusive classroom better accommodates current views on
what giftedness is and how talent develops.** The notion that giftedness
is synonymous with a high level of general ability or 'g', which is innately
determined, fixed, and can be accurately measured by testing, is much less
prevalent today. The case for an expanded view of giftedness and talent
cannot be made within the scope of this chapter, but it is now much more
common for teachers and schools to take a multi-categorical approach to
giftedness and talent (McAlpine 2004). An associated shift in thinking sees
giftedness and talent as a developmental phenomenon rather than as a fixed
trait. In other words, exceptional ability may emerge at different times and
under different circumstances. These two principles would appear to position the inclusive classroom strongly. First, a broader view of giftedness and
talent means that children may be gifted and talented in number of general
areas (intellectually, physically, socially, creatively) and in innumerable
specific areas (science, mathematics, dance, drama, mediation, swimming,
poetry writing). No gifted and talented child will be gifted in all domains,
and in fact most will be characterised by a very 'jagged' profile of abilities.
Alongside exceptional ability, some will have a need for support in another
area. This exposes a weakness in both acceleration and segregation. For
example, do you accelerate to a higher class level a student who is outstanding in mathematics and science but below average in reading and
writing? Do you place in a separate class a student who is highly creative
but academically of more average ability? These questions are less of an issue
in the inclusive classroom. In this environment, a wide range of abilities can
be accommodated and strengths and needs addressed more naturally. It is

much easier in the inclusive classroom to see every child as potentially gifted in some area and to provide access to multiple opportunities to demonstrate this potential. This is far from suggesting that every child is gifted, but it represents a different perception, both by teachers and students, than that which occurs when there is an imperative to judge definitively who is, and who is not, gifted.

- **The inclusive classroom can offer a level of flexibility that is more commensurate with the needs of gifted and talented students.** Some options, particularly those that are part-time and/or short-term in nature, are often quite disconnected from the regular classroom programme. It is not uncommon to hear gifted and talented students complaining that they have had to do two iterations of a single subject on the same day, once in their home classroom and once in their extension or enrichment class. The inclusive classroom, at the primary school level at least, offers the opportunity to integrate the curriculum. Van Tassel-Baska (2003: 175) argues that an integrated curriculum can address 'all salient characteristics of the gifted learner simultaneously, attending to precocity, intensity, and complexity as integrated characteristics that represent cognitive and affective dimensions of the learner'.

- **The inclusive classroom can accommodate both qualitative and quantitative differentiation.** Gifted and talented students need learning experiences that offer vertical and horizontal extension. One of the major weaknesses of year-level advancement or grade-skipping is that it addresses the need for quantitative differentiation (acceleration) but usually not for qualitative differentiation (enrichment). Students who are accelerated very soon discover that although they are working at a higher level, they are still in a regular classroom with an undifferentiated curriculum. In their investigation into gifted and talented students who had been accelerated, Vialle et al. (2001: 16) found that ' ... after the honeymoon period of the initial six weeks in the class, the accelerated students became dissatisfied with the class pace', concluding that this 'demonstrates the need for acceleration options to be accompanied by qualitatively different curricula that are commensurate with the accelerated students' abilities and learning preferences'. The two can coexist very easily in the inclusive classroom, although it must be conceded that qualitative differentiation has dominated provisions in this setting, and there has been wariness about allowing gifted and talented students to progress through the curriculum at a faster pace.

- **The particular needs of gifted and talented students from some cultural groups may be more consistent with the inclusive classroom environment.** For many children, being selected for special programmes that withdraw them from their regular classroom and their same-age peers is validating and rewarding. For others, this separation is unwelcome. In more individualistic cultures, being singled out on the basis of ability is likely to be perceived positively. For cultures where the group takes precedence over the individual, actions that separate an individual from the group can be perceived negatively. In fact, there is some evidence that students from these cultures may deliberately underachieve to avoid this separation. Bevan-Brown (2004: 179), researching Maori perspectives on giftedness and talent, reported examples of children who 'failed, misbehaved or opted out of programmes in which they felt isolated, uncomfortable and unfamiliar'. Although there is little direct evidence to generalise this finding to other cultural groups, inasmuch as Maori have much in common with other indigenous peoples, it is likely that this aversion to being separated from the group is widespread.

- **Viewing every teacher as a teacher of the gifted ensures greater consistency of provision for gifted and talented students.** Educational provisions for gifted and talented students are inherently patchy, both between and within schools. The reason for this is quite simple: the investment in raising teacher awareness and capacity in this area of education has been very weak. This means that the odds are low that a gifted and talented student will be taught by a teacher who possesses the attitude, knowledge and skills to provide an educational experience that matches the student's needs. Unfortunately, where the focus is on provisions beyond the inclusive classroom, there can be a perception that responsibility for meeting the needs of this group no longer resides with the inclusive class teacher. This is extremely flawed thinking, as even the most comprehensive and well planned approach to acceleration or segregation will exclude a significant proportion of gifted and talented students. Interestingly, those at greatest risk of being omitted from selection are creatively gifted students (Moltzen 2009). In selecting students for placement in special programmes, schools often use approaches to identification that are conservative and result in hardworking, achieving, but somewhat compliant students being over-represented. One could argue that the students who could most benefit from a change of learning environment are among the least likely to be selected.

The contention that every teacher is a teacher of gifted and talented students is hardly an extreme idea. If the investment in gifted and talented education is aimed at regular class teachers, not only is this likely to represent the best value for money, it will exponentially increase awareness of the needs of these students and the capacity to meet them.

Including gifted and talented students in the inclusive classroom

In this chapter, a case has been made for an inclusive approach to providing for gifted and talented students. This is not to dismiss the potential benefits of acceleration and/or segregation. In fact, the benefits that can accrue for these students in the regular classroom will not occur unless teachers have the willingness and the prerequisite knowledge to make some significant adjustment to their practices to cater for this group. Advocacy for the inclusive classroom is not advocacy for enrichment over acceleration. Enrichment is a term that is frequently used to describe programmes that are, in essence, more of the same. Any programme for these students that does not attend to their potential to acquire knowledge and skills at a much faster rate than their same-age peers is neglecting a basic need to learn at an accelerated pace.

In the same vein, there are some obvious advantages to gifted students having opportunities to work alongside like-minded peers. There has been a growing awareness more recently of the particular social and emotional needs of this group, which are not necessarily immediately obvious to an uninformed observer. Gifted children can be gifted at masking their feelings. A knowledgeable teacher can be sensitive to these needs, but there is little doubt that some opportunities to spend time with like peers can be very affirming and validating.

There is no recipe for restructuring the inclusive classroom to attend to gifted and talented learners more appropriately. There is not the space here to explore these, but there is a high level of consistency across the literature and research in this field as to what comprises effective practice in gifted and talented education. An excellent book that combines research and practice is *Best Practices in Gifted Education: An Evidence-Based Guide* (Robinson *et al.* 2007). First and foremost, programme differentiation must recognise the individuality of the learner. Gifted and talented students are far from being a homogenous group, even where the concept is defined very conservatively.

Focusing on the inclusive classroom should not be seen as a mandate to discontinue specialist support across or within schools. However, it could lead to deploying such expertise in a different way. For example, a specialist teacher who has been used to take pullout/withdrawal classes might be used to support the inclusive class teacher to work with his or her gifted and talented students within the classroom environment and as part of the class programme.

Conclusion

The case for the inclusive classroom is not made on the basis that the alternatives represent perceived elitism. Nor is it proposed because any provisions outside the regular would seem inconsistent with an inclusive ideology and thus inappropriate on principle. It is not being argued for primarily on the basis of cost effectiveness, even though it is most definitely a better financial investment than the alternatives. If the inclusive classroom is to be an effective context for educating the most able, it must not be seen as a cost-neutral option. In fact, without a significant investment in comprehensive and ongoing programmes of learning for teachers, this option is not an option. Programmes of professional development should be school-wide and enjoy the active support of senior management. School-wide professional development that leads to coordinated and consistent approaches across the school will make a difference. The ideal is for the inclusion of gifted and talented learners to become core business in a school and a natural part of a school's culture, and for every teacher to be viewed as a teacher of gifted and talented students. An acceptance of the inclusive classroom as a viable and a defensible context for educating gifted and talented learners, coupled with effective professional development, has the greatest potential significantly to increase the number of very able students receiving an education that is commensurate with their strengths, interests and needs.

Reflection on values and practice

What are some of the key characteristics of students with gifts and talents that should inform how a teacher might differentiate their learning experiences?

What are the implications of an inclusive class teacher allowing a gifted and talented student to work on curricula at a faster pace?

How might parents of gifted and talented students be facilitated to work collaboratively with their children's teachers?

Resources

Plucker, J.A. and Callahan, C.M. (2007) *Critical Issues and Practices in Gifted Education: What the Research Says*. Waco, TX: Prufrock Press.

Roberts, J.L. and Inman, T.F. (2007) *Strategies for Differentiating Instruction: Best Practices for the Classroom*, Waco, TX: Prufrock Press.

Smith, C.M.M. (2006) *Including the Gifted and Talented: Making Inclusion Work for More Gifted and Able Learners*, New York: Routledge.

References

Bevan-Brown, J. (2004) 'Gifted and talented Maori learners', in McAlpine, D. and Moltzen, R. (eds) *Gifted and Talented: New Zealand Perspectives*, 2nd edn, Palmerston North: Kanuka Grove Press, 171–97.

Colangelo, N., Assouline, S. and Gross, M.U.M. (2004) *A Nation Deceived: How Schools Hold Back America's Brightest Students (Vols 1–2)*, Iowa City: University of Iowa, The Connie Belin and Jacqueline N. Blank International Center for Gifted Education and Talent Development.

Delcourt, M., Loyd, B., Cornell, D. and Goldberg, M. (1994) *Evaluation of the Effects of Programming Arrangements on Student Learning Outcomes: Executive Summary*, Monograph No. 94107, Charlottesville, VA: National Research Center on the Gifted and Talented.

DCSF (2008) *Personalised Learning – A Practical Guide*. London: Department for Children, Schools and Families. http://publications.teachernet.gov.uk

Freeman, J. (1991) *Gifted Children Growing Up*, London: Cassell.

——(2001) *Gifted Children Grown Up*, London: David Fulton.

Kulik, J.A. (2003) 'Grouping and tracking', in Colangelo, N. and Davis, G.A. (eds) *Handbook of Gifted Education*, 3rd edn, Boston: Allyn & Bacon, 268–81.

McAlpine, D. (2004) 'The identification of gifted and talented students', in McAlpine, D. and Moltzen, R. (eds) *Gifted and Talented: New Zealand Perspectives*, 2nd edn, Palmerston North: Kanuka Grove Press, 93–132.

Moltzen, R. (1992) 'The impact of reforms in education on provisions for gifted children', Master's thesis, University of Waikato, Hamilton, New Zealand.

——(2005) 'Realising potential: investigating the life stories of gifted New Zealand adults', PhD thesis, University of Waikato, Hamilton, New Zealand.

——(2009) 'Talent development across the lifespan', in Shavinina, L.V. (ed.) *International Handbook on Giftedness*, New York: Springer, 353–79.

Robinson, A., Shore, B. and Enersen, D. (2007) *Best Practices in Gifted Education: An Evidence-Based Guide*, Waco, TX: Prufrock.

Townsend, M. (2004) 'Models of enrichment and acceleration in developing the talented', in McAlpine, D. and Moltzen, R. (eds) *Gifted and Talented: New Zealand Perspectives*, 2nd edn, Palmerston North: Kanuka Grove Press, 289–308.

Van Tassel-Baska, J. (2003). 'What matters in curriculum for gifted learners: reflections on theory, research and practice', in Colangelo, N. and Davis, G.A. (eds) *Handbook of Gifted Education*, 3rd edn, Boston: Allyn & Bacon, 174–83.

Vialle, W., Ashton, T., Carlon, G. and Rankin, F. (2001) 'Acceleration: a coat of many colours', *Roeper Review*, 24(1): 14–19.

Chapter 10

Challenging students, challenging settings

Jackie Scruton

Introduction

The purpose of this chapter is to help you understand and explore some of the complex issues surrounding challenging situations and behaviour that you may experience in your classroom. In doing so, it aims to help you develop your inclusive pedagogy.

Examining newspapers or searching the internet, you will soon find reference to the challenges of working with children in schools. In 1996 the Ridings School hit the national headlines; and Channel 4 filmed undercover in schools in 2005, running an 'exposé' of the state of behaviour in the classroom. Subsequently, in 2007 Ed Balls, Secretary of State for Children, Schools and Families, was quoted as saying:

> We know that standards of behaviour continue to be a matter of concern
> for parents and teachers, as well as children and young people themselves.
>
> (DCSF 2007: 11)

A survey of newly qualified teachers by the Association of Teachers and Lecturers (ATL) in 2006 identified that pupil discipline was the most important issue for them (www.behaviour4learning.ac.uk). In 2009, a subsequent ATL survey discovered that aggression, not only from pupils but also from parents, has increased. In addition, around half the respondents suggested that pupil behaviour has worsened over the past two years.

So, what can you do to meet such a challenge and help foster improved behaviour? This chapter explores the historical perspectives and changing terminology, and examines the latest debates and research. It moves on to identify some of the current strategies that can be used to help you develop your inclusive classroom practice. It also suggests ways in which you can reflect on your practice, and in so doing compile a set of tips for yourself. A key way of achieving an inclusive classroom is to ensure you are developing an inclusive pedagogical approach. This includes not only behaviour management, but aspects such as environment, resources, and your own enthusiasm for the job – how you engage your children in the teaching and learning that you provide.

Elton (1989) suggested that although 'reducing bad behaviour' was a realistic aim, eliminating it completely was not. At the end of this chapter, I hope you will feel more confident in your own skills and abilities in order to provide a learning environment that fosters positive behaviour and learning.

What do we mean by 'challenging' students?

Trying to define this term can be problematic for a number of reasons, some of which are explored below. However, it is worth noting that what one teacher would deem to be challenging behaviour, another would not. I was recently teaching a group of mature students, all of whom worked in educational settings. I asked each member of the group to make a list of behaviours that they found most difficult to work with. As an example, I indicated that the clicking of pens caused me to become frustrated and created a challenge in dealing with the situation. A member of the group said that he found students who sit on desks the most difficult to deal with. At that time, I was talking to the group perched on a desk! In subsequent weeks, if I sat on a desk he would click his pen – all in the spirit of humour. This anecdote illustrates how behaviour can be experienced quite differently, and may depend on different levels of tolerance and the subjective experience of the teacher.

Thus I suggest that defining the term 'challenging children', and indeed 'challenging behaviour', is difficult. Often in the classroom the two can be seen as interchangeable. Behaviour may be challenging because it prevents the teacher from providing a learning environment in which every child has the opportunity to maximise his or her learning. The challenge may also be for the teacher to alter the ways in which s/he approaches teaching in order to ensure learning takes place. In doing so, the teacher may have to spend time and energy containing and controlling the class, rather than teaching. Particular challenging behaviour may not be aimed at disrupting learning, but may result from other factors, such as difficulties with curriculum content or use and understanding of language and vocabulary.

Some behaviour is aimed at disruption and at undermining the authority and control of teachers. Rogers (1990) suggests that this may be a challenge to the teacher's right to exercise leadership in the classroom. In such cases, it may be difficult for the teacher to determine the causes of the challenge, as these may be very complex. Additionally, in schools today there is an added pressure caused by the need to raise achievement.

Further and more recent definitions have begun to identify a number of possible contributory factors to challenging behaviour, including the social and emotional aspects of learning; possible low self-esteem; and specific special educational needs such as attention hyperactivity deficit disorder (ADHD) or autistic spectrum disorder (ASD). In order to develop further our understanding of some of these complexities, and to provide an in[...] approach in the classroom, we need to explore the two main models o[...] ability: the medical and social models. The medical model has ensured that the 'blame' lies with the child, that there is something wrong with them, that they could be described as dysfunctional or 'ill' and, as result, need to be cured. No account is taken of external factors such as the environment (Frederickson and Cline 2009; Garner 2009). The social model takes a much more inclusive approach, suggesting that the 'blame' lies with society. It is society that creates barriers, which may prevent children from accessing learning opportunities.

I am advocating a move from a medical model to one where we aim to change the behaviour and not the child; one that has a stronger inclusive approach. In attempting to achieve this, we may also need to examine our own behaviour, and we must pay attention to the voice of the child. Increasingly, practitioners across Children's Services are being required to elicit children's views as a fundamental part of their work. This agenda is being driven by government through a number of initiatives such as 'Every Child Matters' (DfES 2003) and the Children Act 2004. Topping and Maloney (2005) draw on children's experiences where they have indicated that a teacher's behaviour affects their own. For example, they argue that if a teacher treats children with respect and has a sense of humour, then children's commitment will increase. They also suggest that a teacher who praises good work will be much more likely to have pupils who are not disruptive and are engaged with the learning process. The lesson for us is that our own behaviour is very likely to have an impact on our classes.

In trying to understand what we mean by 'challenging' children and ultimately in ensuring that we include them, it is important to identify a number of factors, including definitions, the use of language, teachers' tolerance levels, the impact of any specific conditions and impairments, and the 'blame' culture in which we live. This is a complex issue, with which newly qualified teachers will have to grapple.

Behaviour and learning

How do we ensure we provide an inclusive classroom that enables all children to access the teaching and leaning opportunities? We could start by developing our understanding of the links between behaviour and learning.

Haydn (2007) points out that there is an assumption that all children come to school wanting to learn – this is, however, not always the case. He also suggests that many outside the world of education view learning and behaviour as two entirely separate activities, entertaining the notion that a teacher with a new class will 'sort out' behaviour in the first few weeks. Developing and understanding children's 'learning agendas' (Elliott et al. 2001) can be viewed as an important and essential part of a teacher's role in providing an environment that facilitates learning. Steer (2008) suggests that the relationship between behaviour and learning is now widely accepted, and there is an expectation that schools should monitor the impact of this connection.

A significant approach to managing 'challenging' children is 'behaviour for learning'. This theory is based on the idea that a set of three relationships should be in place, which will enable the desired outcome of effective and worthwhile learning (Evans *et al.* 2003). These three relationships are:

- child and self
- child and other
- child and curriculum.

The theory suggests that when there is balance between these three components, a child will learn and behave appropriately. However, if there is an imbalance, learning and behaviour may be affected.

In 2004, the Behaviour 4 Learning (B4L) initiative was established and used as a major component of teacher training, aimed particularly at helping new teachers to develop and foster an environment in the classroom that promotes behaviour for learning.

Policies, initiatives and debates

It is important to recognise the effect history has had on the ways in which we perceive behaviour and work to promote behaviour for learning.

The 1944 Education Act aimed at ensuring that post-war Britain had an education system that all learners could access. This laid the foundation of our current education system. The Warnock Report (Warnock 1978) was ground-breaking in that it marked a move away from a deficit medical model to one that could be described as positive and empowering. This report formed the backbone of various policies and legislation, including the 1981 Education Act, the 1989 Children Act and the 1989 Elton Report.

The Elton Report (Elton 1989) was established to examine and make recommendations regarding what was seen at the time as disruptive behaviour in schools. It made the link between behaviour and learning much more explicit and as a result, the report has relevance today. This report laid the foundations for the Steer Report (2005) and subsequent review (2008). Elton (1989) suggested a whole-school approach to behaviour management through which an atmosphere would be created that would foster and promote learning. This approach would necessitate schools having clear policies and procedures, not only for when things went wrong, but also to highlight and reward 'good behaviour'. It recommended the development of a school-wide ethos with regard to positive approaches to behaviour management. The significant difference in the recommendations when compared with previous behaviour-management ideas was that of a proactive approach to teaching and learning.

National initiatives concerned with supporting children who may experience problem behaviour include 'Every Child Matters' (DfES 2003) and the subsequent Children's Plan (DCSF 2007). Every Child Matters arose following the tragic death of Victoria Climbié in 2000. It highlighted five key areas/outcomes that every child had a right to expect, and that would enable all learners to fulfil their potential. The outcomes are to:

- be healthy
- stay safe
- enjoy and achieve
- make a positive contribution
- achieve economic wellbeing.

When we examine these outcomes, we can see that they all have some connection with behaviour. In particular, the aims of 'enjoy and achieve' and 'make a positive contribution' are relevant to you as a teacher. Furthermore, all five outcomes help to ensure that children are included in schools, and that by providing opportunities in these areas schools are going some way to providing a truly inclusive environment.

As a teacher, you will not be alone in helping children to achieve these outcomes. The focus of the initiative is to develop a multi-professional Team Around the Child. Such a team has the school at the centre, and as a teacher you will play an important part in helping your children, drawing on support from other members of the Team Around the Child such as the youth offending team. We need to be a group – all stakeholders helping children to access education and succeed.

The Department for Children, Schools and Families published *The Children's Plan: Building Brighter Futures* (DCSF 2007) with the aim of continuing to build on the work of Every Child Matters. The route for achieving this is identified though a number of 'headline' ideas, such as greater collaboration between agencies; early intervention such as Sure Start; greater involvement of parents, and 'stage not age' teaching tailored to meet individual needs. One outcome of The Children's Plan was to ask Sir Alan Steer to review the progress made in managing 'challenging' students and in implementing the recommendations he made in his 2005 report.

Steer's review (DfES 2005) has become the centrepiece of the government's plans for tackling what is perceived to be problem behaviour, and suggests some useful strategies. These include highlighting effective practice that allows for the right conditions for good behaviour, and offering practical examples of how to achieve this, for example, parental involvement and effective school leadership. Steer's later report (Steer 2008) identifies what progress has been made and makes 47 recommendations grouped under three main themes: legal powers and duties, supporting the development of good behaviour, and raising standards.

The report's purpose and ideology can perhaps best be summed up by Steer's own observations:

> Consistent experience of good teaching promotes good behaviour. But schools also need to have positive strategies for managing pupil behaviour that help pupils understand their school's expectations, underpinned by a clear range of rewards and sanctions, which are applied fairly and consistently by all staff. It is also vital to teach pupils how to behave – good behaviour has to be learned – so schools must adopt procedures and practices that help pupils learn how to behave. Good behaviour has to be modelled by all staff all of the time in their interaction with pupils. For their part, staff need training and support to understand and manage pupil behaviour effectively
>
> (Steer 2005: 12)

The questions for teachers are, what approach do you take as an individual, and which of the myriad of behaviour management books and resources do you use?

It is helpful for you to be aware of your own beliefs and value sets. These may be different from those of the children you are working with, due to cultural and environmental factors. You will need to be able to identify what behaviours cause you the most difficulty. Once you have identified these, it is important to try and reflect on why these behaviours cause you difficulty, and you may begin to change your own behaviour. At this stage, it is also important to focus on children's positive behaviours and to reflect on how you reward them. Above all, be prepared to embark on a journey that does not have an ending!

In general terms, there are a number of strategies you could consider using in the classroom to ensure you continue to develop your inclusive pedagogy and, as a result, include all your children. These are best used within a framework, which could comprise the following approaches.

- Good communication – this should include positive body language, avoiding long, complex instructions, communicating with other professionals, and listening to learners and their parents.
- Consider your approach to children. They quickly pick up if you "like" them and respond accordingly.
- Being well prepared – Elton (1989) and Haydn (2007), among others, recognised that good preparation of lessons is essential.
- Establish a few simple ground rules that everyone can understand and achieve – do not set the bar so high that achievement is impossible.
- Use the school's policies to support your work.
- Use the Team Around the Child – Steer (2008) indicates that the development of collegiate professionalism and the sharing of good practice should have a significant impact on behaviour.
- Use assessments to check on children's level of achievement, especially in the area of social and emotional development. Try and ensure the activities

you provide are appropriate – that they match the level at which the child is functioning. You may find that overstretching a child exacerbates problematic behaviour.

- Involve parents wherever you can – sharing responsibility and planning can be most effective.
- Decide which behaviours to focus on, and which to ignore.
- Develop your own strategies, based on your developing inclusive practice.
- Refer to the Social and Emotional Aspects of Learning (SEAL) initiative.

This list is by no means exhaustive, but should give you a starting point.

In the final part of this section, I will briefly examine SEAL and three types of provision: inclusion units, pupil referral units and nurture groups. A number of writers (Goleman 1998; Roffey and O'Reirdon 2002) have identified that meeting children's social needs plays an important part in nurturing and fostering an environment that enables them to access the teaching and learning that is on offer, and to succeed as a result. Gardner (1984) discussed the concept of 'multiple intelligences', which identified the importance of being intelligent about our own emotions. Further work was explored by Goleman (1995), who used the phrase 'emotional intelligence' and suggested that emotional and social skills could be seen as more important in developmental terms than raw intelligence.

As we have already identified, there has been concern, sometimes media-driven, about young people's antisocial behaviour. This, together with perceived problematic behaviour in schools (DfES 2005), has prompted the government to develop a programme to support nurturing of learners' social and emotional skills. This has been translated into the SEAL initiative, which was originally targeted at the primary school population, and more recently was developed for use in secondary schools. This initiative can be viewed as being of particular importance for children who are seen as both challenging for schools and at risk of educational failure.

SEAL is based on five broad areas: self-awareness, managing feelings, motivation, empathy, and social skills. In supporting and nurturing these five areas, it is envisaged that children will become more effective learners. In terms of challenging behaviour, it is intended that the initiative will enable children to build a foundation for managing their own emotions, and hence a greater understanding of their behaviour and how it might affect others – in other words, that each child will develop a social conscience. Some schools have chosen to 'deliver' specific SEAL lessons, while others have integrated the concept throughout the curriculum, for example during playtimes and in assemblies. A vast range of materials, which can be used flexibly, are available for teachers to support their work with this initiative.

SEAL is not the only programme available to tackle these issues; other strategies that might help support children's development include nurture groups, circle time, buddy systems, and peer mentoring.

While considering inclusive strategies, it is important that we should also recognise that educational placement has a part to play. By this I mean that some children may be placed, or perceived as 'dumped', within an inclusion/exclusion unit that is part of a mainstream school, or in a pupil referral unit. Inclusion units are a relatively new type of provision, and you may find them called other things, such as a learning support unit or seclusion room. In essence, they provide a physical environment together with short-term tailored programmes aimed at meeting individual needs. There is little guidance on how this type of provision should be run, and as a result schools are left to work out what they believe is right for them. While the aim is to keep pupils in school, it could be argued that the units themselves internally exclude pupils, become a dumping ground for young people seen as 'problems', and as such are not inclusive in the wider sense.

Unlike inclusion units, pupil referral units are an older provision, established in 1996 in order for local authorities to become compliant with their statutory duties, providing suitable education for pupils of compulsory school age who had been excluded from mainstream provision. This type of setting is based within local areas rather than within schools. The aim is to provide short-term intervention and re-inclusion into mainstream provision. During the 1980s, a number of critical reports identified that these units did not enable pupils to progress, and the teaching and learning pedagogy was poor. Pupils, once 'sent' to a unit, rarely re-entered mainstream provision. More recently, pupil referral units have supported pupils in following the National Curriculum, albeit differentiated, providing a flexible approach to meeting individual pupils' needs. They are also increasingly working in successful partnerships with further education colleges, enabling pupils to develop vocational as well as academic skills.

In contrast, nurture groups are viewed by many (Cooper and Whitbread 2007; Binnie and Allen 2009) as being a highly effective *inclusive* method of supporting children's emotional development and improving their behaviour. This approach, originally developed by Boxall in 1969, centres on a small group setting in which children spend flexible amounts of time depending on their individual needs. The focus is on building a nurturing, safe environment that proactively promotes self-esteem, emotional well-being, positive relationships and communication, whilst minimising anxiety and addressing underlying problems that impact on learning. There are now more than 1000 nurture groups in the UK and although these were initiated for young children, their success has led to increasing numbers of secondary schools adapting the approach for older pupils (Colley 2009). Whilst there may be the potential for similar dangers in this approach to that of 'inclusion units' in that pupils may become isolated from their peers, the intention of nurture groups is to support young people's full inclusion in their schools; indeed, many schools report the benefits of such an approach on wider school practice.

How does this type of provision fit within an inclusive culture? It can be argued that it follows the medical model – placing the 'blame' within the child by removing them from the classroom and attempting to 'cure' them, and as such does not follow an inclusive ideology which also considers the role of the environment within challenging situations.

Conclusion

Sharing knowledge and enabling learners to experience success is one of the most rewarding aspects of the teacher's role. However, I recognise that working in a situation where you feel challenged is a difficult task.

Having examined, albeit briefly, some of the issues and strategies that surround the concept of children who may present a challenge, I would like to emphasise that prevention is better than cure (Kyriacou 2001). We have all seen the teacher who makes managing a classroom appear easy. It is highly likely that they achieve this apparent ease by having put in significant preparation behind the scenes.

I also want to stress that you are not alone in developing your skills. There are a lot of published materials to help you, but probably one of the best support mechanisms you can use is effective communication. This works on a number of levels – teacher to child, teacher to teacher, teacher to parent, teacher to other professionals. Listening to and asking for help is not a sign of failure, rather it indicates a willingness to learn and to nurture individuals. DCSF (2009) recognises that, in *Building a 21st Century Schools System*, every school should be working in partnership because no school can do it alone. In recognising this, they are requiring schools to deliver the Pupil Parent Guarantee, which requires schools to work in partnership with the Team Around the Child. This, together with the policies and strategies mentioned above, can help ensure support for all children is in place, and that this support will enable them to succeed in adult life.

Some of the strategies discussed in this chapter will help you develop your own skills and enable you to become inclusive teachers. In order to further develop your skills to support children, keep reading, observing, listening and talking.

Reflections on values and practice

- Think about your own teaching practice. What behaviour strategies have worked for you, and why? Conversely, what strategies have not worked for you, and why?
- How do you deal with the stress of working children whose behaviour you find challenging? Identify your support mechanisms.
- How well do you know the community in which your setting is placed? Consider the impact this may have on children's values and attitudes, and how these relate to your own.

Resources

Bishop, S. (2008) *Running a Nurture Group*, London: Sage.Hunter-Carsch, M., Tiknaz, Y., Cooper, P. and Sage, R. (2006) *The Handbook of Social, Emotional and Behavioural Difficulties*, London: Sage.

Koeries, J., Marris, B. and Rae, T. (2005) *Problem Postcards: Social and Emotional Behavioural Skills Training for Disaffected and Difficult Children Aged 7–11*, London: Sage.

McNamara, S. and Moreton, G. (1997) *Understanding Differentiation*, London: David Fulton.

Mosley, J. (1998) *Quality Circle Time in the Primary Classroom*, Hyde, Cheshire: LDA.

References

ATL (2009) 'Violent pupils and parents make teachers' lives a misery', press release, London: Association of Teachers and Lecturers, www.atl.org.uk/media-office/media-archive/violence-against-teachers.asp

Binnie, L. and Allen, K. (2008) Whole school support for vulnerable children: the evaluation of a part-time nuture group, *Emotional and Behavioural Difficulties*, 13(3): 201–216.

Colley. D. (2009) Nurture Groups in Secondary Schools, *Emotional and Behavioural Difficulties*, 14(4): 291–300.

Cooper, P. and Whitbread, D. (2007) The Effectiveness of Nuture Groups on Student Progress; Evidence from a National study, *Emotional and Behavioural Difficulties*, 12(3): 171–190.

DCSF (2007) *The Children's Plan: Building Brighter Futures*, London: Department for Children, Schools and Families.

——(2009) *Your Child, Your Schools, Our Future: Building a 21st Century Schools System*, London: Department for Children, Schools and Families.

DfES (2003) Every Child Matters, London: Department for Education and Skills.

——(2005) *Learning Behaviour: the Report of the Practitioners' Group on School Behaviour and Discipline*, 'The Steer Report', London: Department for Education and Skills.

Elton (1989) *Enquiry into Discipline in Schools*, London: HMSO.

Elliott, J., Zamorski, B. and Shreeve, A. (2001) *Exploring the Pedagogical Dimensions of Disaffection through Collaborative Research*, Final Report to the Teacher Training Agency, Norwich: HMSO/Norwich Area Schools Consortium.

Evans, J., Harden, A., Thomas, J. and Benefield, P.(2003) *Support for Pupils with Emotional and Behavioural Difficulties (EBD) in Mainstream Primary School Classrooms: A Systematic Review of the Effectiveness of Interventions*, EPPI-Centre/National Foundation for Educational Research.

Frederickson, N. and Cline, T. (2009) *Special Educational Needs, Inclusion and Diversity*, Buckingham: Open University Press.

Gardner, H. (1984) *Frames of Mind: The Theory of Multiple Intelligences*, London: Heinemann.

Garner, P. (2009) *Special Educational Needs. The Key Concepts*, Abingdon: Routledge.

Goleman, D. (1995) *Emotional Intelligence*, St Ives: Bloomsbury.

——(1998) *Working with Emotional Intelligence*, London: Bloomsbury.

Haydn, T. (2007) *Managing Pupil Behaviour. Key Issues in Teaching and Learning*, Abingdon: Routledge.

Kyriacou, C. (2001) *Effective Teaching in Schools: Theory and Practice*, Cheltenham: Nelson Thomas.

Roffey, S. and O'Reirdon, T. (2002) *Young Children and Classroom Behaviour*, London: David Fulton.

Rogers, B. (1990) *You Know the Fair Rule*, Harlow: Pearson Education.

Steer, A. (2008) *Behaviour Review: Paper 3*, www.teachernet.gov.uk/_doc/12743/Steer%20Report%20and%20letter%200708.pdf

Topping, K. and Maloney, S. (2005) *Reader in Inclusive Education*, London: Routledge.

Warnock, M. (1978) *Special Educational Needs: Report of the Committee of Inquiry into the Education of Handicapped Children and Young People*, London: HMSO.

Chapter 11

Teachers working with teaching assistants

Vikki Anderson

Introduction

Effective partnerships between teachers and teaching assistants form an essential part of embracing diversity and enabling all pupils to participate fully in the classroom. However, the impact of such collaboration is highly dependent on the conditions under which teaching assistants operate, and the ways in which their role is interpreted and understood. This chapter explores the changing role of teaching assistants and their effect on inclusive classroom practice, highlighting some of the key issues to consider when working with them in partnership.

The role of teaching assistants

There are currently around 181,580 full-time equivalent teaching assistants in state-funded schools in England – triple the number ten years ago – and this growth has been accompanied by marked changes in their roles and responsibilities (DCSF 2009). Traditionally, they came from parent helper routes, learned on the job, and functioned as classroom auxiliaries who relieved teachers of care and housekeeping-type duties (Clayton 1993). However, changes in educational policy have resulted in them taking on an ever-increasing array of tasks, with many providing behavioural support and/ or playing a significant part in the teaching and learning process. This shift in orientation is highlighted by a teaching assistant in Bach *et al.*'s study of London primary schools:

> I mean we used to be paint washers and just getting stuff ready for the lesson, but we're actually joining in lessons now; we're involved in teaching [Inner school E, TA1]
>
> (Bach *et al.* 2006: 15)

Workforce remodelling (Ofsted 2004) has given teaching assistants the opportunity to develop through a four-level professional career structure, in which level four represents higher level teaching assistant (HLTA) status. In order to reach this level, teaching assistants must meet the appropriate professional standards derived from those for Qualified Teacher Status (Burgess and Shelton Mayes 2009). HLTAs can teach whole classes and have been deployed in a range of roles, some of which were previously undertaken exclusively by teachers, for example pastoral year leader and assistant special educational needs coordinator (SENCO) (Goddard et al. 2007). Although this can be regarded as developing teaching assistants as active participants in teaching and learning, research has shown that, for a number of reasons, they do not all aspire to become HLTAs (Bach et al. 2006; Collins and Simco 2006; Barkham 2008). It is therefore important for teachers to understand that the aspirations of teaching assistants vary, and to aim to develop partnerships based on mutual respect in which they can work to their individual strengths.

The effectiveness of teaching assistants

In some cases, the effectiveness of trained teaching assistants is linked to the fact that they are likely to remain in the job. An example of this consistency is provided by the deputy head teacher of an Inner London primary school:

> I would say that the vast majority of phonics teaching, quality phonics teaching was done by TAs who've been trained because they're the ones who are consistently here. We've had five members of new staff this term, we haven't managed to get all the training in for them yet but we've got TAs who've been doing it consistently and we'll actually use them to demonstrate how to do it when it comes up to initiate new members of [teaching] staff
>
> (Bach et al. 2006: 16)

This transfer of skills forms part of the 'connecting and mediating' role that teaching assistants can play between a variety of stakeholders (Howes 2003: 150). Teaching assistants have been found to be effective in improving contact between home and school, with parents regarding them as more approachable than teachers due to shared values, similar cultural backgrounds, and familiarity with the local community (Collins and Simco 2006; Logan and Feiler 2006). Mansaray's (2006: 179) research illustrates the complexities and subtleties at work within inclusive schools, and how a teaching assistant's work can extend to contexts that are not easily accessible to the teacher:

> Some of the kids we have in our school do not have breakfast. They don't have, – or don't have time to have breakfast, or their parents probably don't get up, and [by] the time they get up it's just in time for them to be at school. ... I know the ones who eat, who doesn't eat, and I just make sure they have sufficient food inside of them.
>
> (Stephanie: TA, Fenton)

This study also shows how teaching assistants from minority ethnic groups use their own cultural and social resources to foster inclusion by correcting stereo-types, developing intercultural understanding and 'creating shared spaces of meaning'. For example, Luke, a Black Rastafarian, describes the advantages of engaging with pupils of African Caribbean heritage in their own vernacular:

> You know, they will try things on, but then I know like the culture, and I know how things are, and I'll be like, 'is that right, yeah?', and they'll be like, 'oh'. ... I know exactly what they're talking about, whereas someone else might not, you know what I mean? ... I don't know, maybe some of them might feel more comfortable coming to speak to me rather than someone else, you know.
>
> (Mansaray 2006: 181)

A major aspect of teaching assistants' work lies in 'bridging pedagogic boundaries' by removing barriers to participation in the classroom (*ibid.*: 178). However, much of the research in this area is based on the views and experiences of teachers and teaching assistants, rather than objective evaluations of practice. The large-scale, longitudinal Deployment and Impact of Support Staff (DISS) project fills this gap by providing a comprehensive assessment of the deploy-ment and impact of teaching assistants across a range of outcomes. In one strand of the study, systematic observations were carried out in 49 primary and secondary schools in England and Wales to investigate the effects of teaching assistants on pupil and adult behaviour in class (Blatchford *et al.* 2009a). In the primary schools, all pupils appeared to benefit from the presence of teaching assistants in terms of better classroom control and more individualised atten-tion, enabling pupils to interact more actively with adults. At secondary level, pupils identified as having special educational needs benefited from more individual attention, together with a significant increase in on-task behaviour, and there were benefits for all pupils in terms of better classroom control and more teaching overall.

The government has proposed that through pedagogical input, support staff should have a direct impact on pupils' attainment as well as behaviour (DfES 2002). Systematic research into the effect of teaching assistants on academic progress has focused mainly on the acquisition of literacy and numeracy skills in the primary school (Alborz *et al.* 2009). However, the DISS project also included a systematic analysis of the impact of the amount of extra support from teaching assistants on pupils' academic progress (Blatchford *et al.* 2009b). This research examined the extent to which the amount of support was related to end of year attainment in English, mathematics and science, controlling for factors that might be expected to explain the relationship, such as prior attainment, income deprivation, English as an additional language, and whe-ther pupils had a statement of special needs or were at School Action or School Action Plus of the SEN Code of Practice (DfES 2001). The results revealed a negative relationship between the amount of additional support and the academic progress of pupils in Years 1, 3, 7 (English and mathematics) and 10 (English), and Years 2, 6 and 9 (English, mathematics and science). In other words, the higher the amount of support, the lower the level of progress.

Drawing upon a range of additional data gathered throughout the DISS project, Blatchford *et al.* (2009b: 133) highlight a number of 'wider factors' that could have affected the relationship between pupils' academic progress and support. These include: insufficient paid time for joint planning and feedback; pupils becoming separated from their teachers and the broader curriculum; the ways in which teaching assistants interact with pupils, and a lack of training for teachers in working effectively with support staff. These are key issues that have also been identified in previous research, and should be considered by all new teachers entering into partnerships with teaching assistants.

Teachers working with teaching assistants

Ofsted (2008) reports that the quality of teaching is enhanced when teachers provide clear guidance to teaching assistants and involve them in planning. Nevertheless, a number of studies highlight a lack of dedicated time for teachers and teaching assistants to plan and evaluate their work together (see, for example, Smith *et al.* 2004; Bedford *et al.* 2008). The Every Child Matters initiative (DfES 2004) identifies the need for a more coherent and flexible workforce, and it is therefore crucial that adults working together in the classroom collaborate effectively. An example of good practice is provided by Fox *et al.* (2004), who describe a situation in which a primary school teacher informed the teaching assistant about the whole day's planning, focusing on the work of the entire class, together with specific planning for a child with Down's syndrome. The teaching assistant recorded her views in the teacher's planning and assessment book at the end of the morning and afternoon sessions, and the teacher used these to differentiate the next day's lessons. In another primary school, teachers and teaching assistants were allocated a weekly slot to engage in reflection and planning during whole-school assembly; and in a secondary school, 'Working Together' slips were created, enabling teachers and teaching assistants to increase communication, plan collaboratively and reflect on their work (Vincett *et al.* 2005).

If teaching assistants do not have opportunities to share their ideas with, seek advice from, and give feedback to, the teacher, the 'voice vacuum' described by O'Brien and Garner (2001: 3) will restrict the growth of a fruitful professional partnership aimed at improving the quality of teaching and learning. It is important, however, that joint planning is not carried out at lunchtime or after school, relying on the goodwill of teaching assistants, but rather that structured, paid time is allocated to it. The responsibility for collaborative working does not therefore rest solely with the class or subject teacher, but is a management issue that requires a whole-school approach.

Concerns about teaching assistants' pay and conditions of service are well documented in the literature. Teaching assistants in Barkham's study point out that the goodwill of voluntary work has been replaced by a climate of professionalism, and that to 'feel valued you have to be paid for what you are doing' (Barkham 2008: 850). As wage rates are set by each local authority, salaries can differ on a regional basis, with some teaching assistants being paid during term-time only, and some with HLTA status being on split contracts where they are paid a higher rate to work with a whole class for part of a week and employed for the remainder as general teaching assistants on a lower rate of pay (Unison 2007). These issues may be resolved by the recently formed School Support Staff Negotiating Body (DCSF 2009) with a new pay and conditions framework for support staff that combines national consistency and local flexibility. However, it is important to note that being valued does not rest solely with financial rewards. Teaching assistants in Mistry *et al.*'s (2004: 134) study commented that they would appreciate 'being thanked occasionally', and those in Anderson and Finney's (2008) research felt that teachers should identify and make full use of their abilities and experience, enabling them to contribute to different areas of the curriculum in addition to core skills.

Teaching assistants are often assigned to pupils identified with learning and/or behaviour difficulties, in the context of either in-class support or small group withdrawal. However, this can result in these individuals missing out on everyday teacher–pupil interaction and becoming separated from the curriculum (Blatchford *et al.* 2009b). The fact that teaching assistants often focus on those who are seen to need 'extra help' may reinforce 'the peer-group label of "dumb"' (Mansaray 2006: 179), and can create dependency on the part of both pupil and teacher. Gerschel (2005: 71) cautions against 'a "Velcro" model' of teaching assistants being attached to single pupils, which can result in emotional dependency on the assistant, and pupils being less likely to be fully included in the class or form relationships with their peers. Emam and Farrell (2009) found that secondary school teachers tended to rely on teaching assistants working with pupils with autism to ensure their participation in, and completion of, academic tasks, and to manage any challenging behaviour. The teachers viewed the teaching assistants as experts in this context, and in so doing, detached themselves from the pupils. Blatchford *et al.* (2009b: 134) argue that pupils experiencing barriers to participation are likely to benefit from more, not less, of a teacher's time, and that there is a danger that delegating responsibility to teaching assistants means the teacher does not feel the need: 'to consider pedagogical approaches that might benefit the whole class'.

It has been suggested by Ofsted (2004) that teaching assistants may be more inclined to keep pupils on-task than to focus on improving their understanding and skills. In the DISS project (Blatchford *et al.* 2009b), teaching assistants were found to prioritise the achievement of outcomes as opposed to promoting engagement in the learning process and the ownership of tasks. For example, they were observed telling pupils what to do, giving them answers, or physically doing work for them rather than prompting them to think for themselves. This type of approach is reflected in studies across the age range (Moyles and Suschitzky 1997; Veck 2009) and may be influenced by unintended messages communicated by teachers about the need to meet targets and get through the curriculum (Audit Commission 2002). It can have an adverse effect on the progress of some pupils (Blatchford et al. 2009b), indicating that schools may need to reconsider the ways in which the role of teaching assistant is conceptualised and put into practice.

Inclusive education involves responding to pupils from a wide range of backgrounds and cultures with different experiences, knowledge, understanding and skills. It is therefore essential for teachers to develop ways of working that will enable them to devote sufficient time and pedagogical expertise to those who require it most. Some innovative approaches are documented in the literature. In a primary school, Rose (2000) observed that teaching assistants played an important role in supporting whole classes rather than concentrating on individuals with statements of special educational needs. For example, a teaching assistant monitored the work of the rest of the class while the teacher worked intensively with a pupil who had speech and language difficulties. In both primary and secondary schools, Vincett et al. (2005) used the models of zoning and room management for collaborative working. Zoning involves arranging the class into learning zones usually structured by the placement of groups (for example, six groups could be split 5/1, 4/2 or 3/3) and allocating these to the teacher or teaching assistant. Within room management, each of the adults in the classroom occupies a clear role – that of activity or learning manager. The activity manager concentrates on the larger group; the learning manager provides intensive support to particular individuals. Staff can take on either role, depending on the needs of the class and the activities to be carried out, and can switch roles during a session if required. With each model, however, the teacher has overall responsibility for the whole class. Both these models were found to have positive effects on pupils' self-esteem and engagement in learning, and enabled teaching assistants to become more involved in the learning experiences of all pupils. Nevertheless, there were some resource implications, as teacher/assistant pairs required training and found that they needed additional paid planning time to work successfully in this way.

In-service training can be critical to the teaching assistant/teacher relationship, and should include opportunities for both partners to reflect on their inclusive aims and values, and the impact these might have on shared classroom practice. It should also focus on strategies for creating responsive learning environments that enable all pupils to feel equally valued, participate actively, and experience success. Additional training may be required if teachers are to become skilled in developing effective working partnerships. It cannot be assumed that the appropriate skills will be well honed in all teachers, especially as some newly qualified teachers have reported feeling intimidated by older, experienced teaching assistants (Barkham 2008), and teaching assistants have expressed concerns about working with new teachers (Anderson and Finney 2008).

Conclusion

Partnership working between teachers and teaching assistants is vital to the inclusion of a diverse range of learners within mainstream schools. If good practice is to occur, an ongoing process of clear, constructive communication and reflective practice is needed, together with supportive organisational cultures that enable teaching assistants to work to their strengths and benefit from joint professional development. Time for planning together is vital, together with teaching and learning strategies to ensure all pupils receive equitable amounts of the teacher's time and do not become separated from their peers. Finally, it is important that the teaching assistant/teacher relationship is based on mutual respect, and that teaching assistants feel valued if they are to play an optimal role in improving educational opportunities for all learners, regardless of difference.

Reflection on values and practice

- Reflect on a relationship you have had with a teaching assistant. What was successful and what aspects could have been improved? How can you use this reflection to build positive relationships with teaching assistants in the future?
- What joint training would benefit both you and the teaching assistant with whom you work, and how might this be pursued?
- How might you work with the teaching assistant so that *all* pupils receive equal amounts of your time and pedagogical expertise?

Resource

Richards, G. and Armstrong, F. (eds) (2008) *Key Issues for Teaching Assistants: Working in Diverse and Inclusive Classrooms*, London: Routledge.

References

Alborz, A., Pearson, D., Farrell, P. and Howes, A. (2009) *The Impact of Adult Support Staff on Pupils and Mainstream Schools. Technical Report*, London: EPPI-Centre, Social Science Research Unit, Institute of Education, University of London.

Anderson, V. and Finney, M. (2008) 'I'm a TA not a PA!', in Richards, G. and Armstrong, F. (eds) *Key Issues for Teaching Assistants*, Abingdon: Routledge.

Audit Commission (2002) *Special Educational Needs: A Mainstream Issue*, London: Audit Commission.

Bach, S., Kessler, I. and Heron, P. (2006) 'Changing job boundaries and workforce reform: the case of teaching assistants', *Industrial Relations Journal*, 37(1): 2–21.

Barkham, J. (2008) 'Suitable work for women? Roles, relationships and changing identities of "other adults" in the early years classroom', *British Educational Research Journal*, 34(6): 839–53.

Bedford, D., Jackson, C.R. and Wilson, E. (2008) 'New Partnerships for Learning: teachers' perspectives on their developing professional relationships with teaching assistants in England', *Professional Development in Education*, 34(1): 7–25.

Blatchford, P., Bassett, P., Brown, P. and Webster, R. (2009a) 'The effect of support staff on pupil engagement and individual attention', *British Educational Research Journal*, 35(5): 661–86.

Blatchford, P., Bassett, P., Brown, P., Koutsoubou, M., Martin, C., Russell, A. and Webster, R. (2009b) *Deployment and Impact of Support Staff in Schools: The Impact of Support Staff in Schools (Results from Strand 2, Wave 2)*, London: Department for Children, Schools and Families.

Burgess, H. and Shelton Mayes, A. (2009) 'An exploration of higher level teaching assistants' perceptions of their training and development in the context of school workforce reform', *Support for Learning*, 24(1): 19–25.

Clayton, T. (1993) 'From domestic helper to "assistant teacher" – the changing role of the British classroom assistant', *European Journal of Special Needs Education*, 8: 32–44.

Collins, J. and Simco, N. (2006) 'Teaching assistants reflect: the way forward?', *Reflective Practice*, 7(2): 197–214.

DCSF (2008) *School Workforce in England (including Local Authority Figures), January 2009 (Revised)*, London: Department for Children, Schools and Families, www.dcsf.gov.uk/rsgateway/DB/SFR/s000874/index.shtml

——(2009) *Joint Circular from the Support Staff Working Group School Support Staff Negotiating Body*, London: Department for Children, Schools and Families, www.lge.gov.uk/lge/aio/1137061

DfES (2001) *Special Educational Needs Code of Practice*, London: Department for Education and Skills.

——(2002) *Time for Standards: Reforming the School Workforce*, London: Department for Education and Skills.

——(2004) *Every Child Matters: Change for Children*, London: Department for Education and Skills.

Emam, M.M. and Farrell, P. (2009) 'Tensions experienced by teachers and their views of support for pupils with autism spectrum disorders in mainstream schools', *European Journal of Special Needs Education*, 24(4): 407–22.

Fox, S., Farrell, P. and Davis, P. (2004) 'Factors associated with the effective inclusion of primary-aged pupils with Down's syndrome', *British Journal of Special Education*, 31: 184–90.

Gerschel, L. (2005) 'The special educational needs coordinator's role in managing teaching assistants: the Greenwich perspective', *Support for Learning*, 20: 69–76.

Goddard, G., Mowat, P. and Obadan, F. (2007) 'One year on: the impact of obtaining HLTA status on teaching assistants and schools', paper presented at the British Educational Research Association Annual Conference, Institute of Education, University of London, 5–8 September. www.leeds.ac.uk/educol/documents/165904.doc

Howes, A. (2003) 'Teaching reforms and the impact of paid adult support on participation and learning in mainstream schools', *Support for Learning*, 18(4): 147–53.

Logan, E. and Feiler, A. (2006) 'Forging links between parents and schools: a new role for Teaching Assistants?', *Support for Learning*, 21(3): 115–20.

Mansaray, A.A. (2006) 'Liminality and in/exclusion: exploring the work of teaching assistants', *Pedagogy, Culture & Society*, 14(2): 171–87.

Mistry, M., Burton, N. and Brundrett, M. (2004) 'Managing LSAs: an evaluation of the use of learning support assistants in an urban primary school', *School Leadership and Management*, 24(2): 125–36.

Moyles, J. and Suschitzky, W. (1997) *Jills of All Trades? Classroom Assistants in KS1 Classes*, London: Association of Teachers and Lecturers.

O'Brien, T. and Garner, P. (2001) 'Tim and Philip's story: setting the record straight', in O'Brien, T. and Garner, P. (eds) *Untold Stories: Learning Support Assistants and their Work*, Stoke-on-Trent: Trentham Books.

Ofsted (2004) *Remodelling the School Workforce: Phase 1*, London: Ofsted.

——(2008) *The Deployment, Training and Development of the Wider School Workforce*, London: Ofsted.

Rose, R. (2000) 'Using classroom support in a primary school: a single school case study', *British Journal of Special Education* 27(4): 191–96.

Smith, P., Whitby, K. and Sharpe, C. (2004) *The Employment and Deployment of Teaching Assistants*, Slough: National Foundation for Educational Research.

Unison (2007) *School Remodelling – The Impact on Support Staff*, London: Labour Research Department.

Veck, W. (2009) 'From an exclusionary to an inclusive understanding of educational difficulties and educational space: implications for the Learning Support Assistant's role', *Oxford Review of Education*, 35(1): 41–56.

Vincett, K., Cremin, H. and Thomas, G. (2005) *Teachers and Assistants Working Together*, Maidenhead: Open University Press.

Chapter 12

Including parents with disabled children

Michele Moore

Introduction

In this chapter I look at positioning parents as allies in the new teacher's project of advancing inclusion from an insider's perspective, by exploring how relationships between parents and teachers can be understood from my point of view as a parent of two children with impairments. In the words of Clarke and Venables (2004), 'an ally is somebody who understands that his or her role is to support somebody else's struggle'. I reflect on my experiences as a parent seeking to work closely with teachers who are willing to see parents as allies. I also write from the viewpoint of a professional working with teachers on best practice in inclusive education, thus trying to weave together contrasting perspectives and agendas. I set out to suggest a theoretical approach to engagement with parents as an academic, and as a parent of disabled children I try to persuade you of its necessity. The approach I suggest, however, works to build productive and comfortable relationships with parents of *all* children at risk of, and at risk from, exclusion. It works as excellent practice for enhancing teaching and learning through closer relations with parents of *any* child, building on the notion that inclusive practice is good for everyone.

Learning through disability studies

I place emphasis on envisioning inclusion of disabled children (but think of inclusion of any child), through the lens of theories and practices which have evolved through the work of disabled people and their allies. Efforts disabled people have made to explain the origins and significance of their own exclusion from school and community life offer many insights for the building of inclusive classrooms schools and communities (Rieser and Mason 1990; Mason 2005, 2008). Disabled people's own ideas on ways of dismantling barriers that create exclusion offer a rich resource to any teacher willing to take seriously inclusive teaching and learning for *all* children.

At the heart of inclusive practice for new teachers lies application of 'the social model of disability'. The model was developed by disabled people, who came together to create a theoretical framework that would enable non-disabled people to understand how the difficulties people with impairment face in their lives are not a product of their impairments, but are the outcome of the experience of living in a disabling world (UPIAS 1976; Oliver 1996, 2009). The social model of disability calls for recognition of material, attitudinal, cultural and the myriad of other socially constructed barriers that limit the lives of people with impairments. Once social barriers to inclusion are identified, they can be dismantled so that children need not encounter disabling schools, communities and identities. It is easy to see that the notion of dismantling barriers holds the key to reducing the risk of exclusion for any child.

'Social model thinking'

I learned through personal experience as the mother of children with impairments, through engagement with teachers, and through people who feel they matter less than their contemporaries, that the social model of disability can function as a 'social model for dismantling exclusion' in any situation. 'Social model thinking' can be applied to assist teachers with reducing the exclusion of disabled children, and can also be applied to dismantling barriers surrounding those at risk of exclusion due to wider politics of inequality; children who are poor, for example, members of cultural or linguistic minority groups, or those at risk of exclusion due to complexities of migration status, and so on.

Social model thinking involves focusing directly on barriers encountered by children; it enables teachers to take a creative approach to dismantling the barriers that create segregation, exclusion and disablement, rather than worrying about specific questions of impairment. To effectively include a child with a hearing impairment in teaching and learning, for example, it is not necessary to have an in-depth knowledge of pediatric audiology, but it is essential to work tirelessly to understand and remove the day-to-day disabling barriers a child faces (Beazley and Moore 1995). Micheline Mason writes of the commitment she made to her daughter, who she describes as 'disabled, feisty, full of life and longing to be in the thick of it':

> I wanted Lucy to go to her local mainstream school and have the support she needed to take part in all aspects of school life.
> Mason, M. (cited 2.1.10) http://www.michelinemason.
> com/topics/inclusion.htm

The quotation shows that parents know support is needed for disabling barriers to be overcome for their child, and so commitment of new teachers to the project of inclusion is vital. The website of the Centre for Studies of Inclusive Education (www.csie.org.uk) evidences widespread commitment among parents to support the participation of their disabled children in mainstream settings. But parents know that:

inclusion is not an easy option. It is difficult because it requires people to examine their deepest held prejudices and fears; it asks people to learn new skills; it means people have to think creatively and design individual solutions for unique people; it means doing things differently and risking failure

(www.michelinemason.com/topics/inclusion.htm)

The imperative for teachers and parents to work as allies in support of inclusive education for children with impairments is plain. Social model thinking enables teachers, parents and children to build inclusive teaching and learning together.

A premise of consultation

In order to apply social model thinking to facilitate inclusion, consultation with parents is required. Recent shifts in policy towards consulting with, and maximizing the participation of, parents in inclusive education reinforce this (DCSF 2009). Emphasis is on 'trying to give parents a much bigger voice in the system', acknowledging that close involvement of parents in their child's education 'can make a profound difference to how parents feel' and is advantageous because very often parents know most about what will benefit their children.

Research repeatedly shows that many parents face a battle to get into a close relationship with professionals, but those children whose parents are in consultation with teachers are best supported and make optimum progress (Beazley and Moore 1995; Cole 2004; Runswick-Cole 2007). Some parents report positive relationships with teachers and others do not; differences can arise even between parents seeking to interact with the same teacher. Consequently, new teachers will wish to continually review their own relationships with parents.

There is hard work involved for new teachers committed to bringing parents into a closer relationship, but the legislative context does assert that all parents, including those with disabled children, should have a strong voice in their child's education. Where they do not, we hear terrible stories from parents (Dunn and Moore 2008). The manner in which disabled children and their parents are brought into consultation with teachers working to support them is crucial (Dunn and Moore 2005). Although the illustrations that follow in this chapter focus on inclusion of disabled children, it emerges that any teacher who can apply social model principles to their work has skills that will facilitate the inclusion of any child at risk of exclusion. The skills of social model thinking quickly inscribe an aptitude for inclusive thinking and practice upon teachers.

Social model language – giving parents cause for optimism

The language teachers use in discussions with parents of disabled children is critically important because of the way in which it positions disabled children in particular discourses and consequent provisions. To illustrate, I refer to my own children as 'children with impairments'. People often ask 'isn't it better' ('kinder' even) to say 'children with disabilities' or 'disabled children?' I am arguing that my children are not 'children with disabilities'; they are children with impairments. 'Disability' is part of their experience only if people impose diminishing or oppressive attitudes upon them, or if environments, resources or opportunities exclude them. It is true that both of my children have impairments: my son is partially ambulant and a sometimes wheelchair-user; my daughter has an auditory processing hearing impairment. Sometimes they *are* disabled children; if a teacher cannot include a wheelchair-user in football practice, then my son is disabled by exclusion from the activity that currently holds most currency with his peer group. If a teacher decides 'Sarah is happy in a world of her own', my daughter is disabled by exclusion from conversation. But Sarah is equally excluded and disadvantaged when a teacher says 'there's no such thing as a left-handed hockey stick'.

What I am trying to get across is that it is not children's impairments that exclude and disable them, but a teacher's limited approach to resources or to enabling curricular activities might intensify the minutiae of exclusions that create disablement (Allan 2007; Slee 2010). What I am hoping to illustrate by the examples of my own children's experience is that it is not physical or sensory (or any other kind of) impairment that disables children – these are determinants of their identity; impairment is a fact of life. I am not embarrassed by my children's impairment and choose to name it. Naming impairment is a direct way of separating the experience of it from the experience of disablement, and I try to teach my children this. To many parents it is essential teachers do not forget, deny, overlook or offer sympathy in respect of a child's impairments. The words of a parent seeking inclusion for her two disabled children are clarifying here:

> When Makia was asked if she felt saddened by 'the pitying way people looked at her children', she replied 'people will look at my children the way I look at them'.
>
> (Al Saleh 2010)

It is not discretion, pity or specialist knowledge of impairment that a new teacher needs when involving parents in responses towards their disabled children, but simply an enabling attitude towards inclusion. This idea, that it is not impairment that creates disability, is the basis of social model thinking for inclusive practice. I argue that any teacher who can make plain social model thinking gives parents tangible insight into how they as the teacher will actively seek to dismantle the barriers that create disablement and exclusion. A parent who hears a teacher talking about 'unblocking the blocks' to their child's participation in school and classroom life starts to feel disablement fall away from their child's experience of education.

On the other hand, a parent who hears a teacher worry about what they do or do not know about the specifics of a child's impairment, hesitate about the 'problems' associated with particular impairments, or stress the numerous difficulties a child will face in the classroom, knows for certain that in this teacher's class their child is on a trajectory leading to construction of disablement. I argue that only teachers who are social model theorists can instil in parents the confidence that they see a child's disability as their teaching difficulty, rather than as a child's learning difficulty. When a parent hears a teacher take the locus of responsibility for their disabled child's education and development away from the child, and place enablement within their own gift, then the distance between teachers and parents is quickly reduced; then parents can be allies in the new teacher's project of inclusion.

Stories of parents and teachers working together to include disabled children

Pahl (2010) stresses the importance of listening to the stories and experiences of parents 'for things that might be missing' so that as practitioners we might 'hear them'. Stories from my own experience vividly illustrate ways in which disability can be reduced when teachers are willing to involve parents as allies.

Michael's impairment involves limb reconstruction through external fixation of bones, typical for children with limb discrepancies, as well as for those with restricted growth. Michael's situation is interesting to any new teacher because he moves in and out of 'disabled child' status depending on where we are up to in terms of surgery. His experience of impairment provides a clear example of how impairment may be a fixed determinant of identity, but disability is not. The beginning of Michael's journey into disabled child status showed he was in a school that could understand disability as a social practice, connect the minimizing of disablement to a commitment to inclusion and valuing the perspective of parents. His headteacher's response was:

> Michael is a Rowan [school] boy. We want to keep him in our Rowan school. We will do whatever we have to do to keep him in. If we have to move Year 5 classrooms downstairs or put in a stair lift we will … [and] we'll just be making provision for other children who come our way in the future.

In this response, Michael's inclusion was seen as an opportunity for the school and its wider community, and inclusion would be the key through which disablement would be minimized. The headteacher remembered her own daughter's medical history as once having jeopardized her inclusion, which brings to mind the observations of Sharma *et al.* (2008) that the more contact pre-service teachers have with children with impairments and their parents, the more confident they are likely to feel about including them in their classrooms.

The school's response to me as a parent seeking inclusion was made easier because I was known to be working in this field; members of staff had taken courses I co-directed. Since first knowing of Michael's impairment, I had been shamelessly building my chances of being seen as the school's ally. I conducted research to assist Governors, for example, and started helping with literacy assessments – facing the risk of my child's exclusion, there was little I would not have done to force the agenda of his continued inclusion. These efforts paid dividends because teachers did talk with me and become familiar with my child's impairment so that Michael's ongoing inclusion was relatively seamless. His class teacher arranged wheelchair access, and children were taught the difference between the consequences of impairment and the consequences of exclusion. Obstacles that couldn't be overcome, such as the lack of an accessible children's toilet, were circumvented by allowing use of staff toilets. Where there were no ramps, the caretaker improvised with boards and children were quick to devise lifting strategies; often strategies to perhaps make a health and safety officer shudder, but these were ordinary everyday solutions to dismantling barriers that create exclusion. Inclusive attitudes enabled a disabled child to be included and their peers to be inclusive. Additionally, the literature asserts that children are entitled to encounter risk, and this offers them many benefits:

> All children both need and want to take risks in order to explore limits, venture into new experiences and develop their capacities.
>
> (Play Safety Forum 2002)

Yet Hasan, who occupied the hospital bed next to Michael, having identical impairment and surgery, attended a school at which the headteacher expressed such fear of litigation that Hasan was effectively excluded. For months, every time we saw Hasan and his parents at outpatient clinics, they told us his school 'couldn't manage him back yet'.

The critical importance of a close relationship between parents and teachers to enable inclusion of disabled children is visible in the different experiences of Michael and Hasan. My own positive experience was facilitated by a particular kind of resource I could offer to the brokering of a strong parent–teacher relationship. Sue Crabtree, also mother of a disabled child, noticed this when she wrote '[teachers] did talk to me because I made myself a nuisance', adding 'I'm a journalist, I'm used to ferreting and checking. I cannot imagine how those with English as a second language cope.' For Hasan's mother, who did not speak English and who had five younger children at home, a teacher would need to take an entirely proactive approach to bring her in to a conversation about how her disabled son might best be included. She was not in any position to battle. Here again, social model thinking would be assistive: what does a teacher need to do to break down the barriers to Hasan's mother's inclusion in her child's education? It is to the difficulty of answering this question that I turn next.

I am relentlessly arguing that consultation with parents is key to inclusion of disabled children. The more teachers and I shared the difficulties of our joint commitment to Michael's inclusion, the more enablement became possible. Over the weeks when Hasan was still not even in school, I watched an initially hesitant teacher begin to include Michael in his wheelchair in PE, and a few days later suggest inclusive strategies to a visiting tennis coach. Sometimes she referred to me, particularly seeking assurance that the level of risk she was taking was acceptable. In these ways, a teacher who was at pains to say she 'had no special needs training' first evolved, and then cascaded, the kind of inclusive practice that diminished disablement. She did it through sustaining a close relationship with me as a parent. I began to know that although my child was struggling with complex impairment and considerable pain, he was included by a responsive teacher looking to apply social model principles to the management of impairment in maximum consultation with parents. The teacher constantly asked herself not 'what are the problems with Michael?', but 'what do I have to do to make sure there are no problems for Michael?' – and if she didn't know, she asked me. I began to realize that ordinary teachers can facilitate the inclusion of disabled children when they are willing to roll out social model thinking. In enabling parents to be co-constructors of inclusion, teachers can raise expectations and outcomes for children with impairments, *and* make parents feel better.

Michael's teacher made him confident about his inclusion; she made other children confident so their parents would still invite him for tea; she persuaded the Scout leader to let Michael attend in the wheelchair – this was inclusion. My child struggled with impairment, but this was not turned into disability by processes of exclusion. Hasan, whose mother was not brought into close contact with his teachers, missed school for six months. He became isolated and unsurprisingly set back in learning and self-esteem. Eventually, following sedentary months at home, his physical recovery was compromised and impairment compounded.

I often hear parents of children with impairments express reluctance to seek out close contact with teachers. They fear being a nuisance or putting their child's problems too closely under scrutiny. A mother recently told me 'I was too scared to go in about Katy's reading because I'm probably a bit dyslexic too and I'm worried I won't really understand what they're saying'. An observant teacher, willing to embed social model thinking into their practice, will spot these barriers to parents' participation and find ways of circumventing them. Later, the same mother was asked to help with her younger son's class lettuce planting. 'One of the teaching assistants,' she said, 'was really friendly and I started asking her a bit about what they do about dyslexia.' I have written elsewhere about how teaching assistants can bring parents into closer relationship with schools, and their role in supporting new teachers is well worth maximizing (Moore 2008).

Positive stories of teachers working with parents of disabled children to promote inclusion offer new teachers good practice pointers (Moore 2010). So too, however, do stories of teachers who exclude parents. A teacher overheard recently was explaining that involving the mother of a disabled child would be impossible, saying '[that group of women] all wear hijab so I can't even tell which one is her mum'. It does not take a leap of imagination to see how investment in social model thinking would compel this teacher to change their practice around inclusion of both this child and her parents. I do see some parents having a terrible time in their relationships with teachers. I tell their stories here because those stories help us to think about ourselves and our practice (Walker 2007).

Stories of parents and teachers *not* working together to include disabled children

This is the experience of the parents of Leigh and Daniel. Behaviour of both children troubled the school from the earliest days, and the more their parents sought inclusion, the more they were seen as seen as refusing to take seriously 'the problem of their child's behavior'. Both sets of parents pursued formal diagnosis of impairment, thinking a label of autistic spectrum disorder would render the school better able to acknowledge their child's needs. However, when diagnosis came, it was quickly recommended the children be moved to segregated schools. The parents were treated as having confirmed a diagnosis their school 'doesn't deal with'. They were told that the support required was not within the remit of the school, so that asking for support positioned them as working separately from the school. Soon, all possibilities of conversations between these parents and their children's teachers started to close down. The parents felt embattled, they started to feel unwelcome and that, indeed, they were a nuisance.

With no dialogue between Leigh's mother and teachers, his behaviour became more challenging and he was put on a differentiated school timetable to reduce disruption associated with his attendance on other pupils. As his mother predicted, patchwork attendance guaranteed that Leigh's behaviour deteriorated as he found it impossible to cope with altered relationships, interrupted routines and missed opportunities for learning. An escalation in unsettled behaviour meant other parents started to say 'it's better if Leigh's not there', seizing upon the segregation agenda as a strategy they perceived as enhancing their own children's experiences of teaching and learning. Leigh's mother talked about the pain of being the parent of a child teachers are finding hard to include. This is not, of course, the same as talking about children who are hard to include. But the fact is that soon afterwards, Leigh was moved to a segregated school.

Daniel's mother took a different approach. She saw the traps of the differentiated day and fiercely resisted attempts to displace the school's behaviour management problems. She felt unwanted in Daniel's classroom, probably, she felt, because she was always at odds with the teacher's proposed intervention strategies. She feared incurring further annoyance. She didn't have any friendly relationships with teachers. She had no 20 minutes of peace in any 24 hours, and was desperate for any kind of short break, but had no expectation of access to universal services such as Scouts or after-school activities, or of being treated as a partner in Daniel's inclusion. Daniel's only friend had been Leigh, because years of focusing on the perceived nature of their impairment, rather than on the dismantling of social barriers that compounded each child's difficulty, meant they had been separated from other children. The school had managed to remove one of the children in the age-old and invidious manner Armstrong (2003) describes. Neither of these children presented the major access complications, special toileting arrangements, physical handling or medical problems that Michael presented. Yet for them, the school's response seemed to be 'inclusion is not the answer', and this extended to allowing inclusion of their parents to fall away.

In the apparently dying moments of Daniel's inclusion, a new teacher was appointed. Her first priority was to invite his mother in, and the two agreed to meet every day for 15 minutes to review his day. To each and every difficulty, the teacher sought a solution in her own practice. Daniel had good days and bad days, but from the moment the new teacher brought his mother into a close relationship, she herself felt better and was able to then co-construct responses to Daniel's experience of teaching and learning with his teacher. Four months later, she was helping to judge the Ball Poach on Sports Day. Her delight at being an included parent was plain to see. She told me that Daniel was nowadays happy and motivated. 'Actually' she said, 'other children can cope with him better *because* he's included.' Because of the sustained efforts of a teacher to bring a parent in to the joint project of inclusion, Daniel, who had been presenting difficult, aggravating, frequently injurious behaviours, had been settled and included so that, from being excluded on an almost daily basis, he had been sent home only twice in a term. Daniel's impairments, howsoever labelled, had not changed or gone away, but a teacher practicing social model thinking had actively brought a parent into the shaping of inclusion, again demonstrating that experience of disability has little to do with impairment.

Conclusions

In these stories, the important focus has been on working with the social model of disability to maximize inclusion of parents in the education of disabled children. In the first story, a close relationship between a parent and teachers greatly enhanced the chances of satisfactory teaching and learning for a child with impairments. It was also seen that not all parents can come easily into relationships with teachers, but that social model thinking helps teachers keep open the options for reducing distance.

The examples in this chapter focus on using social model thinking to involve parents in the education of children with physical, sensory and other named impairments. However, the aim stated at the beginning of the chapter was also to suggest the utility of social model thinking for building relationships with any parent whose child teachers might find difficult to include. For all teachers, in segregated or mainstream settings, inclusive practice is a central requirement irrespective of whether training in special and inclusive education has been undertaken. For all children, social model thinking around their entitlements, combined with a close relationship between parents and teachers, whilst not easy for a new teacher to secure, is essential.

Michael's inclusion still requires an exacting level of exchange between teachers and parents. At secondary school, a concern is how to secure his participation in a Spanish exchange at a time when he will again be a wheelchair-user. It is true that the average training course for modern language teachers does not specifically address inclusion of children with limb deformity or any other kind of impairment. Michael's inclusion lies simply in the willingness of all teachers to facilitate close involvement of parents and to focus solely on dismantling whatever barriers create disablement.

In the UK, teachers beginning their careers in the context of growing conservative forces which openly challenge the link between social justice and segregation, shoulder tremendous responsibility for ensuring inclusive teaching and learning will be available to all children. Cameron and Clegg (2010) insist they will bring to an end what they call 'unnecessary closure of special schools, and remove the bias towards inclusion' paying scant regard to the voices of parents 'who want their children to be a part of their local community' (Bartley 2010). Taking apart and resisting new forces for exclusion, frequently mooted in the name of 'parental choice' will demand a forthright and courageous commitment to keeping open a considered critique of the origins and significance of exclusion in our schools. For new teachers, the task is to engage parents in keeping the agenda for inclusive education open.

I hope this chapter conveys how considerable benefits accrue when teachers privilege involvement of parents and inscribe their work with the principles of a social model approach to dismantling barriers surrounding inclusion. Through these strategies, any child can be welcomed and included in schools and not turned into a child 'with disabilities'. I ask new teachers to think of inclusion of *all* children and their parents as simply a decision and a practice.

Reflection on values and practice

- An important point of reflection for any new teacher working with parents of disabled children is to think about the language and discourse to which you will subscribe. What is the difference between a teacher who talks about 'a child with impairments' and one who talks about 'a child with disabilities'? Why does language matter? How does it shape practice?

- For any new teacher, the presence of disability in your own life may not be too far away. What can you learn from your own experience to enhance teaching and learning in your classroom?
- I ended this chapter by asking new teachers to think of inclusion of disabled children and their parents as 'simply a decision and a practice'. What is the decision required, and what are the practice requirements for you as a new teacher?

References

Al Saleh (2010) 'Including disabled children in Oman', EdD thesis submitted to the University of Sheffield.

Allan, J. (2007) *Rethinking Inclusive Education*, Dordrecht, the Netherlands: Springer.

Armstrong, F. (2003) *Spaced Out: Policy, Difference and the Challenge of Inclusive Education*, Dordrecht, the Netherlands: Springer.

Bartley, J. (2010) That isn't choice? Centre for Studies on Inclusive Education, *Supporting inclusion challenging exclusion*. http://www.csie.org.uk/news/index/shtml#120513 (accessed 30 July 2010).

Beazley, S. and Moore, M. (1995) *Deaf Children, Their Families and Professionals: Dismantling Barriers*, London: David Fulton.

Clarke, K. and Venables, K. (2004) 'Including me in: Can we learn from the voice of disabled children?' in Billington, T. and Pomerantz, M. (eds) *Children at the Margins*, Stoke on Trent: Trentham Books.

Cole, B.A. (2004) *Mother-Teachers: Insights Into Inclusion*, London: David Fulton.

Crabtree, S. (2009) 'I came to see the school as a little corner of paradise', *The Observer*, 20 December 2009.

DCSF (2009) *Lamb Inquiry: Special Educational Needs and Parental Confidence*, DCSF-01143-2009, Nottingham: DCSF Publications, www.dcsf.gov.uk/lambinquiry

Dunn, K. and Moore, M. (2005). 'Developing accessible playspace in the UK: what they want and what works', *Children, Youth and Environments*, 15(1): 331–53.

——(2008) *Transforming Short Break Provision*, Inclusion, Sheffield: Childhood and Education Research Publications.

Mason, M. (2005) *Incurably Human*, London: Inclusive Solutions.

——(2008) *Dear Parents*, London: Inclusive Solutions.

Moore, M. (2008) 'Inclusive relationships: insights from teaching assistants on how schools can reach parents', in Richards, G. and Armstrong, F. (eds) *Key Issues for Teaching Assistants. Working in Diverse and Inclusive Classrooms*, London: Routledge.

——(2010) 'Inclusion, narrative and voices of disabled children in Trinidad and St Lucia', in Lavia, J. and Moore, M. (eds) *Cross-Cultural Perspectives on Policy and Practice*, London: Routledge.

Oliver, M. (1996) *Understanding Disability: From Theory to Practice*, London: Macmillan.

——(2009) *Understanding Disability: From Theory to Practice*, Basingstoke: Palgrave Macmillan.

Pahl, K. (2010) 'Changing literacies', in Lavia, J. and Moore, M. (eds) *Cross-Cultural Perspectives on Policy and Practice*, London: Routledge.

Play Safety Forum (2002) *Managing Risk in Play Provision: A Position Statement*, London: Play Safety Forum.

Rieser, R. and Mason, M. (1990) *Disability Equality in the Classroom: A Human Rights Issue*, London: Disability Equality in Education.

Runswick-Cole, K. (2007) 'The experience of families who go to the Special Educational Needs and Disability Tribunal (SENDisT)', *Disability and Society*, 22(3): 315–28.

Sharma, U., Forlin, C. and Loreman, T. (2008) 'Impact on training on pre-service teachers' attitudes and concerns about inclusive education and sentiments about persons with disabilities', *Disability & Society*, 23(7): 773–85.

Slee, R. (2010) *Irregular Schooling*, London: Routledge.

UPIAS (1976) *Fundamental Principles of Disability*, London: Union of the Physically Impaired Against Segregation.

Walker, M. (2007) Action research and narratives: 'Finely Aware and Richly Responsible', *Educational Action Research*, 15:2, 295–303.

Chapter 13

Working with the 'experts'
Working in partnership with other education professionals

Alison Patterson

Introduction

Support services to schools, offering advice for children identified as having special educational needs (SEN), have existed for almost a century. Although there have been many changes throughout the years, it is the more recent changes in education and inclusion that have been particularly important in shaping the support services that exist today. Support services also vary greatly across the country, in both the way they are structured and the services they offer. This means that if you do your teaching practice in one authority, and then subsequently work in a different authority, albeit a few miles away, you may find considerable differences in the support services on offer. However, in general, local authority support services for children identified as having SEN will include educational psychologists and specialist advisors, who offer support for cognition and learning, physical difficulties, communication, behaviour, hearing impairments and visual impairments. Some advisors may specialise in autism, information technology for children with SEN, or early years children (which may mean offering support from birth). However, it is worth noting that in each local authority, support services extend well beyond SEN. For example, there will probably be support services offering advice for gifted and talented pupils and for children who speak English as an additional language. Much of what is discussed in this chapter may therefore be applicable to your relationship with, and expectations of, these other advisors.

In addition to this, you may receive support and advice from professionals from other agencies, for example speech and language therapists, physiotherapists and social workers. Again, some of this chapter may be relevant, but working in partnership with other agencies can be more complex due to the different priorities and targets that the government sets for each agency (e.g. health may prioritise waiting-list times). Each agency will also have its own funding routes, language and procedures, and there may be ethical differences regarding confidentiality (DH 2003; DfES 2006a; Fitzgerald and Kay 2008). Despite these differences, it is now a requirement of 'Every Child Matters' (DfES 2003) and the subsequent Children Act 2004 and Children's

Plan (DCSF 2007) that agencies work together – so be prepared to be involved in multi-agency work from the start of your teaching career in today's inclusive and diverse classrooms.

The government and support services for pupils identified as having SEN

Requesting the involvement of a support service is part of the *SEN Code of Practice* (DfES 2001), and government guidance after the Code of Practice but prior to the new coalition government of 2010 still clearly supported the notion of support services. For example in *Removing Barriers to Achievement* (DfES 2004a: 48), it stated that support services play 'a key role in supporting the development of inclusive practice' and in Quality Standards for Special Educational Needs (SEN) Support and Outreach Services (DCSF 2008: 4) support services are cited as being 'crucial' in helping schools to achieve the five outcomes of the Every Child Matters Agenda (DfES 2003, 2004b, 2004c). However, during this period, as part of the attempt to drive up standards in schools, the then Labour government also placed great importance on competition and accountability, and support services were included in these government initiatives too.

The drive to create competition for support services emerged in 1998 when the system of funding for support services was radically changed by the Fair Funding Initiative (DfEE 1998). This initiative required local authorities to delegate ever higher percentages of their money for SEN provision to schools, allowing, and arguably encouraging, schools to buy in the support services they required. Shortly after this, Gray (2001) reviewed the role of SEN support services and concluded that this government initiative had resulted in considerable diversity in support services, and in some areas local authority support services competing with services from the private and voluntary sector. This meant that support services were now part of the 'competition agenda' and, although it did not result in the end of local authority support services, it did lead to a focus on accountability, because if support services want to compete, they need to be explicit about what they are doing and why.

With the change of government in May 2010 it would seem that the support services are now more vulnerable than ever. This is partly due to the drive to expand the number of schools being granted academy status (and as academies are independent of local government control they will have to buy in any support services they need) but also because local authorities face financial cutbacks that may impact on support services. Now more than ever, support services will need to grasp the concept of accountability and be prepared to prove that they are making a difference to the outcomes for the child.

Not surprisingly, as a result of all of the changes in the past 20 years, the role of a support service worker has also changed. Years ago, many support service workers would visit schools and withdraw children in small groups or individually, often returning the child to his/her class teacher at the end of the lesson, with the possibility of the nature and content of what they had done remaining the world's 'best kept secret'. Nowadays, their role is much more that of an advisor or consultant, where the support is often 'hands-off', and they may be involved in whole-school improvement work rather than focusing on individual children. Blamires and Moore (2004: 11) describe this transition as part of moving from the 'cupboard' to the 'community', and their model also mirrors the transition from a medical model of disability.

More harm than good?

For some writers, support services sit uncomfortably within the inclusion agenda. They argue that such services help to perpetuate a medical model of disability, as interventions and strategies that centre on the individual child may help to reinforce the idea of the problem residing within the child – in other words, a 'fix-it' approach, where the teacher and support service worker try to get the child to fit the system, rather than expecting the school to make changes (Rieser 2003). However, others argue that support service workers can help class teachers make changes to their pedagogy and whole-class planning and find ways to reduce or remove the barriers the child is facing (Booth and Ainscow 2000), thus indicating a more social model of disability.

This is particularly important because these models of disability will also affect and be reflected in the ethos and culture of the school. This can be illustrated by considering the difference between a school that genuinely welcomes and celebrates diversity, and a school with an ethos of benevolence, where children with SEN are treated in a special way, within a culture that has its roots in sympathy and pity.

This dilemma between medical and social models of disability is also apparent if we consider the use of assessment. For some, assessment links clearly to a medical model of disability, leading to diagnosis and labelling (Thomas and Loxley 2001) and undue emphasis on the individual child, which at worst may contribute to a self-fulfilling prophecy either by the child themselves, or because of the perceptions of those who work with the child. However, others argue that providing an assessment allows a child to 'demonstrate competence and attainment' (Farrell 2004: 142), and that the child is assessed against their own previous achievements rather than normative targets (Rieser 2003), so the assessment may actually help the teacher to break the child's learning down into smaller, more achievable steps, with good quality Individual Education Plan (IEP) targets that have a positive impact on the child's achievements and thus fit into a social model of disability. It is therefore worth considering here the research by Fletcher-Campbell and Cullen (2000), who explored schools' perceptions of support services and found that teachers had often already carried out assessments, and that what they actually wanted was practical help from the support service worker. So maybe the issue with assessments is really about what happens *after* the assessment? For example, if the support following an assessment involves modelling strategies (Ofsted 2005) or discussing good inclusive programmes of intervention with the class teacher (Blamires and Moore 2004), then the assessment might be an important part of an approach that fits a social model of disability within today's diverse and inclusive classrooms.

However, the question about whether support services do more harm than good extends beyond debates about their role within social and medical models of disability. In particular, there is a long-running and important debate about whether the existence of support services encourages the 'expertise myth' (Dessent 2004: 78), perpetuating the idea that the teacher's own competencies are not sufficient to meet the child's needs. The mystique may even extend to the pedagogy, causing the teacher to believe that a 'highly specialist' pedagogy is needed (Lindsay 2000: 45) in order for the child to learn within a mainstream classroom. This may lead to a belief by the teacher that they do not have the skills to monitor the child's progress, plan for the child, or even teach the child. This, in turn, may result in a dependency culture (McNamara and Moreton 1995), so it is important that support service workers always seek to enskill rather than deskill the teacher (Gray 1999; Mittler 2000).

However, the concept of specialism and expertise is not straightforward. Ask yourself whether the existence of support services offering specialist advice really does encourage teachers to believe that they cannot teach children identified as having SEN? Perhaps specialist knowledge, skills and understanding will simply help to further the teacher's understanding of learning, and this may benefit all children. Also, there are some needs that teachers may not encounter very often in their teaching career, for example, a child who uses a wheelchair, making it difficult for teachers to build up specific knowledge and expertise. Clearly, it is important that these teachers feel able to ask for help and advice. Therefore, perhaps specialist knowledge, skills and understanding are simply an essential part of achieving more inclusive schooling (Robertson 2001) in today's diverse classrooms, and the argument of Drifte (2005: 131) that support service workers should be seen as having 'different' expertise rather than 'better' expertise provides a sensible solution and allows expertise to contribute towards inclusion rather than detracting from it.

However, hidden within the arguments about whether support services do more harm than good is the issue of the teacher's own confidence. This must be taken seriously because confidence affects attitude and Ofsted (2004) found that the teacher's attitude was critical to inclusive teaching and learning. Pause and consider the findings by Evans and Lunt (2002: 9), who found that 'a child could be in a mainstream class, yet still be excluded because of the attitude of the teachers or other children in the class'. If this is true, then support teachers have a vital role to play in helping teachers to feel more confident; indeed, Corbett (2001) found in her research that teachers valued having someone to turn to. Clearly, giving advice may be supportive and boost confidence, and given that Croll and Moses' (2000) research found reservations among teachers about their expertise in terms of teaching children with SEN, it is vital to do this. The support may help to change the teacher's attitude and, if the advice is given skilfully, should build capacity rather than dependency.

Your views on social and medical models of disability and the importance (or not) of support services and expertise will almost certainly affect, in some way, your expectations of what the support service worker will do when he/she visits you. However, they will not be the only factors. Your expectations will also be shaped by your own school experience and your initial teacher training, including the attitude of your lecturers and the ethos of the school where you did your teaching practice. Let's now consider some of the issues surrounding the expectations of support services, and remember that this may also be relevant to other professionals and agencies with whom you work.

Great expectations!

It is definitely worth thinking about why you, as a class teacher, have referred to a support service, and what you expect from them, as clarity about what each of you will do is fundamental to the success of the partnership. It may also avoid frustration and disappointment on both parts, particularly if the support service worker believes in a social model of disability and the class teacher is expecting an intervention based on a medical model of disability. For example, are you expecting the support service worker to help you secure more funding for the child, to teach alongside you, to carry out some form of assessment, or to deliver whole-school training? The list is endless. However, is the support service worker expecting to do any of these things? In other words, do you share the same expectations?

It is important to consider what would be realistic to expect. Given that support services exist to offer support and advice, it would seem reasonable to expect this from the support service worker. However, giving and receiving advice is not necessarily straightforward. Firstly, it is important that any advice is set in context, so that the teacher does not feel over loaded (Lacey 2001); secondly, the support needs to make sense within the curriculum and classroom (Fletcher-Campbell and Cullen 2000). But remember that it is also vital that the teacher 'retains ownership of the child's learning' (DfES 2004d: 32) and that they still acknowledge and accept their responsibilities for every child.

These points are partly reflected in a model that McLaughlin (1989: 97) calls the 3Rs. In this model she suggests that support service workers should follow three basic principles in their work:

- respect (for teachers and their work)
- reality (start from where the teacher is at)
- responsibility (this should remain with the teacher, and should be encouraged).

It is interesting to note that while this model is over 20 years old, it still appears to be relevant today, and would probably form a sound basis to underpin the expectations of both teachers and support services workers. Certainly, if the partnership is based on mutual respect and a recognition of what is realistic for that particular teacher, with a clear understanding of roles and responsibilities, then there should be a strong foundation on which to build a successful relationship that leads to inclusive outcomes for children.

So, if the work between teacher and support service worker is to be successful, there is a need for clear expectations; Fletcher-Campbell and Cullen (1999) called for this following their research over ten years ago and in *Quality Standards for Special Educational Needs (SEN) Support and Outreach Services* (DCSF 2008), there are several references to the need for clear information about what service users can expect from services.

However, while written agreements about roles and responsibilities may help to clarify expectations at a service level, remember that it does not automatically follow that the support service workers and classroom teachers understand and share those expectations. In the busy world of education, the class teacher may not have even seen or read any written agreement.

Will I have to change?

In a small research study that I carried out with early years support service workers and Foundation Stage teachers about the expectations they have of each other, one issue that emerged was that the teachers had not anticipated having to make changes, and the support service workers were not explicit enough about the fact that their role is often linked to making changes. Therefore, within the partnership, it is important to have agreement on some of the practical issues that accompany change, and also expectations about the pace of change (Pearson 2001). For example, who will make and supply any new resources that are needed, and when will this happen? The teacher's attitude towards inclusion will also be important here, as teachers have to believe the new thinking makes sense if they are going to try and make changes (Cornwall 2001). This can be particularly relevant if the teacher expects advice and support based on a medical model of disability and the support service worker suggests changes based on a social model of disability. It can result in the intervention being flawed from the start, and may lead to frustration for both individuals. You might therefore like to consider the following ideas about your partnership with the support service worker.

How can you get the best out of working with a support service worker?

How do I make a referral?

Each support service will have its own referral procedure; these vary throughout the country, but you should always discuss the need to make a referral with your SENCO, who will probably complete the necessary paperwork with you. It goes without saying that you will need parental permission and that the parents (and pupil, if they are old enough) will fully understand what is happening and why. It is never ethical to ask an advisor to 'have a quick look at a child' for you while they are in school for another child, and this would be contrary to the *SEN Code of Practice* (DfES 2001) and the principles of Every Child Matters (DfES 2003).

After making the referral, try to find out as much as possible about what the visit will involve. Some questions to ask are suggested below.

How long will the support service worker be there for?

It is not wise to assume that the support service worker will be there for the whole morning or afternoon – they may be timetabled to fit three or four school visits into one day, and may have considerable distances to travel between each visit.

What paperwork will the support service worker want to see?

Under the *SEN Code of Practice* (DfES 2001), it is assumed that the child will have an IEP or targets in some form, and there may also be observations of the child or other reports or assessment documents. Have these ready for the support service worker so that he/she can build on what is already known about the child. There may also be a Common Assessment Framework (DfES 2006b) for the child, and the support service worker will need to know this.

What will the support service worker want to do on the visit?

In particular, you need to be clear about whether they will expect to work alongside the learning support assistant (this would not be unreasonable as they are meant to be empowering staff, not disappearing with the child to carry out 'secret' work in another room). If the learning support assistant is not time-tabled to be with the child at that time, can you make a swap with another teacher so that they are there at the right time? This may be difficult, but remember that it is impossible for support service workers to match their visits to the learning support assistants' timetables of every school they are involved with, and if you can show some flexibility on this, the visit will be far more worthwhile.

The support service worker will almost certainly want to talk to you. They are usually happy to talk through break time, lunchtime, or before or after school, depending on when the visit is scheduled – are you happy to give up this time to chat? If not (and maybe it is not reasonable to ask a teacher to talk through their lunch break), then be clear about this. If it is a first visit, maybe you can ask the senior management team if you can be released during lesson time to talk to the support service worker. This request may seem daunting, but you will gain more from 30 minutes of uninterrupted talk time with the support service worker than from numerous visits when you try to talk while also teaching.

The support service worker may be asking you to make changes to the way you teach or plan, and while it is not fair to ask you to make major changes overnight, do expect to have to make some adjustments. This may be as simple as where the child is seated, or may involve more long-term changes such as making your teaching more visual. See it as part of ongoing development that may help all the children in your class, rather than criticism. After all, you have asked for help and advice for the child, and it is bound to mean a change somewhere. Don't be frightened by the change – the support service worker should support you with it, should be realistic in what they ask you to change, and should be making at least one follow-up visit to see how things are going. It is not reasonable to ask you to spend hours making new resources, but a visit by a support service worker will almost certainly involve some extra work. However, the child will remain your responsibility. The support service worker is not there to wave a magic wand – and remember that inclusion is about removing barriers, not 'fixing' the child.

What can you expect of the support service worker?

Time

The support service worker should make time to talk to you during their visit. If that is not possible due to your teaching commitments, then you should both be clear as to how they will feed back to you – will it be a written report, a phone call, or will they have had a discussion with the SENCO or learning support assistant who will then feed back to you? You should never be left wondering about what they did or found out when they were in your classroom.

Support and advice

It is important that the advice and suggestions are appropriate and useful, but equally they are not necessarily strategies that will work overnight. You will need to make a real commitment to trying the strategy before you can say that it is not useful, and remember to expect the strategy to be focused on removing barriers. However, if it genuinely does not work then you should certainly expect the support service worker to be willing to make further suggestions.

Respect and realism

The support service worker should treat you with respect and be realistic about all the other responsibilities that you have. They should build on what is already known about the child, and should not dismiss what you tell them. If the support service worker wants to carry out further assessments, what will they tell you about the child that you don't already know? It is not good enough for a support service worker to carry out an assessment just because it is a routine procedure for their service.

To be listened to

You are the child's teacher and you will have spent more time with the child than the support service worker. You will know the child better than they do, and what you have to say is very important. Also, don't be afraid to be honest about how you are feeling. Inclusion is complex and the support service worker is there to support you, as an individual, and answer your questions. Remember that mutual respect and honesty are needed to form a successful partnership.

Summary

Local authority support services have changed considerably during the past 20 years, and in some areas may now find themselves competing with other services. They are also operating in a climate of accountability and must find ways to justify the need for expertise and specialist advice for children with SEN in diverse and inclusive classrooms. In the future, their success may depend on whether they align themselves with medical or social models of disability, but it will also depend on formulating mutual expectations with teachers about the roles and responsibilities of both support service workers and teachers. As a newly qualified teacher, it is an ideal time to discuss and explore mutual expectations with your support service worker, and indeed with professionals from other areas of education and other agencies, so that your partnership is built on strong and clear foundations.

Reflection on values and practice

- Are you expecting advice based on a social or medical model of disability? What difference does this make to teaching and learning in diverse and inclusive classrooms?

- Do you understand the 'graduated approach' in the *Special Educational Needs Code of Practice* (DfES 2001) and the implications it has for teaching and learning?
- Do we really need 'experts', and if so, what is their role in diverse and inclusive classrooms?

Additional resource

Gray, P. (2002) 'Custodian of entitlement or agents of dependence? SEN support services in English LEAs in the context of greater delegation of funding to schools', *Support for Learning* 17(1): 5–8.

References

Blamires, M. and Moore, J. (2004) *Support Services and Mainstream Schools*, London: David Fulton.

Booth, T. and Ainscow, M. (2000) *Index for Inclusion: Developing Learning and Participation in Schools*, Bristol: Centre for Studies on Inclusive Education.

Corbett, J. (2001) *Supporting Inclusive Education. A Connective Pedagogy*, Abingdon: RoutledgeFalmer.

Cornwall, J. (2001) 'Enabling inclusion: is the culture of change being responsibly managed?', in O'Brien, T. (ed.) *Enabling Inclusion: Blue Skies … Dark Clouds?*, London: The Stationery Office, 127–42.

Croll, P. and Moses, D. (2000) 'Ideologies and utopias: educational professionals' view of inclusion', *European Journal of Special Educational Needs*, 15(1): 1–12.

DCSF (2007) *The Children's Plan. Building Brighter Futures* (Cm.7280), London: The Stationery Office.

——(2008) *Quality Standards for Special Educational Needs (SEN) Support and Outreach Services*, Nottingham: Department for Children, Schools and Families.

Dessent, T. (2004) 'Making the ordinary school special', in Thomas, G. and Vaughan, M. (eds) *Inclusive Education, Readings and Reflections,* Maidenhead: Open University Press, 77–83.

DfEE (1998) *Fair Funding: Improving Delegation to Schools*, Consultation Paper, London: Department for Education and Employment.

DfES (2001) *Special Educational Needs: Code of Practice*, London: Department for Education and Skills.

——(2003) *Every Child Matters*, London: The Treasury Office.

——(2004a) *Removing Barriers to Achievement. The Government's strategy for SEN*, London: Department for Education and Skills.

——(2004b) *Every Child Matters: Change for Children*, London: Department for Education and Skills.

——(2004c) *Every Child Matters: Next Steps*, London: Department for Education and Skills.

——(2004d) *Learning and Teaching for Children with Special Educational Needs in the Primary Years*, London: Department for Education and Skills.

——(2006a) *Information Sharing. Practitioners' Guide*, London: The Stationery Office.

——(2006b) *The Common Assessment Framework for Children and Young People: Practitioners' Guide*, London: The Stationery Office.

DH (2003) *Confidentiality: NHS Code of Practice*, London: Department of Health.

Drifte,C. (2005) *A Manual for the Early Years SENCO*, London: Paul Chapman.

Evans, J. and Lunt, I. (2002) 'Inclusive education: are there limits?', *European Journal of Special Education*, 17(1): 1–14.

Farrell, M. (2004) *Special Educational Needs. A Resource for Practitioners*, London: Paul Chapman.

Fitzgerald, D. and Kay, J. (2008) *Working Together in Children's Services*, Abingdon: Routledge.

Fletcher-Campbell, F. and Cullen, M. (1999) *The Impact of Delegation on LEA Support Services for Special Educational Needs*, Slough: National Foundation for Educational Research.

——(2000) 'Schools' perception of support services for special educational needs', *Support for Learning*, 15(2): 90–94.

Gray, P. (1999) 'Policy issues raised by rethinking support', in Norwich, B. (ed.) *Rethinking Support for More Inclusive Schooling*, Policy Paper One (Third Series), Tamworth: NASEN (National Association for Special Educational Needs), 129–37.

——(2001) *Developing Support for More Inclusive Schooling: A Review of the Role of Support Services for Special Educational Needs in English Local Authorities*, London: Department for Education and Employment/National Foundation for Educational Research.

Lacey, P. (2001) *Support Partnerships. Collaboration in Action*, London: David Fulton.

Lindsay, G. (2000) 'Summary of discussions', in Norwich, B. (ed.) *Specialist Teaching for Special Educational Needs and Inclusion*, Policy Paper Four (Third Series), Tamworth: NASEN (National Association for Special Educational Needs), 45–48.

McLaughlin, C. (1989) 'Working face to face: aspects of interpersonal work', *Support for Learning*, 4(2): 96–101.

McNamara, S. and Moreton, G. (1995) *Changing Behaviour*, London: David Fulton.

Mittler, P. (2000) *Working Towards Inclusive Education. Social Contexts*, London: David Fulton.

Ofsted (2004) *Special Educational Needs and Disability: Towards Inclusive Schools* (HMI 2276), London: Ofsted.

——(2005) *Inclusion: The Impact of LEA Support and Outreach Services* (HMI 2452), London: Ofsted.

Pearson, S. (2001) 'Inclusion: a developmental perspective', in O'Brien, T. (ed.) *Enabling Inclusion: Blue Skies … Dark Clouds?,* London: The Stationery Office, 143–57.

Rieser, R. (2003) *Everybody In*, London: Disability Equality in Education.

Robertson, C. (2001) 'The social model of disability and the rough ground or inclusive education', in O'Brien, T. (ed.) *Enabling Inclusion: Blue Skies … Dark Clouds?,* London: The Stationery Office, 113–25.

Thomas, G. and Loxley, A. (2001) *Deconstructing Special Education and Constructing Inclusion*, Buckingham: Open University Press.

Chapter 14

Disability, human rights and inclusive education, and why inclusive education is the only educational philosophy and practice that makes sense in today's world

Richard Rieser

"From now on the new paradigm of inclusive education must mark the institution of education, understanding that the traditional education system, as it was conceived and designed, is not only opposed to diversity, but also works against the rights and interests of populations historically excluded."

(Muñoz 2007: UN Special Rapporteur on the Right to Education)

Introduction

This chapter examines some of the main issues you will face in thinking about the values and practices that underpin inclusive education from a global perspective. This is not an academic, but a practical concern, as in every mainstream school and class there are a diversity of pupils, including those from different social classes, cultures and ethnic backgrounds, and with different impairments. A firm understanding of the issues involved in responding to, and celebrating, difference will help you develop effective inclusive teaching.

'Inclusive education' has become a bit of a buzzword, but many who use it, and many who oppose it, do not understand what it requires, and that it involves a process of structural change throughout the education system. Inclusive education requires the transformation of what has been common practice in schools and colleges, to ensure all learners can be successful in achieving their social and academic potential. Historical inequalities exist and have existed throughout human history. A human rights perspective, which has gained support in the years since the UN Declaration of Human Rights (1948), demands that the world move forward to embrace a collaborative future where people and our environments are placed before profits. All are born into humankind, so all have a right to grow up and receive their education together. Breaking down the barriers that prevent this is an important part of human progress and the development of a sustainable future.

The international context

The UN Convention on the Rights of Persons with Disabilities (UNCRPD; United Nations 2006), which the UK has ratified, requires us to develop new thinking about disabled pupils. It demands moving away from a special educational needs deficit view to an empowering rights-based view, which is,

> An evolving concept [...] that disability results from the interaction of persons with impairments and attitudinal and environmental barriers that hinder their full and effective participation in society on an equal basis with others.
>
> (United Nations 2006: Article 1)

Countries ratifying the Convention must address disabling barriers such as lack of accessible transport and buildings, rigid grade-related curriculum and assessment fixed by national government, teachers untrained in inclusive pedagogies, attitudes based on identifying what people cannot normally do, lack of social acceptance and opportunity for employment, and denial of human rights.

In 1994, 92 countries and 20 NGOs came together under the auspices of UNESCO in Salamanca, Spain and adopted the Salamanca Statement, which gave the world community a clear steer towards a more inclusive education system.

- Education systems should be designed and educational programmes implemented to take into account the wide diversity of these characteristics and needs.
- Those with special educational needs must have access to regular schools which should accommodate them within a child centered pedagogy capable of meeting these needs.
- Regular schools with this inclusive orientation are the most effective means of combating discriminatory attitudes, creating welcoming communities, building an inclusive society and achieving education for all; moreover, they provide an effective education to the majority of children, and improve the efficiency and ultimately the cost-effectiveness of the entire education system (UNESCO 1994).

However, most of its suggestions amounted to little more than *integration* of disabled children into mainstream schools, as it did not address structural change. Perhaps this has been one of the conceptual barriers to developing a fully inclusive system.

This certainly was one of the key themes at the recent Global Conference on Inclusive Education: 'Confronting the Gap: Rights, Rhetoric, Reality?' (Inclusion International 2009). The 2009 Salamanca Conference adopted a resolution that clearly sees inclusion as a process of transforming existing education systems by giving support to all pupils to achieve their potential and the removal of barriers. It stated:

> We understand inclusive education to be a process where mainstream schools and early years settings are transformed so that *all* children/students are supported to meet their academic and social potential and involves removing barriers in environment, attitudes, communication, curriculum, teaching, socialisation and assessment at all levels.

This definition of inclusive education is in line with a wider definition adopted by UNESCO (1994), which sees inclusive education as a

> ... process of addressing and responding to diversity of needs of all learners through increasing participation in learning, cultures and communities, and reducing exclusion within and from education. It involves changes and modifications in content, approaches, structures and strategies, with a common vision which covers all children of appropriate age range and a conviction that it is the responsibility of the regular system to educate all children.

This definition is very wide and applies to all groups excluded from education. The thinking about disability outlined above can be specifically applied to education of disabled children.

From medical model to social model – implications for education provision and teaching

In the UK we have moved some way towards inclusive education, but 'medical model' attitudes still lie behind government thinking. This thinking identifies children with different impairments as having varying educational needs, and then provides a range of provision to meet those needs. In some local authorities, parents can choose mainstream schooling for their children who have significant impairments. However, it is assumed that those labelled as having 'profound or complex needs' will attend special schools, and many professionals encourage this view. This is classic 'medical model' thinking, where children's needs are identified by their special educational needs assessment based on what they 'can't do' and different levels of provision are made for them. The medical model sees the problem in the person and their impairment, rather than in the system and its need for restructuring (Mason and Rieser 1994).

In a recent book on *Implementing Inclusive Education* throughout the Commonwealth (Rieser 2008), I put some key ways of thinking about disability together with related forms of education, as in Table 14.1:

Table 14.1 Types of thinking about disabled people and forms of education

Thinking/ model	Characteristics	Form of education
Traditional	Disabled person a shame on family, guilt, ignorance. Disabled person seen as of no value.	**Excluded** from education altogether.
Medical 1	Focus on what disabled person cannot do. Attempt to normalize or, if they cannot fit into things as they are, keep them separate.	**Segregation** Institutions/hospitals. Special schools (with 'expert' special educators).
Medical 2	Person can be supported by minor adjustment and support, to function normally and minimize their impairment. Continuum of provision based on severity and type of impairment.	**Integration** in mainstream: • at same location but in separate class/units • socially in some activities, e.g. meals, assembly or art • in the class with support, but teaching and learning remain the same. **What you *cannot* do determines which form of education you receive.**
Social	Barriers identified – solutions found to minimize them. Barriers of attitude, environment and organization are seen as what disables, and are removed to maximize potential of all. Disabled person welcomed. Relations are intentionally built. Disabled person achieves their potential. Person-centred approach.	**Inclusive** – schools where all are welcomed, and staff, parents and pupils value diversity. Support is provided so all can be successful academically and socially. This requires reorganizing teaching, learning and assessment. Peer support is encouraged. **Focus on what you *can* do**.

Source: Commonwealth Secretariat 2008.

For the vast majority of disabled pupils, their 'needs are met' in mainstream education under School Action/School Action Plus. However, where children receive a statutory assessment leading to a Statement of Special Educational Needs, parents can express a preference for where they want their child educated, and a large minority still want segregated education in special schools (44.4% of 228,900; DCSF 2009a). In some local authorities there is more capacity and support for inclusive education than in others, and a much wider range of disabled children is successfully included. Schools in these authorities demonstrate that where there is a strong inclusive ethos and a willingness to address barriers and find solutions, all children benefit socially and academically.

In a study I carried out for the Department for Education and Skills in the UK to identify best practice in making reasonable adjustments for disabled pupils, we visited 40 mainstream schools and filmed and observed much good inclusive practice. We carried out more than 300 interviews with headteachers, SENCOs, teachers, parents and pupils. They identified the following factors as important in the development of their good inclusive practice (DfES 2006):

- vision and values based on an inclusive ethos
- a 'can do' attitude from all staff
- a proactive approach to identifying barriers and finding practical solutions
- strong collaborative relationships with pupils and parents
- a meaningful voice for pupils
- a positive approach to managing behaviour
- strong leadership by special educational needs coordinators or management and governors
- effective staff training and development
- the use of expertise from outside the school
- building disability into resourcing arrangements
- a sensitive approach to meeting the impairment-specific needs of pupils
- regular critical review and evaluation
- the availability of role models and positive images of disability.

Despite these findings, there are many detractors of inclusive education. A quick examination of the development of special education will help illuminate some of the reasons.

Policy making in a historical context

Disabled people were traditionally invested with meanings from different cultures that saw us as evil, penitent sinners, objects of charity, holy, incapable, and figures of fun or unworthy of life. From the Enlightenment onwards, we became subject to fledgling medical science, so if we did not conform to thinking about 'normal' development of body and mind, we had to be rehabilitated or 'made normal', and if this was not possible, then locked away from society. This process was extended by the false science of eugenics, wishing to breed superior human beings. This held sway from the 1880s to 1950s and led to the sterilization, incarceration or death of millions of disabled people throughout Europe and North America. Psychological testing was often used to justify these practices with dubious psychometric procedures (Rieser 2000a).

Mass primary education was introduced in England in the 1870s. Disabled children, apart from blind and deaf children, who in the late nineteenth century acquired a right to education, were deemed ineducable. Up until the Second World War, a series of measures were introduced that allowed selected groups of disabled children to receive education, usually in separate settings designated for particular categories of impairment and isolated from their non-disabled peers. These settings had a strong rehabilitative and medical emphasis, and were underpinned by highly medicalized and impairment-led perceptions of disabled children and young people, as illustrated by the labels used to describe them ('physically handicapped', 'mildly educationally subnormal').

The Warnock Inquiry (Warnock Committee 1978) recommended that children should no longer be categorized by their impairments (or 'handicaps'), but by their special educational needs and that, wherever possible, disabled children should be integrated into mainstream or ordinary schools. However, Warnock had no conception of inclusion, rather, 'integration' was to be locational (on the same campus in different institutions), social (mixing for assemblies, lunch, play), or functional (in the same class with some support, but with the overall approaches to teaching and learning remaining unchanged). This Inquiry led to the 1981 Education Act, which allowed for the 'integration' of disabled children in ordinary schools, unless they fell under one of three caveats: if it was deemed that their needs could not be accommodated; if their 'special educational needs' would interfere with the education of other children; or if the costs involved were considered an inefficient use of resources.

In practice, as there was no new funding put in place to support this policy, this meant a slow increase in the proportion of the education budget in each local authority going towards supporting disabled pupils, usually by the employment of unqualified teaching assistants, as specified through the newly introduced Statements of Special Educational Needs. Some local authorities, such as Newham and Barnsley, took the 1981 Act at face value and started dismantling special schools and setting up resourced schools and experienced teams of support teachers. In more rural areas, such as Cumbria, Cornwall, North Yorkshire and Norfolk, a higher proportion of disabled children were already attending their local schools in a process of piecemeal integration. However, for the majority of local authorities it was business as usual, and increasingly the caveats were used, often against the wishes of pupil and parent, to assess disabled children as needing special schooling. There were many arguments, and so a later Education Act (1993) introduced an independent Special Educational Needs Tribunal and a much more codified process of assessment and placement, with a statutory Code of Practice (DfES 2001; Rieser 2000b).

In 1997, New Labour came to power with a stated commitment to human rights for disabled people, as exemplified in both the Green Paper 'Excellence for All Children' (DfEE 1997), which appeared to offer support for 'inclusion', and in the 2001 Special Educational Needs and Disability Act, passed after some strong lobbying from disabled people and parents. This removed two of the caveats, leaving only 'interfering in the efficient education of other children', and gave parents a right to choose either mainstream or special schools for their disabled child's education. The 2001 Act also set up a new duty for all schools not to treat disabled pupils 'less favorably' than other pupils and to make 'reasonable adjustments' in admissions, education, associated services and exclusions. The special educational needs assessment and statementing system was left intact to provide the resources, and the school environment had to be made gradually more accessible under the Schools' Access Planning Duty. A similar duty was placed on all post-school provision, meaning that all education settings had to meet learners' needs and remove physical barriers to participation as part of making reasonable adjustments. However, increasing reliance on market principles in the design and culture of education systems and notions of 'choice' have undercut New Labour's stated intentions on inclusive education (Dyson 2005).

Recent policy developments and the international context

Between 2003 and 2006, there was a backlash against the presumption of inclusion as a desirable and achievable goal. Baroness Warnock (2005) decided she had changed her mind and the then opposition, particularly David Cameron, argued for a moratorium on special school closure. This shift appears to have been motivated by two groups: firstly, some parents who felt their children were not getting the support they needed; and secondly, special school head-teachers fighting to maintain the position of special schools. This led the government to build a new generation of special schools and to talk of a 'continuum of need to be met in a continuum of provision'. This missed the point that inclusive schools need to be resourced, and staff trained, to meet the diverse needs of all. Not 'one size fits all', as inclusion has been parodied, but 'all sizes fit in here' (Barton 2005; Disability Equality in Education 2005).

More recently, the UK Government has been putting forward the view that one can have 'inclusion' in special schools. The Tory Party is committed to challenging 'ideological inclusion', building more special schools and introducing 'choice' with vouchers which will further undermine inclusive education (Conservative Party 2010).

The Coalition Government has adopted as a reversal of policy 'the bias towards inclusive education'. The unseemly rush to push through the Academies Bill in the first session of the new Coalition Government, which demonstrated no understanding of the need for Special Education Needs provision in ordinary schools, is perhaps a sign of how the new Government intends to reverse the so called bias to inclusive education. Another consequence of such legislation will be to destabilise the role of Local Authorities and their ability to support disabled pupils. One might ask: what about 200 years of 'ideological' segregation?

The UNCRPD (2006) is the first human rights treaty of the new millennium, and extends to disabled people the human rights proclaimed for all in the 1948 Universal Declaration of Human Rights. Disabled people were not specifically left out of this declaration. They were not mentioned, so it was not seen that human rights should apply to disabled people. This was not malign in the main, but based on traditional and medical model thinking. In short, we were seen as exceptions, as less than human.

The ambiguity of the UK New Labour Government's position on inclusive education is demonstrated by the fact that it was the only country in the world to register a reservation and an interpretive declaration against inclusive education Article 24 of the UNCRPD, when they ratified in June 2009. Article 24 requires state parties to ensure:

all disabled children and young people can fully participate in the state education system and that this should be an 'inclusive education system at all levels'
the development by persons with disabilities of their personality, talents and creativity, as well as their mental and physical abilities, to their fullest potential
this right is to be delivered in local schools within an inclusive primary and secondary education system, from which disabled people should not be excluded
reasonable accommodations should be provided for individual requirements and support provided in individualised programmes to facilitate their effective social and academic education.

(summarized from United Nations 2006)

The UK New Labour Government's reservation in relation to Article 24 reads:

The United Kingdom Government is committed to continuing to develop an inclusive system where parents of disabled children have increasing access to mainstream schools and staff, which have the capacity to meet the needs of disabled children.

The General Education System in the United Kingdom includes mainstream and special schools, which the UK Government understands is allowed under the Convention.

The United Kingdom reserves the right for disabled children to be educated outside their local community where more appropriate education provision is available elsewhere. Nevertheless, parents of disabled children have the same opportunity as other parents to state a preference for the school at which they wish their child to be educated.

(www.un.org/disabilities/default.asp?id=475)

However, more recently the Lamb Report (DCSF 2009b) has made some recommendations, accepted by the then government, to improve the position of disabled children in English schools, support inclusion and develop parental confidence. The Coalition Government are to hold as SEN Review and we do not yet know if they will accept the Lamb Report.

Current contradictions are demonstrated by the global campaign Education for All. World leaders committed themselves to Millennium Development Goals in 1990, including Goal 2: 'that **all** children should complete primary education by 2000'. At the World Education Forum in Dakar in 2000, this was revised to be achieved by 2015. These Statements have been backed by major initiatives from the World Bank, such as the Fast Track Initiative, and have led to many poor countries offering free primary education, with a big increase in those attending school, especially among girls. Yet disabled children have barely been mentioned.

This gap led to the setting up of the UNESCO 'Flagship' Education for All in 2001, which partly took on including disabled children, especially through UNESCO's work. The World Vision (2007) report *Education's Missing Millions* drew attention to the large numbers of disabled children not in education. This is estimated to be between 25 and 40 million out of the 75 million children estimated by the Global Monitoring Report (2009) not to be in education.

Disabled children are often not enumerated or registered in many parts of the world. UNESCO estimates that 10% of the world's population is disabled, but in developing countries they are more likely to identify 1–3%. The One Goal Campaign has been organized around World Cup 2010 in South Africa, with the aim of implementing Millennium Goal 2 (www.join1goal.org/en/about-us). This provides a great opportunity to ensure disabled children are included in these initiatives. Since adoption of the UNCRPD in 2006, the various international agencies are now taking the education of disabled children much more seriously.

In 2007/08 I examined a wide range of examples of inclusive education across the 53 Commonwealth countries (Rieser 2008). Most examples were more to do with placement of disabled pupils in mainstream schools (that is, integration), but there were some examples of teachers and schools restructuring to accommodate disabled pupils. From these, the following criteria at national, regional, district and school levels were drawn up.

What needs to be done to ensure all children are included successfully in school?

Requirements at national level:

- a flexible national curriculum with the means of making the curriculum accessible to all
- assessment systems that are made flexible and meaningful to include all learners
- active encouragement to disabled pupils and their parents to enrol in their local school
- sufficient school places and adequate numbers of support staff and specialist teachers, including those with expertise in visual, hearing, physical, communication, learning or behavioural impairments
- all teachers trained in inclusive teaching and learning
- sufficient specialist teachers for the development of a pupil-centred pedagogy where all can progress at their optimum pace

- sufficient capital for school building and modification
- reduction of class sizes
- media and public awareness campaigns to establish rights-based approaches to disability and inclusive education
- mobilisation of communities to build new schools or adapt existing environments
- sufficient specialist teachers for those with visual hearing, physical, communication, learning or behavioural impairments working with a range of schools.

Requirements at regional/district levels:

- strengthening of effective links between education, health and social services so that they work collaboratively on a joint inclusion strategy
- development of links between schools and local authorities with the support of disabled advisors
- support for ongoing inclusion training for teachers, parents and community leaders
- development of centres with equipment and expertise on techniques that support inclusive education (sign, Braille, augmented and alternative communication)
- ensure all disabled children identified are able to enroll in their local schools
- draw on the knowledge and experience of members of the local community who can support the cultural and experiential interests of pupils
- regular training on inclusive teaching and learning for teachers and for parents and community leaders on inclusive education
- support to help parents of disabled children empower their children
- sharing of best practice in the region.

Requirements at school level:

- sufficient staff and volunteers in place to provide support for disabled children, and teachers who are trained and support each other in planning and developing inclusive practice
- all staff understand and know what is required of them to include *all* learners, including disabled children
- curricula and pedagogies accessible to all, with a range of learning situations, styles and paces
- inclusion is audited regularly and barriers tackled systematically
- school environment and activities are accessible, and information is available in alternative forms as required (Braille, audio, pictures, signing)
- create a school that welcomes difference, and in which pupils support each other – collaboration rather than competition should be the ethos

- assessment is continuous and flexible, and is used formatively to assess what children have learnt
- the school is the hub of the community and encourages the involvement of all its members, regardless of difference.

Given that parents, disabled people, teachers and academics have been demonstrating the efficacy of inclusive education for more than 20 years, one may be tempted to ask why such fundamentally good educational practice as is contained in the paragraphs above is taking so long to be adopted and generalized throughout the education systems of the world. Many arguments have been put forward by the detractors of inclusive education, but these are all easily answered by the evidence and principles demonstrated by the Centre for Studies on Inclusive Education's Inclusion Charter under three key headings: 'human rights', 'good education' and 'social sense', as follows (CSIE 2002/1989).

Human rights

Inclusive education is a human right, it's good education and it makes good social sense.

1. All children have the right to learn together.
2. Children should not be devalued or discriminated against by being excluded because of their disability or learning difficulty.
3. Disabled adults, describing themselves as special school survivors, are demanding an end to segregation – Article 24 of the UN Convention on the Rights of Persons with Disabilities was drawn up by disabled people from around the world.
4. There are no legitimate reasons to separate children for their education.
5. Children belong together – with advantages and benefits for everyone. They do not need to be protected from each other.

Good education

6. Research shows children do better, academically and socially, in inclusive settings.
7. There is no teaching or care in a segregated school which cannot take place in an ordinary school.
8. Given commitment and support, inclusive education is a more efficient use of educational resources.

Social sense

9. Segregation teaches children to be fearful, ignorant and breeds prejudice.
10. All children need an education that will help them develop relationships and prepare them for life in the mainstream. Only inclusion

has the potential to reduce fear and to build friendship, respect and understanding.

Conclusion

We now have the human rights framework. We have the experience around the world to know how to develop and build inclusive education. We have exemplars of how to make inclusive education work. We have the World Bank Fast Track Initiative for Education for All, putting disability centre stage. Yet negative attitudes, fear, the inertia of existing education systems and professionals seem to remain as the major reasons why inclusive education is not developing.

For existing teachers and those entering the profession it is vital that they understand that developing their practice to accommodate all learners, where diversity is valued both in the curriculum and in methods of teaching and learning, underpins a human rights approach, and that inclusive educational practice is the best way of ensuring this.

Surely now is the right time for the development of an inclusive education system that emphasizes collaboration rather than competition – collaboration which involves all children, based on fundamental human values? Surely it is high time to recognize that we are all interdependent, and that a shared understanding of human rights and a commitment to the good of all members of society is crucial to the development of a more just and harmonious society? There is no better place to start developing this understanding than through the collaborative work of teachers, schools and communities.

Reflections on values and practice

- Examine the wording of Article 24 of the UNCRPD and then think of a local authority you know and list the changes that would have to occur for Article 24 to be fully implemented.
- A parent of a child who has a physical impairment and low vision wants their child to attend their local mainstream school. Imagine you are a) the headteacher and b) the class teacher. Describe how you will go about finding out about the changes that may be needed. What might these changes be, and how will you go about implementing them?
- You are in the role of an OFSTED Inspector, and you are inspecting a school known to you. How would you assess the progress disabled children make, how safe they are, and whether they have full equality?

References

Barton, L. (2005) 'A Response to Warnock M. 2005: Special/Educational Needs – A New Look', www.leeds.ac.uk/disability-studies/archiveuk/barton/Warnock.pdf

Conservative Party (2010) Draft Education Manifesto, http://issuu.com/conservatives/docs/drafteducationmanifesto

Commonwealth Secretariat (2008) *Implementing Inclusion*, London: Commonwealth Secretariat.

CSIE (2002/1989) 'The Inclusion Charter', Bristol: Centre for Studies on Inclusive Education, www.csie.org.uk/publications/charter.shtml

DCSF (2009a) 'Special Educational Needs in England: January 2009', www.dcsf.gov.uk/rsgateway/DB/SFR/s000852/index.shtml

——(2009b) 'Lamb Inquiry: Special needs and parental confidence', www.dcsf.gov.uk/lambinquiry

DfEE (1997) 'Excellence for All Children: Meeting Special Educational Needs', Green Paper, London: Department for Education and Employment.

DfES (2001) *Special Educational Needs: Code of Practice*, London: Department for Education and Skills.

——(2006) Prologue, in *Implementing the Disability Discrimination Act in Schools and Early Years* (films available from HMSO), London: Department for Education and Skills.

Disability Equality in Education (2005) 'Warnock challenges the rights of disabled children to inclusion', open letter signed by over 600 people and organisations, advertisement in *Times Education Supplement*, 8 July 2005, www.worldofinclusion.com/res/warnock/Warnock_Ad.pdf

Dyson, A. (2005) 'Philosophy, politics and economics? The story of inclusive education in England,' in Mitchell, D. (ed.) *Contextualizing Inclusive Education: Evaluating Old and New International Perspectives*, London: Routledge.

Falvey, M. (2004) 'Reviewing inclusive education', *TASH Journal* Spring 2004.

Global Monitoring Report (2009) 'Overcoming inequality: why governance matters', Paris: UNESCO, www.unesco.org/en/efareport/reports/2009-governance

Inclusion International (2009) 'Global Conference on Inclusive Education', 21–23 October 2009, Salamanca, Spain, www.inclusion-international.org/en/extras/4.html

Mason, M. and Rieser, R. (1994) 'Altogether Better', London: Comic Relief, www.worldofinclusion.com/res/altogether/AltogetherBetter.pdf

Muñoz, Vernor (2007) *The Right to Education of Persons with Disabilities*, Report of the Special Rapporteur on the Right to Education to the UNHRC A/HRC/4/29, Geneva: UN Human Rights Council, http://daccess-ods.un.org/TMP/9241911.76891327.html

Rieser, R. (2000a) 'Disability discrimination, the final frontier: disablement, history and liberation', in Cole, M. (ed.), *Education, Equality and Human Rights*, London: Routledge.

——(2000b) 'Special educational needs or inclusive education: the challenge of disability discrimination in schooling', in Cole, M. (ed.) *Education, Equality and Human Rights*, London: Routledge.

——(2008) *Implementing Inclusive Education: A Commonwealth Guide to Implementing Article 24 of the UN Convention on the Rights of People with Disabilities*, London: Commonwealth Secretariat.

UNESCO (1994) *The Salamanca Statement and Framework for Action on Special Needs Education*, Adopted by the World Conference on Special Needs Education: Access and Quality, Salamanca, Spain, 7–10 June 1994, Paris: UNESCO, www.unesco.org/education/pdf/SALAMA_E.PDF

——(2004) *EFA Flagship Initiatives: Multi-partner Collaborative Mechanisms in Support of EFA Goals*, Paris: UNESCO, http://unesdoc.unesco.org/images/0013/001356/135639e.pdf

——(2008) 'Messages of Ministers of Education: Sarah McCarthy Fry', International Conference on Education, 48th session, 25–28 November 2008, 'Inclusive Education:

The Way of the Future', www.ibe.unesco.org/fileadmin/user_upload/Policy_Dialogue/48th_ICE/Messages/UK_MIN08.pdf

United Nations (2006) *Convention on the Rights of Persons with Disabilities*, New York: United Nations, www.un.org/disabilities/default.asp?id=259

Warnock, M. (2005) *Special Educational Needs: A New Look*, No. 11 in a series of policy discussions, London: Philosophy of Education Society of Great Britain.

Warnock Committee (1978) *Special Educational Needs: The Warnock Report*, London: HMSO.

World Vision (2007) *Education's Missing Millions: Including Disabled Children in Education through EFA FTI Processes and National Sector Plans*, Milton Keynes: World Vision UK, www.worldvision.org.uk/server.php?show=nav.1780

Index